AUTOBIOGRAPHY
FACT AND FICTION

AUTOBIOGRAPHY
FACT AND FICTION

Edited by

Rosy Singh

Aryan Books International

New Delhi

AUTOBIOGRAPHY: FACT AND FICTION

ISBN-978-81-7305-366-5

First Published in **2009** by:

ARYAN BOOKS INTERNATIONAL

Pooja Apartments, 4B, Ansari Road, New Delhi - 110 002 (India)

Tel.: 23287589, 23255799; Fax: 91-11-23270385

E-mail: aryanbooks@vsnl.com

in association with

DEPARTMENT OF GERMANIC AND ROMANCE STUDIES

University of Delhi, Delhi

Computer Typeset and Printed in India at

ABI Prints & Publishing Co., New Delhi

Preface

Autobiography: Fact and Fiction is a collection of essays with deliberations on the nature of an autobiographical discourse, its multiple semiotic structures, its inherent complexities and contradictions and the new trends emerging in the contemporary world in this genre, among other things. The long tradition of autobiographical narratives from the ancient world through the medieval world to the modern and post-modern worlds, in the Orient and the Occident, as oral and written texts, as verbal and visual signs, is also discussed and interpreted. These reflections and responses of scholars from various parts of the world who came together in March 2005 to participate in the three-day international seminar in the Department of Germanic and Romance Studies, University of Delhi on the theme of 'Autobiography' are presented in this volume.

I thank all the contributors who sent in their papers at a short notice and cooperated in the editing process.

March, 2008 **Rosy Singh**
Delhi

Contents

ROSY SINGH

Introduction

This issue of *germinal* presents the proceedings of the seminar on "Fact and Fiction: Autobiography after the Death of the Author" held on 10–12 March 2005 in the Department of Germanic and Romance Studies, University of Delhi.

The essays in the book are broadly organized into two sections: one, where an individual, considering himself a part or a representative of a whole, records the experiences of a marginalised group in the society; and two, where the individual and his/her set of unique existential experiences dominate. The former category is of fairly recent origin, flourishing more in the non-western world with crass inequalities and injustices, not always of their making. In this case, the autobiography becomes the testimonial voice of a people, be it in terms of race, religion, caste, colour, gender or physical challenges, with the protagonist in the role of a victim or a witness or both. The last two decades have seen the emergence of new minority autobiographies such as those by sex workers and terminally ill cancer and AIDS patients. In case of AIDS autobiographies, the author, a dying HIV-AIDS patient, records his last agonizing days as a new social outcast. Hence, in this category the textual space addresses group memory, functions as a frozen image of a particular historical period or society and contributes, in this manner, to communal consciousness. The pent-up emotions find an outlet and telling one's story translates into a cathartic experience or political resistance, as the case might be. The latter category comprises, more often than not, literary writings, often marked by a refined language and a sophisticated mode of presentation par excellence, typical of the European tradition where the individual has been the focus of attention in the modern era. Revealing the ups and downs of one's personal and/or professional life and confessing the 'sins' committed may provide a therapeutic release from guilt as well as give some egoistic pleasure. Many of these self-explorations are today considered classics. In this category of autobiography, 'word' is the yardstick whereas in the first, aesthetics takes a backseat to the veracity of the statements. The two also criss-cross. Anna Frank's diary describes two years in the life of a Jewish school girl hiding in Amsterdam from the Nazis before she is discovered and left to perish in the concentration camp in Bergen-Belsen. Her diary gives a rare and moving insight into the little known world of a thirteen-year-old girl entering puberty — her aspirations, fantasies, frustrations and her way of looking at the world of grown-ups. "… nobody can understand that a thirteen year old girl is all alone in the world," Anna Frank tells her only friend, Kitti – her diary. In the backdrop looms the dark shadow of the Holocaust. The diary has a child-like sincerity as well as a literary quality outstanding for a child. Is it then the universal voice of adolescents or is it what is clubbed together as the Holocaust literature or is it rather a specific discourse of a specific being articulated in a specific manner?

There is a sub-category in the second section — in contrast to the 'pure' form, the autobiography is dispersed in various works (essays, stories, poetry, letters, paintings, films, photographs, music or any other form of art) of an artist or a philosopher. For instance, painters often paint themselves in various disguises, sometimes even including themselves as a face in a crowd. Picasso disguised himself as a harlequin in his series on circus. Sometimes dedications and acknowledgements at the beginning of a book are deeply personal and autobiographical, even camouflaged. In such disguised autobiographical texts the critic functions like an archaeologist excavating a site, collecting fragments and putting them together. According to Federico Fellini, a renowned Italian film-maker, all art is autobiographical; the pearl is the oyster's autobiography. Picasso also felt that painting and maintaining a diary were akin. One must understand the complexity of these propositions, for personal experiences of an artist are indeed a point of departure for his art, but art cannot be an exact reproduction of those experiences. A good writer would try to camouflage or cover his tracks. Equally true is that man forgets his signifiers but the signifiers never forget him. The hidden or buried signifiers get restructured and manifest themselves in dreams, jokes or slips of the tongue, the pen or the brush. They emerge with or without the conscious permission of the referent. For the critic it is indeed a complex situation, as in the process of tracing these tracks, the boundary between the biography and the autobiography invariably becomes diffused.

The Romantics used the trope of *Bergwerk* or 'mining' to describe the urge to dig deep into the inner self. A century later, Freud called it the 'talking cure'. The most intriguing signifier of autobiographical writing is the first person "I". Introspection of "I" begins, according to Lacan, with the Mirror Stage when for the first time a child looks at its own image in the mirror. The dialectics of the "real" self and its "appearance" (*Gestalt*) in the mirror makes the infant realise itself across the mirror. It is captivated by its own image and this moment of identification of the self vis-à-vis the adult other marks a turning point in its development, for it is the birth of the tricky problem of identity. Self-representation or interpretation becomes henceforth, frankly and critically speaking, narcissistic. At the same time, historical, cultural and political deposits flow into it, reflecting the *zeitgeist*. But if the autobiography is treated as a literary text, it must not be reduced to a footnote to social sciences which are by definition deductive, empirical studies. Further, an autobiographical discourse is full of paradoxes. In the story of his life *Beim Häuten der Zwiebel* (*Peeling the Onion*), in the year 2006, published by Günter Grass at the age of 78, which Grass prefers to define as the story of the becoming of an artist, memory is compared metaphorically to an onion whereby one can peel, one by one, the layered pages of life. But as a certain critic sarcastically remarked, with obvious reference to Grass's rather belated admission of his Nazi past, that it took Grass an inordinately long time (sixty years!) to peel his onion, this "peeling" or telling-all is not all that simple a process. After all, it is entirely up to the cook to decide how much and how finely he would like to peel the onion! For instance, certain images from the memory are enlarged whereas others are allowed to lie dormant, in deep freeze. This is linked with the human tendency to boast and the other side of it: shame and disgrace. Boasting in terms of highlighting and exaggerating one's successes may come easily to an author but how far can one be truthful in describing one's failures and painful details of life. Then there is the dialectics of remembering (what and how) and forgetting, both of which can be intentional rather than natural, selective rather than chronological. Going back and forth in time and space is also not a simple affair. The mystery of time has always fascinated poets, philosophers and painters. Marc Chagall often painted flying clocks with heavy, rocking pendulums. At times he painted clocks upside down. Salvador Dali's famous painting, *The Persistence of Memory* (1931) also called *Melting Clocks* or *Soft Watches*, depicts time not as a 'frozen' but a 'soft' entity. Ants eating away a clock becomes a surrealist metaphor for erosion or disintegration of time. The persistence and disintegration of the reservoir of memory go hand in hand, at one and the same time. Above all, perception, based on the individual author's mental universe, invariably plays tricks on the reception of reality. The German term for perception is *Wahrnehmung*, i.e., there is, indeed, an element of *Wahrheit* or truth in the perception. However, truth and perception of truth merge and submerge into each another, leading to a realignment of empirical reality. The "I" is all the time in a flux and it is also possible that in one and the same person there are more than one perceptions of the same object. In view of these contradictions, the autobiographical discourse evolves into a complex conceptual and formal totality where subject and object, truth and perception, reality and imagination, remembering and forgetting, reflection and the nuances of language freely intermingle and in the process, facts get transformed into artefacts. This distinctiveness of creative writing is what I would like to emphasize. For an author, 'to write' is an intransitive verb, says Roland Barthes. The creative author does not construe the 'word' as a means to an end but an ontological end in itself. The artist and the society, in linguistic terms the *parole* and the *langue*, in philosophical terms the microcosm and the macrocosm, interact and intersect, like a Being standing at a junction, but the artist, unique and solitary by nature, does not dissolve into the collective. S/he stands within and without the collective.

All the essays in the book focus on modern texts from the twentieth century and even very recent postmodern autobiographical texts although due cognizance is taken of the age-old European scholastic tradition of autobiographical writing from St. Augustine's *Confessiones* (AD 397-398), *Letters of Abélard and Héloïse* (1132-1140), Pope Pius the Second Enea Silvio Picolomini's *Commentarii* (1464) and *Family Books* of the mercantile class during the Renaissance period in Italy to the Romantic autobiographies of Rousseau, Wordsworth and Goethe, to cite but a few examples. After all, there are bound to be ideological inter-linkages between the past and the present. It is a fact that many ideas of modernity are not really products of modernity. They are received from the past and have been reworked to suit the contemporary world. The question is: Why has the (ancient or medieval) oriental autobiographical writing not found a voice in the book? There do exist famous narratives like *Babarnamah (Memoirs of Babar)* (1530) in Turkish by Babar, the founder of the Mughal Empire in India and *Bichitter Natak (Resplendent Play)* (1730-1732) by Guru Gobind Singh, rendered in verse in early Braj bhasha (today considered a regional dialect). But these examples are few and mostly in poetry form. Should we then conclude that there is no established oriental tradition of autobiography, that autobiography is not an indigenous oriental genre but a genre borrowed in modern times from the West, just like the genre of novel? The classical autobiographical genre based on introspection of the self and confession does, indeed, appear to be very Christian in letter and spirit. I would argue that the Orient has different autobiographical practices. Autobiographical material is not available in the Orient as clear-cut texts in prose but it is realised in forms like poetry, travelogues, letters or historical accounts. Lyrical poetry, particularly, has deep roots in the Orient and that is where the autobiographical urge finds its partial or full expression. This issue, however, needs to be explored in greater detail.

The participants of the three-day seminar on 'Autobiography' now have definitive texts to reflect upon. The readers may like to contest some of the theoretical positions proposed in the essays. It is not really my task to draw a balance sheet of the papers although I have attempted to give direction to the discussion around the definition and the scope of the genre of autobiography. Interesting propositions are propositions that make you think. The point is not to provide the right answers but to formulate the right questions. If these deliberations help the readers conceptualize and consolidate their own theoretical positions on autobiography as a genre and, in the larger context, literary or artistic discourse, as such, then this intellectual exercise was indeed one worth undertaking.

ARTICLES

Let me give a brief account of the papers included in the journal.

I

'In the beginning was the word', the spoken word, and thus we begin symbolically with an essay on oral narration. Alessandro Portelli's *Autobiography, Plural Authorship and the Death of the Author* illustrates situations where authorship and writing are disjointed, i.e. one person narrates and another writes. Termed as "as-told-to autobiographies", this is a method of data collection used by historians and folklorists for reconstructing history through oral narratives. This kind of cooperative writing has its own peculiarities. The power relationships between the narrator and the recorder, the narrator's modesty or arrogance, his spontaneity or shyness, recorder's mediation and censorship, the commercial interests and image-making in case of music and films, etc. are some of the motifs discussed. The focus of the essay is on slave/Afro-American narratives like *The Autobiography of Mother Jones*, *Coal Miner's Daughter* and *The Autobiography of Malcolm X*. It is not a coincidence that black autobiographies, aboriginal autobiographies and *dalit* (untouchables) autobiographies underline similar mechanisms of exploitation and dehumanisation. In fact, some noted scholars have termed casteism in India synonymous with racism in other parts of the world.

Abhai Maurya applies Propp's model to autobiographies by *dalits*. Propp collected Russian folktales and proved that many of them can be reduced to a single plot, because they are products of the same historical and economic period in the Russian history. Similarly, the *dalit* autobiographies have, despite some differences at the manifest level, identical structures at the immanent level because the historical and social conditions that produce these texts are more or less identical. Many of these autobiographies are maiden attempts by the then non-celebrities at writing, reflecting the first phase of *dalit* emancipation. Mulk Raj Anand's autobiographical novel in English, *Untouchable*, published way back in 1935, also deserves mention in this repertoire, for it was the first serious work in this field that drew national and international attention to the oppression of the *dalits* who are at the *nadir* of the Indian society. The author also makes intertextual comparisons between *dalit* literature and nineteenth century Russian literature (Chekov's *Vanka* and Pushkin's *Village*), underscoring his method of analysis where similar historical situations make comparisons across cultures possible. Suchitra Mathur's paper *De-Scribing the Indian Woman: New Autobiographical Ventures by Indian Women Writers in English* focusses on two autobiographies, Nayantara Sahgal's *Relationship: Extracts from a Correspondence* and Mrinal Pande's *Daughter's Daughter* respectively, which appeared on the Indian scene in the 1990s. These autobiographies move away, at least to some extent, from the earlier attempts of situating Indian women within the larger nation-building paradigm, treating instead life as a series of existential experiences. The "fourth wave" of the Indian feminist movement, in fact, questions both "nation" and "woman" as singular entities recognizing the diversity of women. There is a shift from documentation of suffering towards the more vexing search for identity and the realisation of one's being. By highlighting the predicaments and contradictions within the *dalit* and women's movements in the Indian context, the above two papers demonstrate that the pitfalls of such social movements are often the same.

II

Sharmistha Lahiri's *Family Lexicon of Natalia Ginzburg: Re-living Life in Words* is a chronicle of Ginzburg's Jewish family in the turbulent times under Mussoloni, but "should be read as if it were a novel". Ginzburg candidly confesses the discrepancy between the "experiencing self" and the "narrating self". So, the choice of the novel for the articulation of her world is deliberate as it gives her "the freedom to select and exclude". In any case, she accepts that one can reconstruct a life story only "partly". The novel draws structurally on the Italian tradition of maintaining Family Books in which family events were meticulously recorded during the period of Humanism and Renaissance, particularly amongst the mercantile class in Tuscany. It is indeed intriguing how particular words and expressions, values and myths, insignificant from the point of view of others, acquire a semiotic significance for a family as a unit, forming "lasting depositions" in the family memory or family lore. Ginzburg aptly states: "Any one of those phrases would have us recognize each other even inside a dark cave, among millions of persons."

Remo Ceserani's *Autobiographies of Contemporary Intellectuals: What to Make of Them* draws on the biting critique by a young turk, De Costro Rocha, of the "fashion" among university professors of literature, like Terry Eagleton and Edward Said, to pen down their autobiographies wherein they display "an excess of vanity". Despite their comfortable jobs in prestigious universities, these famous men of letters attempt to create an impression of exile. These postmodern autobiographies are mostly "entertainment", where the distinguished academics transform themselves into popular film stars or football players, or certain sections of their autobiographies loudly push and promote their political agendas. The paper also refers to some other autobiographies by contemporary intellectuals like Prof. of Italian Literature Alberto Asor Rosa, Prof. of Semiotics Ceasre Segre and the French-Hungarian-Jewish Prof. André Lorant. One wonders if this autobiographical itch among the learned professors has something to do with the impulse to write freely, at least once in life, without the burden of footnotes, and in the process elevate themselves from Barthean critics into authors!

Manfred Stassen's *Reflections on Christa Wolf's Post-Wall Autobiography "What's Left"* also reveals the hypocrisy of intellectuals. It revolves around the controversial musings of a German writer attempting to come to terms with her privileged life in the former East Germany and the heated debate that the book triggered on its publication in 1990. Does one understand this autobiographical narrative as the repentance of a collaborator (she has been discredited with names like the 'state poet'), a sort of *apologia pro vita sua*? Is she a victim of a totalitarian state or a turncoat or both, like "Stasi-amese twins"? In terms of intentions, comparisons have been drawn with St. Augustine's *Confessions* and Solshenytsin's *One Day in the Life of Ivan Denissovitch*. In the essay, Christa Wolf has been compared to the legendary Rosa Luxemburg, a martyr to the lost cause of socialism. The German title and its rendering into English have also been discussed. German history will continue to fascinate generations of scholars within and outside Germany. Margit Köves essay on Peter Esterházy's *Corrected Version* is a continuation of the issues raised in the previous paper on Christa Wolf: bad faith of artists and intellectuals in supporting dictatorships, police surveillance as a way of life in the Soviet-bloc countries, in this case Hungary and the question of guilt. Esterházy spends a year in the police archives, painstakingly copying and reconstructing every detail of his father's dubious role as a police informer. *Corrected Version*, structured as Errata of his novel, *Harmonia Caelestis*, is a son's confession of his father's double life, the *doppelgänger* motif. In the process of writing, outright denunciation similar to Kafka's *Letter to the Father* gradually turns into understanding, exoneration and finally reconciliation. It reveals oedipal anxiety in all its complexities, but the leitmotiv is that of the classical autobiographical genre where confession leads to healing. In the process, the aristocratic Esterházy family, condemned by previous leftist regimes as "class enemy", is rehabilitated in the post-1989 Hungarian society and that probably is the real correction.

Carmen Ulrich's *Mended Holes of Memory. The Meaning of Pictures in Elias Canetti's Autobiography* addresses some tricky questions in the genre of autobiography — the interplay of past and present, facts and fiction, selection and silence, authenticity and aesthetics, metonymy and metaphor and, last but not least, the personal and the collective. Canetti's childhood experiences of seeing, speaking and hearing coagulate as mental *Bilder* or pictures before he moves on to the next stage of observing, perceiving and reflecting. Some of these images get transformed, after a considerable period of churning, into words. Canetti's fascination with *Masse* or crowd (rather mob) instincts and death masks are some motifs specific to this massive three-volume autobiography in German of the Nobel laureate (1981) with a Jewish-Bulgarian background who lived in exile in London. The Jewish-German symbiosis has produced excellent writers and thinkers and despite everything, the Jewish love for the German language does not appear to have diminished. The main thrust of Dorethea Jecht's paper on the contemporary Austrian writer, Peter Handke, *At the Border of Autobiographical Writing: Peter Handke's Report of a Consciousness* is on the architectonics of his text *Das Gewicht der Welt (The Weight of the World)*. Perceptions in the form of gestures, thoughts and impressions, real or abstract, light or heavy, are recorded more as instant responses than ideas arrived at through solemn reflection and contemplation. The recordings are always short and crisp. Awkward moments are also recorded. It is entirely up to the author to decide what is worth recording. Dorethea categorises it as "Protocol of Consciousness", an autobiographical subgenre distinct from diary or aphoristic writing. Since Handke perceives the world through the medium of language, the moments of perception are invariably the "moments of language". Handke's entries have been compared to the eighteenth century German scientist, Lichtenberg's diary *Waste Books*.

Dirk Wiemann's essay on Bob Dylan's autobiography, *Chronicles: Volume One* (2004), takes us through the flamboyant and the rebellious sixties and seventies in which Dylan played a major role as a musician along with the Beatles. It is "the story of Dylan's exceptional career as a pop superstar" beginning with his change of name (but there is no reference to his conversion from Judaism to Christianity!), the first recording, his relation to his producers and fans, his ambivalent relation to folk music, so on and so forth. The various Dylans — a private person, a cult figure, an artist and a chronicler — produce a blend of multiple identities that disclose and conceal at one and the same time and, despite the game of hide-and-seek, the autobiography only deepens the legend of Dylan. The title itself mischievously suggests that more volumes are in the pipeline. The paper also discusses the genre of chronicles in the middle ages.

III

The contributions that follow focus on autobiographies in the absence of a traditional autobiography. So how does one go about extracting autobiographical strands from the works of a writer?

Romit Roy takes up this challenge in his paper as he sifts through Theodor Adorno's theoretical works, his language, his recurring themes and examples that inadvertently betray his existential universe. Roy uses the term "involuntary autobiographism". The article reconstructs with the help of this material (*Dialektik der Aufklärung*, *Amorbach*, *Minima Moralia*, *Philosophie der neuen Musik*, interviews, correspondence with Walter Benjamin and others) some moments and dilemmas in Adorno's turbulent life in Germany, in exile and finally in post-war Germany. Some of the questions discussed in the essay are: How do the personal and the subjective come together in theoretical formulations without undermining the objectivity of the object of enquiry? How does an essay on European music bear an inscription of the theoretician's personal life and how does this microcosm contain the macrocosm within itself? The next essay by Rosy Singh, *Kafka's Letters to Felice Bauer: A Lover's Discourse*, also proceeds theoretically on somewhat similar lines. The author attempts an insight into Kafka's world and universe through his letters. The postal romance or one can say the Prague-Berlin hotline shows that amorous relationships can survive world's grimmest historical upheavals. It also reveals the less known, romantic side of Kafka, otherwise the undisputed master of the Absurd and the Grotesque. The paper borrows its title from Roland Barthes' *Fragments d'un discours amoureux*. But how can you justify a peep into private letters that were never meant for publication in the first place, even if they are literary masterpieces?

Patrizia Raveggi's essay draws on Giorgio De Chirico's writings *Hebdomeros, Mr Dudron* and *Memories of My Life* and his self-portraits, 1945 in seventeenth century costumes. The self-portraits express clearly his rejection of the avantgarde surrealist and abstract art flourishing in France, of which he too had been initially an ardent supporter. The prodigal son returns to the classical Italian style like a victorious Roman Emperor! De Chirico's autobiographical texts from two different semiotic systems, writing and painting, give interesting insights into an artist's emotions, inspirations, visions and revelations that contribute to the enigma that is a work of art. For instance, has the enigmatic city of Turin any role to play in Nietzsche's mental breakdown? De Chirico's friends and foes, intellectual rivalries and the aesthetic debates in the post-World War II period are the other issues discussed in the essay. De Chirico's outbursts leave the reader wondering about the autobiographical intentions of this eccentric writer-painter. Are they to be interpreted as a *mea culpa* or "a great laugh"? Sanja Roić's *Autobiographical Paradox of Alberto Savinio* explores the world of De Chirico's younger brother, Andrea De Chirico, who adopted the pseudonym, Alberto Savinio. The change of name itself is a significant autobiographical gesture comparable to liberation or rebirth. The "I" in this case becomes all the more difficult to define. Alberto's *Tragedy of Childhood*, wherein his autobiography is "scattered" like "patches of fabric", gives priority to childhood. (It reminds us of Sartre's *Words*, which covers the first ten years of his life!) The shift from the first-person to the third-person protagonist is deliberate. An important aspect of the autobiographical research is exploring the words and their etymologies, as used by a writer, because this is an echo of his conceptual world. Savinio was also a writer-painter like his brother and some others of his generation.

Swantje Lichtenstein's *Lyrical Autobiography: Life, Death and Self in Lyrical Poetry of Heiner Müller and Thomas Kling* is broadly based on Paul de Man's theoretical framework. Müller's *Krieg ohne Schlacht. Leben in zwei Diktaturen*, *Herzkranzgefäss* and *Ich kaue die Krankenkost der Tod* revolve around the dialectics of life and death in terms of the dissected and diseased body. The lyrics describe the cold examination and diagnosis of the doctors using machines which are sophisticated, but not sophisticated enough to conquer death and the fear of death. Kling's lyrical texts like *Gesang von der Bronchoskopie* and *Inhalator* (2005) also reflect similar pathological motifs. Kling died of lung cancer in the same year and Müller died in 1995. Poetry thus becomes the site for *poetische Beichte* or poetic confession. These authors literally play out Barthes' notion of "the death of the author" by recording the trajectory of their fatal diseases. Of course, the last and final entry will always be missing but that is true of any autobiography.

Kathleen Kerr-Koch analyses in her essay *Autobiography as Critique: De Man and the Realists* Paul de Man's critique of autobiographical texts, with special reference to Rousseau's *Confessions*. Further, de Man makes the connection between the author and the text in the form of a comparative study of Saint-Preux's twenty-third letter to Julie in Rousseau's *La Nouvelle Heloise*, sections of Book VI of Wordsworth's *The Prelude* and Hölderlin's *Heimkunft*. From eighteenth century Romantic autobiographical texts, the essay moves to the strikingly different mode of presentation and aesthetics of post-colonial oral autobiographies like the slave narratives as also the controversial Nobel prize winning *testimonio I Figoberta Menchu: An Indian Woman in Guatemala*, 1983 (it is worth noting that this Nobel prize is for peace and not literature!) and Mahasweta Devi. The essay thus traces the changing forms of autobiography and the dilemmas associated with it.

Last but not least, Amy Wai-Sum Lee juxtaposes in her essay *The "I", "Tibuta" and the "Black Witch" in Maryse Condé's Postcolonial-Feminist-Fictional-Auto/Biographical Song,* the sister genres of biography and autobiography. Tibuta, a slave from the Carribeans in the seventeenth century and a survivor of the Salem witch trials, is the protagonist of a novel written in 1986 as a first-person narrative. There is, hence, a playful criss-crossing of the two apparently related yet conflicting ideas. Comparisons are drawn between Tibuta and Hester, the ostracized and humiliated heroine of *The Scarlet Letter.* The author has added her own autobiographical note to the essay by describing how for a teacher, particularly in Social Sciences and Humanities, the classroom is often the space for disclosing, consciously and sometimes through Freudian slips, the story of his/her own life.

On this autobiographical note that touches us all, I take leave of you.

ALESSANDRO PORTELLI

Autobiography, Plural Authorship and the Death of the Author

I begin with two points. First: In the preface to *Moll Flanders*, Daniel DeFoe points out that no one can write the entire story of one's life, unless one writes after one's death. Therefore, if autobiography means the self-written narrative of a life, it is by definition always unfinished – unless, ironically, it is written by someone else. In other words, unless it stops being *auto*biography and becomes something else.

This evokes the second point. According to Philippe Lejeune, we can speak of *autobiography* when the name of the author on the cover, the name of the narrator, and the name of the protagonist are the same.

The word auto\bio\graphy is a composite of three terms: self-authorship (*auto*), life (*bio*), and writing (*graphy*). I would like to speak of some hybrid types of life writing, in which *authorship* and *writing* are disjointed – in which one person narrates and another writes.

This disjunction is the result of another condition for the writing of autobiography. There is always an element of arrogance, of self-promotion, in speaking about oneself, and therefore the autobiographical act requires a legitimacy of some kind. This can derive either from the importance of the life, as in the case of the autobiographies of public figures, or in the mastery of writing, as in more literary autobiographies, or, as is the case of most successful autobiographies, both: an important life well told. Often, however, one of these conditions is lacking: a public figure may not have the ability or the time to write her own life; or a private person may not feel that his life is important enough to be told in public. When this occurs, the result is a fascinating artifact: a dialogic life narrative, in which the narrator and the protagonist are one person, the *writer* (as *scripteur*) another, and authorship is split and divided in a number of ways.

Briefly, I would like to comment on two genres of this dialogic life narratives: *as-told-to* autobiographies and oral history. In both cases we have a passage from the oral to the written; but the power and professional relationships are different. In the former case, a public figure *hires* a writer to compose the story of her life, while in oral history (as well as in classic slave narratives and Native American autobiographies), a scholar or journalist who has access to the public sphere *collects* the life story of a private person who might otherwise remain unknown.

I

Let us start with the less academically disreputable of the two modes: oral history and its predecessors.

There is no oral history before the encounter of two different subjects, one with a story to tell and the other with a history to reconstruct. We tend to forget, however, that the first person who speaks in an oral history interview is usually not the interviewee, but the interviewer.[1] In a very concrete sense, the source's narrative can be seen always as a response to the historian's initial question: "When were you born?", "Tell me about your life.", "Who was the union secretary at that time?"

By opening the conversation, the interviewer defines the roles and establishes the basis of narrative authority. In fact, although an oral autobiographical narrative may look on the surface very much like any other autobiographical *text*, it constitutes a very different autobiographical *act*. The basis of authority is different: autobiography (especially if written for publication) begins with a person's decision to write about herself or himself; but in the case of the interview the initiative is taken by the interviewer, from whom the legitimacy to speak is ostensibly derived. The right to speak, especially about oneself, is not automatically assumed, especially among the socially disadvantaged groups to which oral historians most frequently address themselves. In folklore, authority is derived mainly from tradition; in literary or historical autobiography, it is derived from the person's sense of her or his own importance or ability, which justifies the implicit breach of modesty. In oral history, however, the construction of legitimacy is more complex. Typical beginnings – "I have nothing to say", or even "What do you want me to say"[2] – may be coy manoeuvrings, but may also indicate that the narrator feels entitled to speak only because of a mandate from the interviewer: "I only speak because you ask me to." (And, often, "I will say what you want to hear.")

Thus, first-person narratives beginning with "I was born" belong in fact to very different genres, because they are the result of very different processes of authorisation.[3] When we compare Benjamin Franklin's "I have ever had a pleasure in obtaining any little anecdotes of my ancestors (. . .)" with Giuseppina Migliosi's "To begin with everything I know: my folks moved from Cesena to Terni," we cannot ignore that the former is a statesman and scientist who has spoken in public all his life (and coyly pretends to be writing a private letter to his son), while the other is ostensibly speaking, in her private parlour, only because her niece and a polite visitor have insisted that she do. When we take this aspect into account, then we recognize the importance of the fact that Franklin begins with "I", while Migliosi begins with "my family": the basis of legitimacy is different. Again:

> I was born in the city of Cork, Ireland, in 1830. My people were poor. For generations they had fought for Ireland's freedom. Many of my folks have died in that struggle.
>
> Let us begin with this business. Well, I was born in Terni. Son of a railroad man; son of a railroad man. And, I lost my father at the age of ten.

In the former example (an as-told-to autobiography), the great radical Irish-American unionist, Mary "Mother" Jones, boldly talks about herself because she feels that her long and brave life entitles her to do so. In the second example, as the deictic expression "this business" suggests, the anarchist factory worker, Riziero Manconi, is responding to an external stimulus, namely, my question:

> We would like you to tell us about your life; your personal and political development; what the environment in which you were born and grew up was like, then go on to your working life and your political activity.[4]

It is questions like these that set the agenda for the interview and begin to shape its form: the chronological order, the relevant themes (work, politics), the interaction of individual and society ("the environment in which you (. . .) grew up"). Of course, a political activist and class-conscious worker like Manconi would have spoken about these things anyway (he also talked about things I had not asked about, such as his literary efforts). But, and this is the point, if a different person had opened the conversation with a different question, he would have done so in different words and in a different order.

Both subjects bring to the interview an agenda of their own, which is constantly renegotiated in the course of the conversation. In the case of Giuseppina Migliosi, for instance, I did not want to hear her hospital story, but she felt that, history or not, it had to be told. Maggiorina Mattioli wanted to talk about her love story and I wanted to hear about anti-Fascism; and, once again, she was right. Of course, interviewees *will* talk about really irrelevant private matters. But we should listen and wait, before we judge: for the oral historian, an interview is always a learning experience.

Though oral history is relatively recent as a self-conscious historical and narrative practice, yet the question of collecting and publishing life narratives of subjects located at the margins of legitimate speech is centuries old. The first century of African American autobiography is almost entirely founded on transcribed oral narratives and co-authored texts. A wonderful image on the cover of William Andrews' *To Tell a Free Story* shows the white gentleman in top hat sitting down by a rustic fireside, pencil and notebook in hand, to take down the narration of a hatless black man with a blanket on his shoulders, while a black woman sits in the background with a baby in her arms.[5]

For a long time, literary critics and historians sought in vain to identify "the real authorial authority"[6] and recover the *authentic* unadulterated voice of the slave from the "spurious" presence of the person who enabled us to "hear" that "voice" in the first place.

Different texts, generated by different modes of production, however, have different types of reliability and respond to different scales of values. Rather than dismissing them because they do not comply with a standard of individual authorship and textual authority – increasingly questioned by post-structuralist criticism anyway – we would be better off if we took their dialogic mode of production, their *betweenness*, as the starting point for a different kind of analysis. This is what Arnold Krupat has suggested with regard to the autobiographies co-authored by Native American oral narrators and white editors and amanuenses, which he reads as "collaborative efforts" at "original bicultural composition". These texts, Krupat argues, are "the result not only of the confrontation of two individuals", but equally, in Frederic Jameson's words, the confrontation of two distinct social forms and modes of production (. . .) a collective as well as an individual encounter.[7]

Thus, in the photographs taken while Geronimo and Yellow Wolf were telling their lives in two classic "Native autobiographies," we see two subjects engaged in the creation of an autobiography, and between them the interpreter, the embodiment of Tedlock's *betweenness.* This, Krupat writes, is "the ground on which two cultures met," that is, "the textual equivalent of the frontier"; not a gala dinner, therefore, but an unequal, expansive *line* punctuated by war and genocide. As Krupat points out, the Native narrators in these texts are losers at war like Yellow Wolf or Black Elk, prisoners in captivity like Black Hawk or Geronimo.

Slave narratives are the result of another bicultural composition, the textual equivalent, perhaps, of something like miscegenation, an illicit encounter between black and white that is anathema to all those who have a stake in keeping the races, and their discourses, separate. Again, like the frontier, miscegenation is not an encounter between equals; likewise, the collaborative effort that produces early African American narratives is also rooted in inequality: the slaves are prisoners, and even free African Americans were second class citizens.

Yet, if we recognize hybridity as multiplicity and complexity rather than exorcising it as impurity and contamination, we discover a number of fascinating issues. When John Marrant and Reverend W. Aldridge compose their collaborative narrative, is it Marrant who is speaking *through* Aldridge, or is it Aldridge "writing" himself upon Marrant, using Marrant as material for a frustrated desire to write? Or was it both, the black servants and ex-captives and the white gentlemen, using each other in mutual, though unequal, exchange? And if so, who manipulates whom? How far do white editors tamper with the slaves' words, and how far do the black servants manipulate their narratees' expectations and credulity?

Therefore, rather than seeking an irretrievable authentic individual authorship, we might re-read these texts as the contested location of *another* type of authenticity, an authenticity of dialogue and strife, of an antagonistic cooperation that continuously re-articulates power relationships.

All three genres are about an encounter with otherness; in all three, otherness is represented by an oral expression that is incorporated in the space of writing, but also segregated, or removed, to a separate space of discourse. The gentleman and the backwoodsman, like the white editor and the black or Indian narrators, speak in the same *context* but not in the same *text;* they must be represented separately, speaking one *after* the other, one about *the other,* hardly ever *to* one another.[8]

II

Let us move on then to the other end of the range, a commercial as-told-to autobiography, *Coal Miner's Daughter*, by country and western singer, Loretta Lynn.

There is a scene in Robert Altman's *Nashville*, in which a singer with long wavy black hair steps on the stage at Opryland, sings a song and then, as the band starts vamping for the next number, breaks into a rambling speech, which soon turns into a loose reminiscence of childhood:

> I think there's a storm a-brewing. That's what my granddaddy used to say before he lost his hearin' and sometimes he'd say, "Oh gosh," or "Durn it," or "My word" (. . .) My granny, she'd go round the house clickin' her false teeth to the radio all day. She was a lot of fun, and always cooked my favorite roast beef and she was a sweetheart. She raised chickens, too. She, uh - in fact, did ya ever hear a chicken sound?[9]

This scene is a fictionalized account of the most famous crackup in country-music history: that of Loretta Lynn in the early '70s. An authorized version of the same episode appears in a later film, Michael Apted's *Coal Miner's Daughter*, based on Loretta Lynn's autobiographical book by the same title (the episode, however, is not discussed in the book). Both films concur in showing the breakdown as an eruption of private memories: a compulsive autobiographical act.

The book takes its title, in turn, from Loretta Lynn's best and most successful song, "Coal Miner's Daughter". The song appears at first hearing as another autobiographical act, containing many features of Lynn's later descriptions of her own life: the sentimental cliché ("We were poor but we had love"), the precise description of background details, the relish in the sound of vernacular speech. In her book, Lynn says:

> I'd always wanted to write a song about growing up, but I never believed anybody would care about it. One day I was sitting around the television studio at WSIX, waiting to rehearse a show (. . .) I went off to the dressing room and just wrote the first words that came into my head. It started: 'Well, I was borned a coal miner's daughter (. . .)', which was nothing but the truth.[10]

Loretta Lynn was indeed born a coal miner's daughter in the mid-Thirties in Western Kentucky; she barely learned to read and write, married at thirteen, followed her husband to Washington state, worked hard, lived poor, had four children by the time she was eighteen (was a grandmother at twenty-nine), and never thought of a career in music until she was twenty-four. Since then, she has moved to Nashville, had two twin daughters, and worked her way up to be the most successful female country singer and one of the most successful entertainers in the history of show business.

It was more than a year before Lynn and her entourage could bring themselves to issue "Coal Miner's Daughter" as a record. The time in which the song was "kept (. . .) in the can" seems like a metaphor for a repressed autobiographical urge. Lynn says that she did not think that people would be interested in a song about her life; in fact, the first important decision in autobiography is always accepting that one's life is worth telling in public. Once the song hit the charts, however, all doubts were removed, and the floodgates of autobiography were thrown open. In further songs, interviews, ceremonies, and finally in a book and a film, the story of the coal miner's daughter, the Washington housewife, the Nashville Opry star was told over and over, in a variety of media but with remarkable consistency.

Now, if we look at the front and back cover of a paperback edition of *Coal Miner's Daughter* (in this case, the 1977 Warner paperback), we find there one of the most concise statements of the nature of autobiography anywhere. The two pictures – the glamorous star on the front, the bucktoothed little girl on the back – are the same person, and yet two different people. The contrast shows the distinction between past and present selves, public and private lives, which creates the inner tension in the autobiographical genre; and it also underlies that this contrast takes place within what is, after all, one and the same person.

Structurally, this means that autobiography has much in common with metaphor. A metaphor is the discovery of similarity in a context of difference: "Achilles is a lion" makes sense as a metaphor precisely because Achilles is not a lion. Jean Starobinski has pointed out that one reason to write an autobiography is that there must have been a change, a dramatic development in the subject. I would stress the fact that the change is only significant because the subject remains the same. The difference between the narrating and the narrated self is worthy of our attention because these two selves happen to belong to the same person.

This is true also at another level. Autobiography is a public performance; but the storyteller is expected to reveal the private self in it. At one level, the autobiographer is supposed to abolish the difference between public and private self; at another, this act is only relevant inasmuch as the reader is constantly reminded that the two selves are logically distinct.

This double metaphorical structure is best expressed in the autobiographies of stars. Their success story enhances change, but they always strive to prove continuity and identity insisting that success has not changed them; they build an elaborate public image, but must persuade their fans that it also coincides with their private selves. Country music as a genre claims sincerity to a very high degree, linking it closely with autobiography: "A hillbilly is more sincere than most entertainers," Hank Williams used to say, "because a hillbilly was raised rougher." "When you're looking at me, you're looking at country," sings Loretta Lynn. In fact, the ideal country star must be born in a cabin and live in a mansion, like Loretta Lynn; and, as she does, must travel back and forth between them, at least in imagination. Most importantly, they are expected to live in a mansion as they would in a cabin. Stars must look dazzlingly glamorous on the stage, declaring distance; but must open their homes to visiting fans and tourists, stressing familiarity. No wonder autobiography is also a thematic staple in so many country songs.

In her book, Lynn presents herself as a regular housewife (an image doubled by her Crisco commercials), who has some problems with her husband but still understands and loves him, who hangs drapes and even worries about where the money for the children's braces is coming from. "When you're lookin' at me, you're lookin' at country," she sings; "I was Loretta Lynn, a mother and a wife and a daughter, who had feelings just like other women," she says (p. 151). And yet – if she were just another housewife, mother, and daughter, who would buy her book and see her movie? But then – *who* is she? As in most autobiographies, the answer is blowing somewhere along the continuum of past and present, public and private.

Let us begin with public and private. *Coal Miner's Daughter* opens in the bedroom; there's another bedroom scene two pages later, and early in the book Lynn describes her wedding night in detail. These, however, are not love scenes. In the opening episode, she has a nightmare and winds up bloodying her husband's nose with her wedding ring; the next thing she mentions is the gun her husband keeps on the night table. The wedding night scene, though ostensibly humorous, describes a rape: "He finally more or less had to rip off my panties. The rest of it was kind of a blur." (p. 78)

At one level, Lynn is grappling with inner dreams and deep-seated fears; at another, she is casting herself in the folksy role of the country girl whose mother never told her about the facts of life and who, "just like other women", had to find out the hard way. The autobiographical urge merges with the commercial image-making: Lynn takes her fans into her bedroom, but then resents the invasion and hides.

A similar contradiction occurs in the relationship between past and present. Being a coal miner's daughter is both an inner identity actively sought and a mask imposed by business associates and fans. Fidelity to roots is an authentic part of herself as well as a role imposed from outside. Thus, in order to play up continuity she is forced to repress the changes that make her what she is. She speaks dialect freely and spontaneously, but a critic has noticed that "from time to time, she will repeat a word which she has pronounced correctly, only to repeat it *incorrectly* (as *born* to *borned*), almost as though she were reminding herself."[11]

Thus, the same sets of signs designate truth and fiction, spontaneity and manipulation. Loretta Lynn does artificially what comes naturally – like speaking dialect – and does naturally what comes artificially – like wearing a mask.

III

One of my favourite quotes from Emily Dickinson goes like this: "When I state myself, as the Representative of the Verse, it does not mean me, but a supposed person." All the theory and practice of autobiography revolve around the meaning of the first person pronoun, "I". The question is: what does Loretta Lynn mean, to what exactly does she refer, when she uses that word?

Let us consider the songs first. When she sings "I was borned a coal miner's daughter," she is using the autobiographical first person; but when she sings "I'm a honky tonk girl," her first hit, she is using the fictional-lyrical first person of a popular song. These two meanings of "I" interact intensively in her work. Because she uses autobiography so much, many songs that are not about herself have been taken for autobiography: an exchange favoured by the fact that, in all her repertoire, Lynn consistently projects a character based very much upon herself, the spunky woman who does not question the system but won't take no nonsense from nobody – "Don't Come Home a-Drinkin' with Lovin' on Your Mind" because "Your Squaw's on the Warpath Tonight".

The interaction of autobiographical and fictional-lyrical "I" generates intermediate forms: first-person songs, written by herself, but not autobiographical; first-person songs, written by others, but based on aspects of her life. She wrote "The Pill", a song about contraceptives which was one of her most controversial hits, though she says she hardly ever used it herself (it would have been harder to write, and sell, a song about her husband's vasectomy, which she talks about in the book). On the other hand, "One's on the way" – a vivid description of a housewife with four kids, a careless husband, maybe twins on the way, the pot boiling over, and the doorbell ringing – is based on recollections of her early married life, but was written by Shel Silverstein. There is even another Shel Silverstein song, called "Hey, Loretta", in which Lynn sings to herself as if she were somebody else.

To further confuse matters, there is the problem of performance. Singers, like all oral performers, present even the most impersonal material through their body and their voice, thus making it intrinsically personal. Even when she performs someone else's songs, Lynn steps closer to an autobiographical act, although it might not be technically described as such.

In conclusion, there are at least four meanings of the word "I" as used in Lynn's repertoire and performances, going from the purely autobiographical to the purely fictional-lyrical, through at least two intermediate forms. Each of these forms shades or may turn into another, through the processes of performance and reception.

Much the same can be said about the book. A capsule definition of autobiography is based on the coincidence between the hero and the narrator inside the book's covers and the author outside: they all have the same name. But if we look at the cover of *Coal Miner's Daughter*, we see that the names on the cover are split: "by Loretta Lynn with George Vecsey". *Coal Miner's Daughter* is one of those "as told to" autobiographies in which famous people delegate the writing to a professional when they are too busy or unable to take care of it themselves. Although these books are billed as autobiographies, the person who says "I" in them is not the same person that does the actual writing. Loretta Lynn makes no pretence about it: George Vecsey is frequently mentioned in the text as "my writer", in the third person. In quite a postmodern fashion, Vecsey writes about himself in the third person, about somebody else in the first, and enters his own text as a character in someone else's story: while he writes his own name, he pretends that this is Loretta Lynn talking about him. One assumes that when the "I" character is different from the author, we are dealing with fiction. *Coal Miner's Daughter*, however, is supposed to be factually straight. The only fiction about it has to do with the uses of the first person.

With the film, we take another step. By definition, there can be no autobiographical film in the strict formal sense. When a book is turned into a film, the first consequence is the disappearance of the first-person narrator: films are always in the third person. In the movie *Coal Miner's Daughter* (whose credits are reproduced on the back cover of the paperback) the "author's" name on the cover is Michael Apted, filming a screenplay by Tom Rickman based on the book written by George Vecsey as told by Loretta Lynn. The face and voice on the screen belong to Sissy Spacek. Yet, the name is still Loretta Lynn: the film is clearly intended as a "true" statement, largely meant to "set the record straight" after *Nashville*. Many side characters in *Coal Miner's Daughter* actually play themselves, reinforcing the "documentary" overtones.

We come full circle when we turn to the paperback and discover that the film has been incorporated into the book. First of all, as we have already pointed out, the book displays the film credits, making it look as if the book was a novelisation of the film: the written autobiography is somehow validated by having been the subject of a fictional movie. In the second place, the images from the film are also included in the book.

In the book, indeed, Loretta Lynn tells her story not once, but three times: with words, with photographs from her family album and with stills from the movie. The two sets of photographs are almost interchangeable: the family album's captions, however, are in the first person, while those of the movie stills are in the third. But the pictures themselves are sometimes hard to tell apart. The picture of Loretta Lynn in her first stage outfit is so similar to the one of Sissy Spacek wearing the replica of it that they perform a sort of reversal of the autobiographical process: while the pictures on the cover portray two different people who are yet the same person, those two photographs inside portray one character who is in fact two different persons. It may not be irrelevant in the book's rhetorical structure, that the film stills come before the family album: it looks as though Loretta Lynn's photos were patterned after Sissy Spacek's. This, of course, has been the problem all along: which of the two, the image or the person, is the real one, which one comes first?

IV

I would like to end with a few comments on another as-told-to autobiography, which, however, ranks much higher that Loretta Lynn's in the historical and literary canon: *The Autobiography of Malcolm* X, written by Alex Haley.

When we speak of autobiography and the death of the author, we mean it as metaphor, but in the case of one of the great autobiographies of our time, the phrase must be taken literally: Malcolm X was killed before his autobiographical narrative to Alex Haley was completed, and was therefore unable to verify its finished form.

Like all dialogic narratives, the *Autobiography* is the result of a complex interaction, a negotiation between two subjects, with distinct agendas. On the one hand, Malcolm X states that he only trusts Alex Haley seventy-five percent; on the other, Haley learns to respect and admire Malcolm as a person. But he retains an integrationist agenda that is much less radical than Malcolm's, and that agenda, in many ways, shapes the text that was published after Malcolm's death.

These two agendas overlap and coincide mainly in the first chapters, which in fact Malcolm X was able to revise in manuscript before he was killed. Both he and Haley are interested in radicalising the story as a moral allegory. Malcolm accentuates his own degradation and marginalisation in order to further dramatize his redemption; Haley is interested in telling a fascinating story, a highly readable narrative. Thus, Malcolm claims that he was expelled from high school, but his unauthorized biographer Bruce Perry shows that he graduated regularly. Perry also casts doubts over Malcolm's version of his father's murder and the burning of their home. The most significant omission is the fact that Malcolm X had already visited Africa and Mecca in 1959, on behalf of Elijah Muhammad. His 1964 epiphany and conversion, then, are less sudden and dramatic than the *Autobiography* leads us to believe (another silence concerns a 1961 meeting with spokesmen for the Ku Klux Klan, in order to explore a common separatist agenda). Both Malcolm X and Alex Haley share an image of "manhood" that can serve as an icon for the black masses, which is why there is no mention in the book of Malcolm's possible homosexual experiences suggested by Perry.

In the final section, after Malcolm's break with the Nation of Islam, and in Haley's added epilogue, the two agendas part ways. These in fact, are the parts of the book that Malcolm was unable to see before he was killed. Haley tries to construct a less threatening, more acceptable Malcolm than he actually was. Of course, he cannot claim him as an integrationist: the final text of the book still retains Malcolm's insistence on the fact that black people need a separate organisation of their own. But Haley cancels out Malcolm's specific political and organisational agenda. As Manning Marable points out,

Haley expunged from the book no less than three chapters in which Malcolm outlined the vision of a broad black united front, from the Nation of Islam to the civil rights organisations.

Ultimately, Malcolm X was more concrete, more complicated, and less amenable than he appears in the book. Yes, even in its pages, he remains unpacified and militant to the end; here, rather than in details and silences, lies the authenticity of this narrative. If, as in Frederick Douglass or Rigoberta Menchú, biographic punctuality is at times sacrificed to the creation of the message and the icon, this finally results in a text and a symbol that have become essential to our sense of history and politics.

NOTES AND REFERENCES

1. I have always used the term "speaker" to refer to the interviewee, not the interviewer. See Ronald J. Grele, "History and the Languages of History in the Oral History Interview: Who Answers Whose Questions and Why?", in McMahan and Rogers, eds., *Interactive Oral History Interviewing,* (Hillsdale, New Jersey Hove: Lawrence Erlbaum Associates, 1994), pp. 1-17, and his afterword, *ibid.*, pp. 163-64.
2. Michael Palmer *et al.*, "'Haven't Anything to Say': Reflections of Self and Community in Collecting Oral Histories", in *International Annual of Oral History 1990*, ed. Ronald J. Grele (New York: Greenwood, 1990), pp. 167-90.
3. The distinction between self-authorisation and authorisation from others is especially important in the genre of slave narratives, some of which are taken down by white editors while others are written directly by the ex-slaves themselves. See John W. Blassingame, "Using the Testimony of Ex-Slaves: Approaches and Problems" and Robert B. Stepto, "I Rose and Found My Voice: Narration, Authentication, and Authorial Control in Four Slave Narratives", both in Charles T. Davis and Henry Louis Gates, Jr., eds., *The Slave's Narrative,* (Oxford: Oxford University Press, 1985), pp. 78-98 and 225-42.
4. *The Autobiography of Mother Jones,* (Chicago: Charles H. Kerr, 1972); Riziero Manconi, b. 1984, Terni, July 7, 1980.
5. Andrews credits the image to Charles H. Wesley, *In Freedom's Footsteps* (1967). The picture, incidentally, is also representative of gender issues in interviewing. Too often, I had a hard time persuading interviewees that I was as interested, or more interested, in the wife's narrative as in the husband's. In the case of Mrs. Cowans's interview, she only began to speak after her husband had spoken for about an hour. Thus, which way the interviewer faces (in this case, towards the man), and where the microphone is placed, are crucial issues in the creation and authoring of an interview.

6. James Olney's "'I was born': Slave Narratives, Their Status as Autobiography and as Literature", in *The Slave's Narrative,* p. 173, n. 14.
7. Arnold Krupat, *For Those Who Come After. A Study of Native American Autobiography,* (Berkeley: University of California Press, 1985), pp. 31-39. Krupat also writes: "Strictly speaking, therefore, Indian autobiography is a contradiction in terms. Indian autobiographies are collaborative efforts, jointly produced by some white who translates, transcribes, compiles, edits, interprets, polishes, and ultimately determines the form of the text in writing, and by an Indian who is its subject and whose life becomes the content of the 'autobiography' whose title may bear his name." (30).
8. This is apart from the few words that are necessary to get the encounter going. The only sentence addressed by the frame narrator to the folk character in Augustus B. Longstreet's *Georgia Scenes* (1850) begins with "Come back, you brute!" It is perhaps the verbal equivalent of the *native words* introduced in monologic anthropological texts as tokens of the contact between the anthropologist and the natives.
9. *Nashville*, screenplay by Joan Tewkesbury (New York: Bantam Books, 1976), no page numbers.
10. Loretta Lynn with George Vecsey, *Coal Miner's Daughter,* (New York: Warner Books, 1980), p. 201. All further quotations will be indicated in the text with page numbers.
11. Dorothy A. Horstman, "Loretta Lynn", in Bill C. Malone and Judith McCulloch, eds., *Stars of Country Music,* (Urbana: University of Illinois Press, 1975), p. 32.

ABHAI MAURYA

Autobiographies of *Dalit* Authors and the Question of *Dasha* and *Disha*

A whole multitude of definitions of the word *dalit* have been offered by *dalit* writers and thinkers themselves. In the words of Om Prakash Valmiki, one of the most eminent *dalit* writers in the field of Hindi literature, a *dalit* is:

> [one] who has been oppressed, suppressed, persecuted, exploited, humiliated, subjected to hate, trampled under feet and crushed, destroyed and deprived of the will to live and subjected to deprivation.[1]

Sohanpal Sumanakshar propounds that *dalits* are those "who have been deprived of human rights over the ages, who in the name of religion and *Manusmriti* have been forced by vested interests to accept false and barbaric values."[2] Sharan Kumar Limbale identifies *dalits* by the values and bondages to which they have been subjected:

> *Dalits* must reside outside the precincts of a village, their names are associated with ugly things and ominous phenomena, they must not accumulate any wealth, they are to rear only donkeys or dogs, they are to wear clothes made from coffin cloth only, they must not study or even read *Vedas* or learn Sanskrit (. . .)[3]

In my opinion, the most important element that condemns one to the category of *dalit* is birth in the caste of *Sûdras* — the untouchables, the last in the strict hierarchy of castes existing outside the pale of Indian civil society. This caste is treated as the riff-raff of Indian society and it is subjected to utter contempt and disgust coupled with ruthless economic and social exploitation. If born of untouchable parents, there is no end to one's miseries and sufferings in a society that is based on values bequeathed by the ancient Indian law book *Manusmriti*.

The literature created by members of the *dalit* community has come to be known as *dalit* literature. The emergence of *dalit* literature has thrown up numerous problems as well as challenges for mainstream Indian writing in terms of the theory and aesthetics of literature. A plethora of questions is being posed by the emerging *dalit* literature: Who is a *dalit* writer? What is *dalit chetna* (*dalit* consciousness)? Can a non-*dalit* writer, writing from the *dalit* perspective, be considered a *dalit* writer? What are the aesthetic principles of *dalit* literature? Can mainstream and *dalit* literatures co-exist?

Indeed, fierce discussions are still on as to what *dalit* literature is. A large number of *dalit* and non-*dalit* writers, scholars and thinkers have put forward their views, trying to define the character of *dalit* literature. In the words of Dinesh Ram, firstly, "the literature created by *dalits* themselves is *dalit* literature" and, secondly, "literature related to the life of *dalits* is *dalit* literature." Having discussed various aspects of the problem, Dinesh Ram lays down certain essential parameters of *dalit* literature:

> 1. *Dalit* literature is part of *dalit* movement (. . .) 2. *Dalit* literature can be created only by *dalits* and not by non-*dalits* (. . .) 3. (. . .) A *dalit* [writer] must be conscious of *dalit* identity (. . .) 4. Ambedkar and his thoughts must be the sources of inspiration for *dalit* literature.[4]

A number of Marathi thinkers like M.B. Chitnis, Baburao Bagul, Arjun Dangle and others have attempted to define the contours and content of *dalit* literature in quite pithy terms. Sohanlal Sumnakshar's views are outright militant:

> *Dalit* literature is a revolutionary literature which has been waging a pen war against discrimination between human beings, untouchability, hatred, humiliation, injustice, inequality, slavery, orthodoxy, ritualism, conservatism and *brahmanism*. It militates against the belief in rebirth, fatalism, god, sin and virtue and religion (. . .). It spurs on man towards development, welfare, faith in himself and introspection. So *dalit* literature is a collection of explosive thoughts which will lead the exploited people to a new life of emancipation, progress and development.[5]

Sharan Kumar Limbale affirms rather dramatically: "The *dalit* movement is a war and *dalit* literature is an epic [about it]."[6] On a more thoughtful note, Limbale asserts: "*Dalit* literature means artistic portrayal of sufferings, slavery, degeneration, poverty and mockery to which *dalits* have been subjected."[7] Om Prakash Valmiki is of the opinion:

> *Dalit* literature basically rejects conservative values. Born as it is out of struggle, it, naturally, has a sense of equality, freedom and brotherhood as its hallmarks and it opposes tooth and nail the system of *varna* and castes.[8]

While discussing the evolution of *dalit* literature, it may be recalled that even in the 14th and 15th centuries the caste system had come under criticism, although mild in nature, in the poetry of *sufi* and *bhakti* poets like Ravidas, Kabir and others. In early 20th century, stray voices of protests against the injustice could be heard, again rather spasmodically in the poetic form. For instance, in 1904 a hermit poet Swami Achhutanand Harihar writes:

> *Manusmriti* has been causing us immense hurt day after day,
> Instead of allowing us to rise it has been driving us down the gutter.

In 1914 a poem by an untouchable, Hira Dom, was published in the journal "Saraswati" in which the poet complains of the injustice perpetrated on the *sûdras*.

> The upper castes do not see our suffering,
> They do not hear our prayer. (. . .)

I

Vladimir Propp, an outstanding Soviet folklorist, published a monograph in 1928 under the title *Morphology of the Folktale* (*Wondertale*). Propp was of the view that the great diversity of Russian wonder tales "is reducible to one single plot, that the elements of this plot (thirty one in number) are always the same and always follow one another in the same order and, finally, that only seven different characters should be taken into consideration."[9]

Let us follow Propp's method to analyse *dalit* autobiographies. In modern times, the *dalit dasha* (material and existential condition) finds expression, first of all, in the autobiographies written by several *dalit*s. Indeed it is in the autobiographies of *dalits* that we should see the first sprouts of *dalit* literature. These works, in most cases, are the real life stories of the authors. The first and foremost unit of *dalit* autobiography is manifested in their very titles, laden as they are with metaphors: *Achhhoot* (*Untouchable*) by the Marathi writer Daya Pawar, *Uchakka* (*The Thief*) by Laxman Gayakwad, *Chora Kolhati ka* (*The Youth of Kolhati*) by Kishor Shantabai Kale, *Akkarmashi* (*The Bastard*) by Sharan Kumar Limbale (all in Marathi, also translated into Hindi) and *Joothan* (*Leftover Crumbs*) by Om Prakash Valmiki, *Trishkrit* (*The Insulted and Humiliated*) by Suraj Pal Chauhan, *Apne-apne pinjre* (*The Cages of Different People*) by Mohan Das Nemisharai, *Dohra abhishap* (*The Double Curse*) by Kaushalya Vaisantri (all in Hindi), *Santapt* (*Persecuted*), a kind of second volume by Suraj Pal Chauhan, *Changya rukh* (*A Pruned Tree*) by Balbir Madhopuri and others.

The second unit in the morphology of *dalit* autobiographies is that the *dalit* writer had absolutely no prior claim to fame or eminence which, in most other cases, lends legitimacy to the autobiographies. In the context of the *dalit*s, autobiographies turned out to be the maiden attempts of their authors at writing anything at all in their life. Indeed, before publishing their autobiographies, most of these authors had been unknown persons, not only in literary circles but also in their own social milieu. It is only after the publication of the autobiographies that they began to be recognised as persons of some name and fame.

The third unit in the morphology of *dalit* autobiographies is the strong desire to document the suffering. Their experiences were vividly engraved in their memory as if their whole being had become branded. *Dalit*s took to this genre because it was the perfect literary space for highlighting their plight. It gave them confidence and strength to tell their experiences without any inhibition in the form of autobiographies. Indeed, autobiographies gave space to their heart-rending cries. These cries were not aimed at evoking pity, but they were voices of protest aimed at arousing a sense of dignity among the *dalit*s, thereby generating waves of *dalit* consciousness and identity. At the same time, the autobiographies became stepping stones for the *dalit* authors for launching themselves as writers in the field of *dalit* literature. Most *dalit* autobiographers attained the stature of well-known writers, authors of stories, novels and poetry only after they had first tried their hand at autobiographies.

Fourthly, it seems to us that the canvas of *dalit* literature is identical across the country in its basic elements or aspects. The diversity exists due to minor differences in the names of castes, modes of life or customs determined by climatic or geographical differences in different parts of India. By way of example, one could mention the *Mahar* caste which is not found in North India. In Maharashtra, the members of this community used to dispose off dead animals, a job carried out by *Chamars* in North India. Similarly, sweeping and scavenging are usually carried out by *Bhangis or Chuhras* in North India. However, when it comes to the hardships and sufferings that the *dalit*s have been subjected to all over the country, we discern a striking commonality. Firstly, most *dalit*s faced immense hardships in meeting the three basic needs, pragmatically called *roti, kapra aur makan* (food, clothing and shelter). In most autobiographies there is a graphic description of the difficulties faced by the *dalit*s in procuring these three basic needs at a minimal level.

The next important element in the morphology of *dalit* biographies is the double or triple exploitation and subjugation of *dalit* women which I shall highlight in the next part of my paper. Apart from this, it is the social position of *dalit*s that should cause consternation in a sensitive mind: the struggle for basic education, the open humiliation and discrimination as well as the subtle forms of discrimination in the society. Most autobiographers address these concerns in great detail in their autobiographies. However, one can also discern striking differences in the treatment of the issues at hand by different authors. We shall dwell at some length on a whole range of these and other issues addressed by individual writers.

The last unit in the morphology of *dalit* autobiographies is discernible in the fact that in these works most authors describe their experiences at rather youthful stages of their lives.

II

The description of indignities heaped on the *dalit*s is terrifying. Each writer describes the shabby, tottering and dilapidated make-shift shelters (huts, etc.) that saved them neither from sun, nor from rain, nor from cold. *Sûdras*, the forefathers of modern day *dalits*, were forced to carve out some godforsaken corner outside the precincts of their villages according to the dictates of the *Manusmriti*. The autobiographies of *dalit* writers situate these places near the garbage heaps, invariably home to creatures like pigs, dogs, mosquitoes and flies. *Dalit*s are still not allowed to draw water from village wells monopolised by upper caste villagers. They are forced to take water from dirty and muddy ponds where buffaloes owned by the upper castes float around, defecating and urinating in the pond waters. Most authors describe how they and their families had hardly anything to cover their bare bodies with. Be it rainy, summer or winter seasons, they had to always go around bare-footed in tattered dirty rags.

The most traumatic episodes in these autobiographies are those in which authors describe how they starved most of the times or what they ate by way of food. Indeed, the title *Joothan* (*Leftover Crumbs*) of the autobiography written by Om Prakash Valmiki refers to the tragedy of the *dalit*s who were perpetually on the verge of starvation. Valmiki, for instance, narrates that his mother, sister and other female relatives worked as scavengers in the cattle sheds of *brahmana* families:

> In the shed of every *taga* (a *brahman*), there generally used to be 10 to 15 cattle (cows, buffaloes and oxen). The dung of these cattle had to be removed to a garbage heap that was situated far away outside the village (. . .) During the night, the dung and the urine would spread everywhere in the shed, over the dry sugarcane leaves or hay, which used to be changed only once in fifteen days. The mixture of dung and urine extracted from underneath the rotten leaves and hay would stink so badly that the scavengers would feel dizzy.[10]

But what does the author's mother get in return for such a cumbersome dirty job? Only 12-13 kilograms of grain for the whole year! Sometimes they would get crumbs of stale bread left in the plates of the *brahmana*s after they had eaten their food (termed *joothan* by the author). Similar *joothan* they would get after the feasts of marriage parties in lieu of the entire cleaning and scavenging work done by the author's family on such occasions. On top of this, all kinds of insults and abuses used to be heaped on the author's mother while the *brahmana*s and other upper caste members gave the *joothan* to her.

Almost all the authors describe how they survived by eating the oddest things like the tree bark and grass. Kanwal Bharati in his book, *Role of Dalit Discourse,* writes about the condition of *dalit*s in the villages of Uttar Pradesh, the biggest state in North India. In this state, upper castes would give *gobraha* (grains extracted from cow or buffalo dung), to the untouchables for the work they did on their farms and houses. The untouchables would wash the dung and extract grains and then grind them and make bread from it. Limbale, in his autobiography, *Akkarmashi* (*The Bastard*), describes how once he tasted bread made of such grains:

> They [*roti*/bread] were freshly baked. [My grandmother] had already served us the bread made from normal flour. But she herself was eating bread made from grains extracted from dung (. . .) She would never give that bread to me. Once I fought hard and snatched a crumb from her. I put the crumb into my mouth and tried to chew it. Oh my God! The bread had the taste and the stink of cow dung![11]

Starving *dalit*s in villages often had to eat meat of dead animals at the risk of catching deadly diseases. So much for the most essential human needs of life, i.e., food, clothing and shelter!

What about their social life: the life in school, at their work places, in social gatherings? All the authors narrate horror stories about the journey of their life in Hindu society. When the authors went to school (that too by some odd quirk of fate), they were constantly taunted by the upper caste schoolmates, teachers and village *kulak*s. They were invariably made to sit away from other school children, near the shoes of schoolboys or near the doors of the classrooms. They were subjected to all kinds of abuse by upper caste teachers. The authors portray how at each step they had to face caste discrimination and persecution. In cities they often survived by concealing their actual castes. Valmiki narrates that he had become very friendly with a *brahmana* family while staying in a hostel in Bombay. The young girl, Savita, was in love with the author, notwithstanding his reticence about the relationship because of his caste. But when the girl made decisive advances towards the author, he revealed his caste lest he should be accused of deceiving her. The girl was, at first, bewildered and refused to believe him. On his insistence, she began crying inconsolably and left him for good, directing him not to tell her parents about his caste as it would hurt them immensely.

She, of course, was least concerned how deeply the author was hurt by her reaction. Valmiki encounters many such humiliating situations. He laments: "One could sustain oneself through poverty, but it is not easy to liberate oneself from the stigma of caste." Or: "One may get rid of one's community, but not caste till the very end of one's life."[12] One of the dreams of Valmiki's father was that his son should be able to get rid of the stigma of caste. The dream remains unrealised till date.

To return to the theme of *dalit* women: Women and young girls are often raped by upper caste goons and landlords with impunity, particularly in villages. Sharan Kumar Limbale writes in his *Akkarmashi*:

> Thanks to the power accruing due to the higher *varna* and the wealth passing from generation to generation, the members of upper castes, particularly landlords and village chieftains, have always been exploiting *dalit* women working on their fields. They have been using them as their mistresses, turning them ultimately into prostitutes. Innocent *dalit* girls become victims of their lust more often than not (. . .) Bastard children are often born from this exploitation (. . .)[13]

The description almost resembles what Russian poet Pushkin had written in his poem "Village" way back in 1819:

> Here young girls ripen
> For the lust of heartless tyrants. [my translation]

Sharan Kumar Limbale, indeed, describes the contents of his autobiography bitterly:

> The powerful people of upper castes have always perpetrated barbarities on the helpless women. They have the backing of wealth, society, culture and religion. But what will happen to that woman? She has to carry this rape in her womb. She had to give birth to this rape, she had to rear it. And then this rape begins to live a life. The pain of that very life forms the content of this autobiography.[14]

The consequences of this rape beginning to live a life have been disastrous for the author, as he had to live through this stigma all his life, carrying it like a millstone around his neck. Because of this blot nobody was ready to give him a girl in marriage. The author often finds himself asking the questions: "How many eyes must have looked upon her [his mother] as a prostitute? (. . .) What is my surname?"[15] Indeed, the author had to face immense embarrassment when he was being admitted to school and the teacher asked his father's name. Limbale is extremely bitter about the situation that is not of his own making. He writes:

> The life which I have lived is undoubtedly terrible (. . .) I am a shattered man as I have no village, no language, no mother, no caste, no religion. Due to my personality being amorphous, my existence has always been stigmatised as that of a bastard. (. . .) my identity has been raped. My life is like that of a raped woman. The social institutions have treated me like a criminal.[16]

Daya Pawar's autobiography, *The Untouchable*, displays in places flashes of adventure. His vivid description of the plight of *dalit* women, their maltreatment by their men folk, his extremely painful struggle for education, his escape to the city of Bombay and hardships faced there owing to his being a *dalit* and so on is quite powerful. Moreover, description of intra-*dalit* schism, i.e., casteism being practised by the community of *chamars* vis-à-vis the *mahars* is bewildering: "But the *chamars* never drank water of our well. They consider the water from the *mahar* well untouchable."[17] The author laments that even the communists, who should have been the natural friends and well-wishers of *dalits*, did not respond adequately to the plight of *dalit* community in Maharashtra.

However, throughout the book Daya Pawar remains inhibited, rather overawed, by the formidable adversities thrown up by his low social status as a *dalit*. He is forced to make compromises on numerous occasions in social, political and even personal domains. He neither tilts towards the left nor to the right. As if the striker of his pendulum got stuck in the middle! He indeed becomes what in *Mahabharata* has been described as *Trishanku*, i.e., somebody whose fate hangs in balance. Coming from the caste of *mahar*s in Maharashtra, he could neither remain a Hindu nor could he convert into a Buddhist. The quintessence of his personality we see after his wife, Sai, leaves him for good. He is an impotent, useless and insignificant man or non-man.

Needless to say, *dalit* cause cannot be served by such protagonists. He willingly performs all the Hindu rituals in marriages and child's name-giving. He seems helpless even to help himself. Clearly Daya as a *dalit* character cannot be termed a role model for *dalit* aesthetics. His life may be a bitter truth, an unmitigated reality. But he should have been able to get rid of the fetters chaining him and taken flight to romantic heights, i.e., towards the final liberation of the community. Daya in *The Untouchable* is an object of *daya*, i.e., pity and not someone who could lead the struggle for liberating his society from the age-old scourge.

Suraj Pal Chauhan also portrays in his autobiography, *Tirashkrit* (*Insulted and Humiliated*), the common elements mentioned above in the life of *dalit*s. In initial stages of his life, he flirts with the right-wing *manuvadi* political forces. He attends the meetings and conferences organised by the writers' wing of the *sangh parivar*. But on seeing the *parivar* from close quarters, Chauhan distances himself from it. At one stage he says:

> Today everybody has suddenly become aware of existence of *dalit*s. Till yesterday most upper caste Hindus considered *dalit*s as mean and untouchable creatures. Upper caste people and their forefathers have been treating *dalits* worse than animals. They were not allowed to enter temples. But today they feign as if *dalits* are their brothers and sisters. This has happened because the upper caste people have realised that they cannot rule the country without the votes of *dalits*. Is it not a big fraud used for perpetuating the rule of the upper castes?[18]

Ultimately Chauhan is forced to say:

> After having understood their [*Sangh Parivar*] ideology I almost began to hate myself. I was thinking, 'I am a *dalit* and in my writings I have been busy trying to win over the patronage of the upper castes which I shall never get'."[19]

Chauhan, like Daya Pawar, gives a vivid description of casteism rampant among the *dalit*s themselves. The people belonging to the caste of *chamar*s or *jatava*s are shown to be practising untouchability vis-à-vis *chuhra*s or *bhangi*s. Another widespread malady is the over-ambition of the *dalit* youth who, it seems, is in a desperate hurry to cast off his caste and cross over to the higher castes, severing all ties with his own community. In Chauhan's autobiography, his nephew Jai Prakash, for example, suffers from inferiority complex because of his *dalit* background. He tries to speak only in English as he believes that English is the language of the upper castes. He tries his level best to hide the fact that his father is a *Safai-karamchari* and that his mother is a dark-complexioned and an illiterate woman. In his desperation to rid himself of the stigma of his caste, he betrays even his uncle, i.e., the author Surajpal Chauhan and destroys, in the process, his family and its reputation.

Surajpal Chauhan also describes the predicament of the *dalit*s, who have managed to study and get white collar jobs thanks to the government policy of reservation. He describes graphically how he faces subtle discrimination in his place of work and detects a hidden revulsion for him amongst his upper caste colleagues and superiors. However, when it comes to the question of ultimate liberation of the Chauhan community, he too is at a loss to provide answers.

In the next volume of his autobiography, *Santapt*[20] (*The Persecuted and Tormented*), Chauhan seems to have fallen prey to the ravages of market economy. Firstly, there was no need for him to have written the second part of his biography, because in this volume he does not give, rather he could not have given, any qualitatively new dimension to what has already been conveyed by him in *Trishkrit.* It would have been better if he had fictionalised in the form of a novel or a long story the bizarre things that he has narrated in the form of an autobiography. In *Santapt* he has filled in some of the gaps that might have remained in his first volume, *Trishkrit.* But in *Santapt* not only do many episodes border on pornography, but also they do not fit in the framework of *dalit* issues. It is quite possible that he was ill-advised by his publishers to stuff this volume with sexually explicit scenes so that it would sell like hot cakes. Suraj Badattya has correctly concluded, "There are several episodes which have been forcibly stuffed into the book [*Santapt*]. They have been included in the book with a view to make it more interesting [read 'hot' – Abhai Maurya]. The author should have avoided it."[21]

Descriptions of *dalit* women, loose in their sexual behaviour, or the author's father, nephew and wife appearing almost as sex maniacs would not win any laurels for the *dalit* community. Indeed, *manuvadi* forces must have got a golden opportunity to laugh their hearts out exclaiming: 'See, how dirty, mean and vulgar these so-called *dalit*s are! They deserve what they have been getting for centuries!'

Packing his accounts in *Santapt* with details from his personal life should certainly lead to a barrage of questions: How do family problems of the author become part of *dalit* discourse? Why should one wash one's dirty linen in public? Does it not show lack of discretion on the part of the author?

It is incomprehensible why the author of *Santapt* chose to indulge in a reckless character assassination of several *dalit* writers and thinkers with unsubstantiated and wild allegations – Om Prakash Valmiki, Tej Singh, Sheoraj Singh Bechain, Vimal Thorat – all are at the receiving end. Even the well known *ajatshatru* kind of a *dalit* story writer, Ajay Navaria, is shown presenting a bouquet of flowers to the mercurial Dharamvir which in fact is loaded with a not so innocuous concomitant message. Only Dharamvir and Tulsi Ram have been spared. This unnecessarily brings out into the open the schism prevailing in the ranks of *dalit* writers, which could hardly serve the *dalit* cause. Moreover, this is likely to unleash accusations and counter-accusations from the aggrieved targets of the vilification campaign. In short, *Santapt* is ill-equipped to serve the *dalit* cause in any tangible manner. In a way the 'autobiography' will certainly fall outside the ambit of the morphology of *dalit* autobiographies.

Lakshman Gayakward in his autobiography, *The Thief*, tells us that he comes from the caste of *Uthaigir,* i.e., a shoplifter or a thief. In Telegu the name of the caste is *santamuchar,* which literally means a thief. In the revenue records this caste was declared a criminal caste by the British. The stigma hangs even today on the name of this community. Nobody is prepared to give them work because of the label of a 'criminal caste'. As a result, the members of the community are forced to become thieves. Gayakward describes how he suffered merciless thrashing at the hands of all his family members right from his childhood. The intention was to prepare him for a situation when he might be caught by the police. His training was meant to help him through the tough interrogation so that he does not crack and reveal the names of other members of the gang. He saw with his own eyes the other members of his family being beaten brutally by the police, so much so that he would often urinate in his knickers.

Describing the frequent stints of starvation, Gayakward tells us that in such situations he and members of his family survived by eating roasted rats, frogs, dogs, bark and leaves of trees or other such things. Children of this community were often sold and purchased for paltry sums of money.

There is a moving description of how he is sent to school and how this non-descript event kicks up a huge scandal within his community which objects that sending a child to school goes against their traditions and customs. The matter comes to a head and it is discussed in the community *panchayat* at the end of which a fiat is imposed on Lakshman's parents to the effect that either his family should immediately withdraw Lakshman from the school or face the wrath of the community in the form of total social boycott of his entire family.

Lakshman somehow manages to continue with the school but he has neither proper dress nor food which he could eat during the lunch recess. He has to go hungry while his classmates were having food from their tiffin boxes. Lakshman describes his situation in the school in the following words:

> All the boys of his class would open their tiffins. I would sit in a corner in the class and cover my face with a book pretending to read. But I suffered bouts of pain because of my empty stomach. It was impossible to read the book (. . .), my classmates, understanding my situation would not come near me. They would avoid my gaze and eat with their back turned on me thinking that if I, by chance, saw them eating, they would have stomach ache. This they would say loud enough to be clearly audible to me. My friend Ankush would collect the leftover crumbs from my classmates and then bring them to me so that I could pacify my hunger.[22]

Gayakward describes his plight in a very touching manner which could be compared with the little boy Vanka in A.P. Chekhov's story of the same name, writing a letter to his address-less grandfather about his miserable plight as a babysitter in a rich trader's house. Gayakward writes this naive letter to Indira Gandhi in the following words: "Dear *mataji*, I am writing this letter to you. Please forgive me if I make any mistakes (. . .)" He further writes:

Something should be done for the poor people. They should be given some clothes to cover their body with. Probably that is why Mahatma Gandhi did not wear a shirt. When will Mahatma Gandhi's dream be realised? Please, see to it that the poor people got at least two square meals a day." Then Lakshman writes the address: 'Shrimati Indira Gandhi, the Prime Minister of India'.

This irresistibly reminds us of Chekhov's Vanka writing the address of his grandfather: "To grandpa's village".[23]

Gayakward repeats the refrain of other *dalit* auto-biographers that they had to carry the stigma of their caste like a mill-stone hanging from their neck. People do not let them forget the name of castes even when the *dalit*s try very hard to do so. Gayakward's account of his life reveals the shocking fact that the members of the community of *dalit*s were mired in complete darkness and they had been performing the rituals and customs of Hindu religion much more devoutly than the upper-caste Hindus themselves. Probably due to the deeply inbred ignorance, they would resort to sacrifice of animals and even children in order to satisfy the whims and fancies of the gods that be.

Going through the excruciating journey of poverty and deprivation, Lakshman ultimately manages to become a worker in a textile mill. His brother ends up as a thief and a beggar. Due to his ignorance, Lakshman is often hijacked by opportunist trade union leaders or fanatic Hindu zealots. They would succeed easily in their design of using Lakshman to further their ulterior motives.

Lakshman describes the miserable life of workers of the mill who are exploited by the mill owners no end. Here he comes in contact with a local communist lawyer who indeed becomes his saviour. As a result of his interaction, many cobwebs are removed from his thinking. In the Marxist philosophy Lakshman sees a ray of hope for the ultimate liberation of his community. But, unfortunately, the Marxists are not able to deliver immediate results and relief to the suffering community of untouchables, which is why Lakshman, once he becomes a *dalit* activist, is easily hijacked by the casteist *dalit*s who put him up as their candidate for election to the state assembly. But even this flirtation with so-called *dalit* leaders does not bring him the desired succour. Lakshman is hounded out of his job and he has to work as a tea-stall vendor, a hawker, a petty contractor and what not. He gives a vivid portrayal of all kinds of exploitation that are rampant in these professions. He describes the thievery resorted to by police, the notorious system of fixed percentages taken as bribe in the world of contractors and that of the *babudom*.

Like other *dalit* writers, Gayakward also does not see any light beyond the tunnel for his accursed community. At the end of the day he is still clueless about the path of *dalit* emancipation, hoping for the dawn of a brighter future to break out some day on its own.

III

One comes across a recurrent refrain in all the autobiographies of *dalit* authors that they may be able to escape poverty by getting jobs with the help of the policy of job reservation in the government sector. But one is constrained to note that most *dalit* authors are painfully conscious that they would still never be free from the stigma of their caste. They face it at every step of their life. For example, they cannot get a house on rent, they are discriminated at the place of work by upper caste members, their children are mocked at in schools and they face undeclared social boycott universally. The scourge let loose by *Manusmriti* two thousand years ago continues to haunt them till date.

Sharan Kumar Limbale has aptly stated: "The story of *dalit*s is a story of suffering."[24] This hard-hitting phrase is loaded with an important message that the *dalit* autobiographies have adequately dealt with while negotiating the *dalit dasha* in Indian society. The autobiographies discussed above more than substantiate this conclusion. More importantly, the autobiographies have succeeded in accomplishing the uphill task of bringing the *dalit* problem into a very sharp focus of public attention not only in India but the world over. But here, the Marxian dictum inexorably comes to mind, to the effect that philosophers have explained the world enough, the question is how to change it.

The autobiographies discussed above should invariably lead to the conclusion that the situation in which the Indian *dalit*s have been languishing hitherto cannot be allowed to continue any longer. The circumstances that give birth to the phenomenon of *dalit*ness have to be eliminated lock, stock, and barrel. The socio-political system, the social customs and practices must change radically for "annihilating" the scourge of casteism in the Indian society. Thus the question, as Marx put it, is that of eliminating the root cause sustaining this disease for more than two millennia. Hence the question arises as to what is the path that could lead to the total emancipation of *dalit*s, to their liberation from the age old curse of *jativad* (casteism)? What should be the *disha* (direction) of the *dalit* liberation movement in days to come?

It is true that the *dalit* autobiographies have neither tried nor provided any answers to this vexed question. Probably, this was neither expected of them nor was it possible for them at the very outset of the first words of *dalit vani* uttered through the autobiographies. But now many *dalit* scholars are of the opinion that the tasks of first phase of the movement stand accomplished and the second phase of *dalit* movement has set in. It is now the right time to address the question of *disha.* But what are the tasks that the *dalit* thinkers claim to have achieved with the *dalit* movement till now? Here opinions differ. Om Prakash Valmiki is of the view that the first tasks were the eradication of inhuman practices like *joothan* (*dalit*s' eating crumbs of food left by upper castes), *salaam* (newly married *dalit* couples paying obeisance to upper caste families by visiting their homes), disposal of dead animals, as well as giving up religious rituals and witchcraft, fatalism and blind faith in God. In Valmiki's opinion, all these tasks could have been accomplished completely through the spread of education among the *dalit* community. But by now even Valmiki must be convinced that despite the significant increase in the number of educated or literate *dalit*s, the eradication of casteism in its entirety in India is nowhere in sight. If anything, the vision of *dalit* liberation stands much more blurred today than it had been in earlier times.

There are other *dalit* thinkers and authors who have come to rather bizarre conclusions about the first phase of *dalit* movement. For instance, Dharamvir in his very slim volume published recently under the sensational title *Who is the Author of Joothan?* has made stunning observations:

> I am overjoyed. We accomplished two tasks for achieving this [happiness]. Firstly, we introduced the people to the name and deeds of Babasaheb Ambedkar. Secondly, we rescued *dalit* thinkers and scholars who were under the sway of Marxism and democratisation and restored them to their roots.[25]

It seems there is a set of *dalit* thinkers which has launched itself on an unbridled splurge of sensationalism, probably with a view to stealing the limelight at all costs. Firstly, Dharamvir and his ilk do not explain why Marxism has been detrimental to the *dalit* cause. Secondly, what are the roots of *dalit*s to which they are claiming to have restored the *dalit* thinkers 'redeemed' from Marxism. The roots of *dalit*s, it should be as clear as day light, lie in the system of casteism. Does it not follow from here that Dharamvir is dragging the *dalit* community into the mire of casteism in the name of so-called *dalit* identity? No wonder they have been openly eulogising *jatavavad, chamarvad* and so on, both by word of mouth and words in black and white. The logical journey from here would be looking down upon the *dalits* of other castes like *mahar*s, *khatik*s, *bhangi*s and others. Will it not sow seeds of discord among the *dalit* ranks with an enormous concomitant loss to the *dalit* cause? All this is obviously happening; it is there for all to see. But Dharamvir and his ilk care two hoots for it. Why should they? They are already 'librated', wallowing as they are in the most comfortable cushions of the new princely caste of Indian Administrative Service (IAS) and their upper class fringes in the soothing shadow of the *bahubali parivar* which has plenty to spare for anyone ready to serve them. For the scholars of this brand, the *dalit* cause has become a way of their personal ego messaging, aggrandisement and staying in the limelight.

What baffles one is that in the pursuit of one-upmanship, for *dalit* thinkers like Dharamvir and Co., no holds are barred in their campaign of demolishing *dalit* scholars, writers and thinkers who fail to toe their line. For instance, in the above cited volume *Joothan ka lekhak kaun* (Who is the Author of Joothan?) Dharamvir fails to display a sense of propriety as he not only dubs Valmiki a fake author of *Joothan*, but he also declares that *Joothan*, as an autobiography, is merely breast-beating and it offers no alternative to the plight of the author. The following observation should amply prove the point: "Having read *Joothan*, one irresistibly feels that the writers in the field of literature have become beggars."[26] Strangely enough, Dharamvir not only connives at the infelicities committed by Surajpal Chauhan, similar to the ones that have been falsely attributed to *Joothan*, but also he praises him no end. Indeed, one is amused to find an article based on *Santapt* titled "Suraj Pal Chauhan and Jawaharlal Nehru" published in the *Dalit Sahitya – 2007* under the editorship of Jai Prakash Kardam. Dharamvir's disdain towards the community of *bhangi*s is not concealed, his avowed aim declared in the subtitle (*Jai bhangi, jai chamar*) of the volume under reference notwithstanding. At the most it has turned out to be an oxymoron par excellence.

One recurrently comes across remarks like: "The people belonging to the community of *bhangi* are so backward." One hears about the letters circulated earlier selectively among *dalit* activists wherein Dharamvir has allegedly vowed not to have anything to do with the members of *bhangi, khatik* and other such *dalit* communities. Even the above subtitle is suggestive of the fact that the *dalit*s not belonging to the communities of *bhangi*s and *chamar*s are doomed to remain outside the pale of *dalit* movement or community. Of course, by publishing books and articles under sensational and provocative titles like *Joothan ka lekhak kaun*, *Samant ke munshi . . .*, *Surajpal Chauhan and Jawaharlal Nehru* and others will certainly ensure publicity and short-lived limelight for the author and his ilk. But it will not do any good to the *dalit* cause whatsoever.

There is another path, another *disha* on which *dalit* thinkers and masses had been pinning their hopes, i.e., the path of Kanshiram and Mayavati, even though most *dalit* autobiographies have refrained from making any reference to this phenomenon. But the latest twists and turns in this path have horrified many a *dalit* activist. It would not be out of place here to quote Jai Prakash Kardam, one of the most sedate and balanced *dalit* writers today. There was a time,

> when Kanshiram used to thunder from public platforms that if any *brahmans* and *thakurs* were present in his meeting they should leave the place forthwith. Obviously, he [Kanshiram] did not distinguish between a *brahman* and *brahmanism*, a feudal and feudalism. Where there is a *Brahman*, there certainly will be *brahmanism*. Where there is a feudal person, it is inconceivable that feudalism will not be there. The slogan, *Tilak, taraju aur talwar, unko maro joote char* (Shun with all the disdain at your disposal, bearers of the four symbols, i.e., tilak – a small smear on the forehead used by *brahmans*, *taraju* – weighing balance used by the *baniyas*, a community of traders and money lenders, *talwar* – a sword supposedly used by *kshatriyas*, a caste of feudal lords and a power-wielding community – AM) was born around this time. But subsequently, with the opportunistic power sharing in Uttar Pradesh with Bharatiya Janta Party, a party universally recognised as one representing *brahmanism,* feudalism and capitalism, there was an influx of *brahmans* and *kshatriyas* into the party. It [Bahujan Samaj Party] died its natural death.[27]

Concluding his remarks in his editorial Kardam writes:

> Kanshiram was ailing and he had been in coma hitherto, but he had been a great mainstay of *dalit* politics. Today after his demise a question has arisen quite acutely as to what will happen to BSP or *dalit* politics in future? At a time when on the one hand BSP is getting *brahmanised* at a rather fast pace, while on the other Damocles' sword of court in connection with the Taj corridor issue is hanging over Mayavati's head, this question assumes tremendous significance. (. . .) If the vacuum created by Kanshiram's demise persists for some more period of time, it will have serious bearing on *dalit* politics.[28]

It is clear from Kardam's observations that those pinning some hope on Mayavati brand of *dalit* politics are in for a big disappointment sooner than later. The writing on the wall should be clear for all and sundry that *brahmanisation* of BSP will sound a death knell for this path of *dalit* liberation in the near future. The path of *Sarvajana hitaya* will inexorably lead to *sarvapunjipati* and *sarvamanuvad hitaya*. The throne of Delhi through this route will remain a perennial mirage. In any case the throne is sought by an individual who is desperately trying to grab it riding on the crutches of *brahmana* brigade. The community at large is unlikely to gain its liberation through this opportunistic alliance. Unfortunately a huge majority of *dalit* community is intoxicated by the idea of capturing the Delhi throne through the route of *sarvajana hitaya*. But the damage done will be enormous by the time *bodhisattva* will dawn on them.

Under the circumstances what should be the *disha* of *dalit* movement? Even in literature, the rightist and revivalist forces are defending the caste system in Indian society most vociferously. Nirmal Verma's views in this context are more than symptomatic:

> Our progressive intellectuals often criticise the caste system prevailing in the villages. But they forget that under this very system there was an age old tradition of 'rights and duties', under which people had been feeling quite secure and tension free, notwithstanding the fact that they might have not been so very well off.[29]

The political mentors of Nirmal Verma and ilk, i.e., Sudarshan, the *Sarsanghchalak* (Commander-in-Chief) of Rahstriya Swayamsewak Sangh also had stated in no uncertain terms that the caste system in the Hindu society was not so bad. The Hindustan Times of 28th January, 2006 published a news item as follow: "The old caste system not all that bad: Sudarshan."

RSS chief K. Sudarshan, who raised a storm by asking the Christians to Indianise the Church and more recently he asked Hindus to produce not less than three children, has now said that "the mutual respect and culture in villages (in ancient times) was such that nobody used to feel the untouchability."

Addressing a function to mark the centenary celebrations of Dada Saheb Apte, the founder of multi-lingual news agency *Himdustan Samachar* and the Vishva Hindu Parishad (VHP), Sudarshan said that the earlier caste system was "non-discriminatory" and every caste was given "job reservation" under it. He said:

> The caste system used to be like a fence around the farm. Those who violated it were ostracised. It was not discriminatory. Rather it provided for job reservation. Every caste was given reservation in a particular job. A mason could not do carpenter's job and carpenter could not do a sweeper's job.[30]

IV

Under the circumstances what is the alternative before the *dalit* movement? Critically analysing Abhai Maurya's novel *Mukti-path*, one of the most eminent *dalit* thinkers Kanwal Bharati writes:

> The most significant point that is the leitmotif of *Mukti-path* is that casteism or the heinous practice of casteism cannot be eliminated until the interference of religion in the society will not be ended fully and irrevocably. And this interference of religion will not end until there is socialist revolution in the country. In India the caste system is intimately linked with religion, in particular with Hindu religion.[31]

Bharati further writes:

> The question of unity, of creating a common front of *dalits* and left forces has been brought into a very sharp focus by Abhai Maurya in a very natural way. In the context of question of unity between the *dalits* and left forces it would be of utmost importance to understand that already for a considerably long period of time virulent campaign has been carried out to a design to the effect that Dr. Ambedkar had been an anticommunist leader. And under this very conspiracy a kind of ideology has been imposed on the *dalit* rank and file that any one who advocates the cause of *dalit*-left unity is subjected to a campaign of all kinds of calumny among the *dalit* masses. Truth is that Babasaheb Ambedkar had been so much influenced by the ideology of Marxism that, according to him, the only path of *dalit* liberation was socialism, i.e., state socialism under which education, industry, agriculture, insurance – all these branches of economy should have been nationalised. Therefore, the system of *varnas* could not be abolished lock stock and barrel by letting the feudal system to continue in Indian villages.[32]

R.D. Anand in his monograph *Dalit Chintan aur Communism* (*Dalit Thought and Communism*), is also concerned about the negative attitude of a section of *dalit* thinkers and activists to Marxism:

> Even today most of the Ambedkerites are wary of Marxism, they consider it an obstruction on the path of eradication of casteism. (. . .) All this is happening because they believe the hearsay more, rather than undertaking a serious study [of Ambedkar]. They do not do deeper thinking over it.[33]

From here on Anand lets loose a barrage of questions albeit via Kanwal Bharati:

> If the *dalits* believe that Ambedker did not believe in God, he was not a fatalist, he did not subscribe to the notion of rebirth, did not believe in blind faith and ritualism, he did not support mysticism, human sacrifice being practised during religious ceremonies and that being so, what was he if not a communist? Dr. Ambedkar was all for development and modernisation, he acknowledged the role of economic forces in history, wanted the establishment of classless society, he was for social and economic democratisation, he also had been demanding the nationalisation of education, industry and insurance. In that case if he wasn't a communist then what was he? If *dalit*s accept the fact that Dr. Ambedkar had through a memorandum submitted to the Constituent Assembly demanded the establishment of national socialism, he had advised all the members of working class to read 'Communist Manifesto', he was of the firm view that working class was capable of providing able leadership to the country. That being so, what was he, if not a communist?[34]

To this observation Anand adds his own assessment:

> The thinking of Dr. Ambedkar is objective, the process of resolution of any problem is quite realistic and revolutionary. On occasions his world view seems to be conveying a message opposite that of Marxism. But when he comes to the stage of implementation of the resolution of any given problem he struggles like a true Marxist.[35]

The difference between Marxism and Ambedkarism lies in the fact that Ambedkar wanted the "annihilation" of caste before the socialist revolution could be ushered in. But the question of questions has been as to how to eradicate the scourge of casteism? In answer to this question, following Ambedkar, *dalit* thinkers have been consistently propagating the view that caste could be eradicated through inter-caste marriages. Now, more than fifty years after Ambedkar's death can *dalit* leaders claim that any headway has been made towards ending the caste system in Indian society? Indeed, in practice, inter-caste marriages, particularly the ones between the *dalit*s and so-called *savarnas*, do not depend on the sweet will of *dalit*s. The reluctance on the part of majority of non-*dalit* members of society to have inter-caste marriages with *dalit*s is all too well-known. In Delhi University, for instance, four-five cases of *dalit*-non-*dalit* marriages have come to our notice and invariably the non-*dalit* partner in these alliances has been a person of leftist convictions. It is thus amply clear that people with a leftist perspective have been able to overcome their casteist mentality almost entirely. It has not happened with other members of our society. Hence, the final solution lies in the synthesis of Marxism and Ambedkarism.

Even the conversion to any other religion including Buddhism may not turn out to be the solution because you will still be surrounded by casteist people all the time, you will be like a poor helpless small fish in an ocean seething with sharks. Your survival itself will be an extremely grim prospect. Sharks will try to gobble you up all the time as it has been happening for more than two millennia long history of aggressive casteism in India. The way out, thus, is taming the sharks into becoming beautiful human beings devoid of any religious labels. And that can be realised by only converting them all to a Marxist perspective (*Savarnas* would not easily agree to get converted to Ambedkarism). This is precisely why we agree with R. D. Anand's conclusion about *dalits* converting themselves to Buddhism:

> One does find deliverance from God in Buddhism, but doesn't Marxism incorporate into its ambit the essence of Buddhist philosophy? One question bothers me a lot, i.e., even after the long history of prevalence of Buddhism in several countries, the humanist principles like equality, freedom and brotherhood have not been realised thus far in these

countries. Not only all the three principles have not been established, but also not even one out these three has been realised.

Anand continues:

> Today it is not possible for *dalits* to achieve their complete liberation by embracing Buddhism. On the contrary in the struggle for realising our goal it will be tantamount to surrendering ourselves into the hands of reactionary forces. *Dalit*s should undertake an extensive propagation of scientific outlook, exchange of views, historical mode of thinking, inculcation of humanist values through seminars, symposia and all other kinds of forum. *Dalit* thinkers, therefore, should squarely face the question that when a communist talks of humanist values and proletarian culture doesn't he have all-round development of human beings in mind, which Dr. Ambedkar had termed as 'brotherhood'?[36]

If yes, then it is absolutely essential that *dalit*s have people with a leftist perspective undertake the uphill task of snuffing out the scourge of casteism by creating a just society based on equality, brotherhood, freedom for all the toiling masses of society. Such a society will inherently be the most humane commune of people free of exploitation of man by man and of humiliation of man by man. We deem it appropriate to end the paper by quoting the clarion call given in 1928 by Bhagat Singh to the *achhoots* (the untouchables) of India:

> You are the real proletariat! Organise yourself! You have nothing to lose. Only the fetters of slavery will be smashed. Rise in rebellion against the existing system. Nothing substantial will come out of the gradual reforms. Create the revolutionary conditions through social movement and get ready for the political and economic revolution. You are the mainstay of the country, the real force. You the slumbering lions! Rise in a powerful rebellion![37]

NOTES AND REFERENCES

1. Om Prakash Valmiki in *Dalit sahitya ka saudriya shastra* (*Aesthetics of Dalit Literature*), (Delhi: Vani Prakashan, 2000), p. 13.
2. Sohan Lal Sumnakshar in *Dalit Sahitya* (*Dalit Literature*), (Delhi: Bharatiya Dalit Sahitya Akademi, 2007), p. 1.
3. Sharan Kumar Limbale in *Dalit sahitya ka saudriya shastra (Aesthetics of Dalit Literature)*, op. cit., p. 31.
4. Dinesh Ram, *Dalit mukti ka prashan aur dalit sahitya (The Question of Dalit Liberation and Dalit Literature)*, (Ghaziabad: Shri Sahityik Sansthan, 2002), p. 35.

5. Sharan Kumar Limbale, op. cit., p. 3.
6. Limbale, *Akkarmashi* (*The Bastard*), (New Delhi: Grantha Akademi, 1997), p. 28.
7. Ibid.
8. Valmiki, *Dalit Sahitya*, p. 15.
9. Anatoly Liberman in Propp, Vladimir, *Theory and History of Folklore*, (Manchester: Manchester University Press, 1984), p. xii.
10. Om Prakash Valmiki, *Joothan* (*Leftover Crumbs*), (Delhi: Radhakrishan Paperbacks, 1999), p. 19.
11. Limbale, *Akkarmashi*, p. 48.
12. Valmiki in *Dalit sahitya ka saudriya shastra*, p. 14.
13. Limbale, *Akkarmashi*, p. 27.
14. Ibid., pp. 27-28.
15. Ibid., p. 78.
16. Ibid.
17. Pawar Daya, *Achhoot (Untouchable)*, (Delhi: Radha Krishan, 2001), p. 62.
18. Surajpal Chauhan, *Triskarit* (*Insulted and Humiliated*), (Delhi: Anubhav Prakashan, 2002), p. 77.
19. Ibid., p. 148.
20. Surajpal Chauhan, *Santapt* (*The Persecuted*), (Delhi: Vani Parkahan, 2006).
21. Suraj Badattya, *Netikta ka kupath aur dalit athmkatha* (*Nasty Lessons of Morality and Dalit Autobiographies*), in *Dalit Literature*, op. cit., p. 73.
22. Laxman Gayakwad, *Uchakka* (*A Thief*), (Delhi: Radhakrishan paperbacks, 2001).
23. Ibid., p. 60.
24. Limbale, *Devata Aadmi* (*An Angel of a Man*), (New Delhi: Pratibha, 1994), p. 7.
25. Dharamvir, *Joothan ka lekhak kon?* (*Who is the Author of Joothan?*), (Hapur: Muhim Prakashan, 2006), p. 7.
26. Ibid., p. 65.
27. Kardam J.P., *Dalit Literature*, op. cit., p. 14.
28. Ibid.
29. Nirmal Verma, cited by Vikas Narayan Rai in *dalit athmkathai – anubhav se chtintan (Dalit Autobiographies – from Experience to Contemplation*), (Allahabad: Itihasbodh Prakashan, 2006), p. 13.
30. Hindustan Times, 28th January, 2006.
31. Bharati Kanwal, *Manuvad ke khilaph saada ladai ka abhiyan* (A Narrative about the Common Struggle against *Manuvad*), in *Dalit Sahitya*, op. cit., p. 387.
32. Ibid., p. 390.
33. R.D. Anand, *Dalit chintan aur communism (Dalit Thought and Communism)*, (Rampur: Boudhisattav Prakashan, 2006), p. 63.
34. Bharati Kanwal, "Ambedkarvad and Marxism – from the point of view of Coordination", cited from Anand, ibid.
35. Ibid., p. 63.
36. Ibid., p. 36.
37. Cited from *Jaati kyon nahin jaati? (Why caste does not go?)*, (ed.) Subhash Chandra, (Udbhavna Prakashan, 2005), p. 79.

SUCHITRA MATHUR

De-scribing the Indian Woman: New Autobiographical Ventures by Indian Women Writers in English

The writing of an autobiography is a deliberate act of self-representation within the public sphere. However, the so-called autobiographical pact between the autobiographer and the reader, which privileges the self-evident truth value of this life narrative, tends to gloss over this very deliberateness, the choices that are made with respect to narrative form, and the ideological imperatives that overdetermine any such choices. The growing field of autobiographical studies has foregrounded the autobiographical narrative itself as a site of investigation, analyzing its spatial and temporal contours, and questioning the politics of its inclusions and exclusions. Such an analysis does not necessarily negate the truth value of autobiography, but it does render this notion of truth partial and particular, dependent upon prevailing notions of subjectivity that frame the articulation of the autobiographer's sense of self. And as changes in the socio-cultural milieu transform existing life-scripts, one can reasonably expect a corresponding shift in autobiographical narratives. In fact, the latter might be seen as sites of struggle and negotiation that not only reflect but also actively participate in the larger cultural dynamics, reformulating the complex interrelationship between individual and society within the parameters of personal life stories.

My argument in this essay is premised upon such an understanding of autobiographical narratives. The last couple of decades have seen significant shifts, both material and ideological, in the category of the "nation." While the economic imperatives of globalization have led to forms of de-nationalization (and the emergence of sub-nationalisms as a sort of inverse reaction), the dominance of post-structuralist theories within academia has encouraged a questioning of the very concept of "nation" – its unity and integrity as it is embodied in the nation-state, and more fundamentally, its feasibility and utility as a form of social organization. Such deconstruction of "nation" has particular relevance for countries such as India that have, relatively speaking, only recently established themselves as sovereign nation-states, and where nationalist discourses have been pivotal in shaping a sense of identity at both the societal and the individual levels. What happens to these nationalist discourses when the nation itself becomes an unstable category? And more importantly, how do notions of identity, of selfhood, change in relation to such de-stabilizations of nation and nationalist discourses? In this essay I would like to argue that this period of post-nationalism has resulted in a weakening of the nationalist imperative, at least in certain sections of society, which, in turn, has enabled a re-conceptualization of women's gender identity in ways that have significant feminist implications. I will focus on two women's autobiographical narratives published during the 1990s, *Relationship: Extracts from a Correspondence* (1994) between Nayantara Sahgal and E.N. Mangat Rai, and *Daughter's Daughter* (1993) by Mrinal Pande, to exemplify this new direction in the life-scripts available to Indian women.

Before I do so, however, I would like to outline briefly the ideological imperatives that have historically overdetermined Indian women's autobiographies, especially those written in English. The genre of autobiography, as it is defined by the dominant western tradition, appeared on the Indian literary landscape in the nineteenth century. Its emergence as a distinct literary genre during this period is linked to the consolidation of British colonial rule in India, which "produced the old colonial subject who had a chance to enter the struggle for individualism".[1] However, according to Partha Chatterjee, nineteenth-century Indian autobiographies do not adhere to all the demands of this western literary genre. Instead of focusing on the "exploration of individuality and the inner workings of personality," these autobiographies are dominated by "facts of social history and the development of new cultural norms for the collective life of the nation".[2] "The 'new individual," Chatterjee finds, "could represent the history of his life only by inscribing it in the narrative of the nation".[3] Chatterjee reads these autobiographies as part of the emerging discourse of anti-colonial nationalism, which was shaped by the fact that the colonial regime, while creating the "individual subject," denied it full citizenship. Consequently, nationalist ideology developed a distinction between the inner spiritual world and the outer material world. While the latter was surrendered to the dictates of the colonial regime, the former became the site for the development of an indigenous identity through the hegemonic discourse of nationalism. Thus, autobiography as the narrative of the inner self became the story of the emergent nation. And since this nationalist ideology was inscribed primarily on the body of the woman, who was deliberately re-fashioned during this period to become the embodiment of an inviolable "Indian" identity, the notion of subjectivity in women's autobiographies was tied, even more so than in the men's, to the life of the nation. Written usually as memoirs, "what held these stories together into a single narrative was not the life history of the narrator or the development of her 'self' but rather the social history of the 'times'".[4] The patriarchal gender politics underlying this conflation of literary genre with nationalist politics is further emphasized by the perception of memoir as an "artless form" that is most appropriate as an "authentic 'feminine' literary voice" which makes it best suited to the expression of an authentic national identity.[5]

Indian women's autobiographies, then, from the nineteenth century through the post-independence period appear to be overdetermined by nationalist life-scripts. Such overdetermination does not of course indicate an unquestioning acceptance of patriarchal nationalisms by these women writers; in fact, Indian feminist scholars have pointed out numerous instances of conflict between individual women and the nationalist re-fashioning of Indian womanhood in these autobiographies. For example, in her reading of Rashsundari Debi's *Amar Jiban*, which many consider the first 'modern' autobiographical text by a woman in India, Tanika Sarkar foregrounds Debi's intense narrative focus "exclusively upon herself, by abstracting herself from her concrete world."[6] While this reading does challenge Chatterjee's claim that women's autobiographical writings privilege the life of the 'times' over the life history of the narrator, it is still aware of how instrumental a role is played by the idea of the nation in the self-conscious narrativisation by Debi of her own identity:

> 'I came to Bharatvarsha (India), and spent a long time here. This body of mine, this mind, this life itself have taken different forms.' She lived out her life in two villages. They are, however, absent, except as mere names (. . .) There is no local time, village time, family time. She gives herself nothing less than a whole sub-continent and almost an entire century to live in (. . .) Rashsundari needed this large context to abstract herself from her actual lived life. She transcended its narrow limits and its inability to intersect with grand historical narratives by giving herself the largest possible temporal and spatial frames that she could relate to.[7]

While in this case it is the general idea of India as a unified political space that structures the sense of self, a more direct influence of specific nationalist discourses is highlighted in Meera Kosambi's study of the personal narratives of two nineteenth-century Marathi women, Anandibai Joshi and Kashibai Kanitkar:

> When these pioneering women worked out individual solutions to new dilemmas and cut trails through uncharted terrain, these very individual acts were informed by a consciousness of the 'sisterhood of women.' The concept probably emerged in the lifetime of these two women and a handful of their contemporaries who formed the first generation of educated women in Maharashtra, and were products of the male reformers' view of (upper caste) women as objects of reform.[8]

These 'male reformers' were very much a part of the nationalist enterprise to create the new 'Indian Woman', and though these women combined "conformity and subversion, conventionalism and quiet rebellion" in responding to this re-fashioning, its impact in their articulation of selfhood in autobiographical writings cannot be ignored.[9]

In post-independence twentieth-century women's autobiographies, the continuing influence of nationalist discourses is evident in the articulation of conflicts between the private and the public, the claims of home and nation, where the nation is seen as an extended version of the domestic sphere which requires service from women as daughters, wives, and mothers.[10] The shifting terms of these conflicts from the nineteenth century to the post-independence period mark shifts in nationalist discourses, but in all cases, to a greater or lesser degree, women's personal identity is negotiated against the backdrop of the nation. In fact, it may be argued that the semblance of a single unified sense of self that is found in these autobiographies may be linked to the nationalist construction of India as a single unified nation. And at both the individual and the national level, this representation of a coherent identity is achieved through suppressions and silences that negate the existence of difference, of any heterogeneity that cannot be melted into a homogenous mass. The conflicts that are acknowledged are those that do not question the basic ideas of nationhood / good womanhood; tradition versus modernity, home versus the world are oppositions that offer different perspectives on the idea of nation and woman without challenging their integrity as concepts.

This intimate connection within women's autobiographies between the narrativisation of female subjectivity and discourses of nationalism makes this genre of life-writing especially fruitful as a site to investigate shifts in notions of self and nation. In the political arena, such a shift has been obvious through events in the past two decades – the consolidation of a fundamentalist Hindu national identity during this period has once again been inscribed on the body of the woman, and this re-inscription has led to a concentrated resistance that may be seen as the fourth wave of the Indian feminist movement.[11] It is in the context of this history that I would like to examine a new kind of autobiographical writing by women that appeared on the Indian literary scene in the 1990s, which, I argue, is simultaneously a product of and an active agent in the transformative feminist politics characteristic of contemporary India. This wave of Indian feminism is characterized by a fundamental questioning of both "nation" and "woman" as singular concepts that can offer an enabling sense of personal and political identity to disparate Indian women. In its place, contemporary Indian feminism is engaged in the process of recovering and reformulating alternative scripts that do empower individual women without collapsing them into the homogenous category of "Indian womanhood." This process is clearly not one of creation – there is no "new woman" of fourth wave Indian feminism; instead, it is the articulation of carefully negotiated subject-positions that are based upon a re-evaluation, rather than outright rejection, of existing models of female subjectivity. *Daughter's Daughter* and *Relationship* exemplify this process of reformulation since both are works by well-established Indian writers, and yet, they mark a significant departure from the usual mode of writing adopted by these two authors. As such, they represent the need for re-evaluating the past which is the defining characteristic of fourth wave Indian feminism.

For both Pande and Sahgal, the texts under consideration mark a major shift in at least two respects – for Pande, a well-established Hindi writer whose work is overtly feminist in its concerns, *Daughter's Daughter* is significant for being a text written in English that uses a child's perspective to describe a group of female relatives who never question the patriarchal social structures governing their lives. For Sahgal, who is an English-language writer and who actually has two more traditional autobiographical texts to her credit,[12] *Relationship* marks a change in basic conceptual terms – its dual authorship and the fact that the choice of letters to be included as well as their placement in the text was left up to the publishers, undermine the ideas of creative control and integrity of voice that characterize her earlier works. In addition, the subject matter, which is the extra-marital relationship between the two letter writers and its consequences, makes public as "truth" an aspect of Sahgal's life that she had hitherto hidden behind the veil of fiction. *Daughter's Daughter* and *Relationship*, then, can be seen as texts speaking through silences; they are personal narratives that articulate linguistic and sexual identities that had been suppressed by nationalist imperatives. They reclaim aspects of the personal that do not fit easily into acceptable public discourses, and as such, may be read as betrayals of both nationhood and womanhood.

By using English to write about her family, Pande violates the dictates of linguistic nationalism as well as family loyalty. According to a cousin, who took umbrage at such autobiographical outpourings, Pande used "the unfair advantage of being the one who could write and had therefore, chosen to shove aside claims of loyalty and chosen to put it all down as [she] saw it."[13]

Similarly, Sahgal has been accused of seeking salacious publicity by publishing a set of letters that have no larger public significance. In both cases, it is the privileging of a purely private perspective, without any sustained attempts to place the personal within a larger socio-political framework that is criticized. Interestingly, both texts, while undoubtedly reclaiming the personal for its own sake, do hint at possible political implications of such revelations. Though Pande warns that "there is no advice . . . nor any lessons in these stories", she also hopes that "the stories may only prove once again how each survival is a case in itself and that hard decisions are born not out of a crusading zeal or ascetic idealism, but only because the choice at that moment was between fighting back or being wiped out."[14] And Sahgal concludes her introduction to *Relationship* with this comment: "How one woman reacted under stress, what she thought, felt, did, may interest other women in what is still a man's world. But ultimately sharing these letters is a celebration of the relationship they brought to birth."[15] The larger political purpose in both cases is explicitly feminist – the authors present their personal lives as possible grounds on which a feminist alliance may be built with the audience. And yet, this feminist alliance is not made prescriptive – it "may" happen, but it is not held up as the primary aim of either text. This tentativeness is very much a part of fourth wave Indian feminism, which has deliberately distanced itself from the feminist/nationalist nexus that subscribes to a discourse of women's rights that glosses over differences within its constituents and variations in its political agenda. Instead, fourth wave feminism recognizes "discrepant dislocations" characterizing women's lived realities and the need for partial theories that do not exercise hegemonic control over the term "feminism".[16] The texts of both Pande and Sahgal may be read as being situated within this feminist context as strictly personal and, therefore, necessarily limited narratives of Indian womanhood.

It is not surprising, then, that these two texts, though autobiographical in content, do not take the form of the traditional memoir; the generic innovations, I would argue, signify a deliberate rejection of the nation–woman connection that underpins traditional Indian women's autobiographies. In form and content these two texts refuse to act as the voice of the proper Indian woman, not only by rejecting the "woman as nation" paradigm, but also by exploding the idea of either nation or woman as a self-contained unified entity. The forms of both texts foreground the partiality of their perspectives. *Daughter's Daughter* is written as seven short vignettes, each of which could function as a self-contained short story. Though the characters as well as the narrative voice remain largely consistent throughout the text, and the text does follow a linear chronology, there is no attempt to construct a coherent sense of female subjectivity through the course of the narrative.

In every section, the large cast of female characters prevents any easy identification of the paradigmatic "Indian woman" – the rigidly traditional grandmother, the young romantic aunts, the mother who encourages her daughters to read rather than cook/embroider, the good older daughter who is always willing to help her aunts, and the younger daughter, the narrator, who is characterized by her tomboyish behaviour, are all equally Indian women. And since there is no single role model, the narrator's sense of self is also not constituted by a single script. Each vignette presents the narrator from a slightly different angle, and there is no attempt to link up the various portraits through a chain of developmental causality. The Tinu who in the first section argues that "you were noticed, therefore you were,"[17] is also the precocious young girl who in the very next section claims, "I can read, therefore I am."[18] While the use of second person in the first declaration denotes a sense of self rooted in a specific familial community, the assertive first person observation in the second vignette signifies Tinu's access to a modern individualist subjectivity. This modern sense of selfhood, however, does not replace or build upon the familial identity. Rather, the two, along with several others, exist simultaneously as discontinuous overlapping scripts that together constitute the narrator's complex and, at times, fragmented sense of self. As Pande herself points out in her author's preface, "men and women are not always socially constructed by other men and women who have been put together in the same way."[19] The many different ways in which people, especially women, can be put together is the subject of *Daughter's Daughter*, which thus undermines the singularity of the category "Indian woman".

In *Relationship*, the idea of a self-contained individual identity is questioned through a focus on the multiple identities of the correspondents, each of which is a result of a different relationship. Sahgal's letters in this collection represent her as wife, mother, lover, and writer, with each of these identities impinging on the others. The separation between public (as a writer) and private (as wife/mother/lover) identities is completely undermined, not by making the private public, but by removing the gendered nationalist boundaries that separate the two. Here, for example, is the entire text of one of Sahgal's letters to Mangat Rai:

> We got back from Delhi last night. There were crackling brown leaves all over Mummie's lawn and I wanted to tread on all of them, only there wasn't time.
>
> I was quite used to not having a relationship like this. Sometimes I almost don't want it. I cannot bear the luxury of it for myself alone. It doesn't seem fair or right (in this "socialist pattern of society"!) that I should have so much. Why can't Gautam have this too? Why can't Champa, or my sisters, or so many people I know? What have I done to deserve this? There's no rhyme or reason to it.

Are you right when you put so much emphasis on the "Muslim" aspect of Kashmir? I think in time Pakistan might quite willingly part with its Bengal bit and be glad to be rid of a burden, but will never give up the Kashmir issue because it is an emotional involvement.[20]

The three paragraphs take Sahgal from being a daughter, to a lover, and finally a political commentator, without any attempt to link these identities together within a broader framework of national identity. In fact, the letter actually inverts the process, making the political personal, by explaining the Kashmir problem in terms of an "emotional involvement" that is as complicated as Sahgal's relationship with Mangat Rai.

A more radical subversion in Sahgal's text is seen with respect to gender identity. Since the letters are not separated by author, and frequently do not have an opening address or closing signature, it is sometimes difficult to determine if the writer of a specific letter is Sahgal or Mangat Rai. The letters merge into each other signifying a slippage of gender identity that refuses to be contained by the trope of "woman" or "man." And this affect of gender-blurring is enhanced by the appearance of similar concerns (one's relationship with one's nation, for instance) in letters by both Sahgal and Mangat Rai. "After all," ends one letter, "this society, this poverty, this squalor has fed me, made me, and maintained me in my special way for fifty years. And I could almost see its skeleton fingers stuffing bread into my mouth."[21] Without any opening or closing salutation, the next begins: "I went to Jeh and Thelly's party for the BOAC chief. The talk among the Indians was bitterly, deadly anti-Government, even to a point of farce and unreality (. . .) What was I doing there?"[22] During such interchanges, which may be seen to privilege a shifting almost androgynous model of subjectivity, the only visible indicator of a change in correspondent is the local address that appears at the beginning of each letter. Identity thus gets tied to place, but not in the rigid formulation of India = Indian Woman. Place, in these letters, is not only always defined in local rather than national terms, but is also ever-shifting since both correspondents are constantly on the move. This fluidity, like the multiplicity in Pande's text, then, signals these texts deliberate subversion of the nationalist paradigm and its monolithic "Indian woman" corollary.

The texts, however, do not offer any easy resolutions to these problematics of female subject-constitution. Recognizing the multiple patriarchies that constantly delimit women's existence, both texts challenge received definitions of "Indian womanhood" and try to disentangle women from nation by focusing on relationships that are not easily contained within existing nationalist life-scripts. But neither text ends on a sanguine note. Instead, they end with the breaking of bonds / relationships rather than their consolidation. In *Daughter's Daughter*, the mother can no longer turn to the grandmother, who is herself dependent on her son, as a refuge, and the narrator's close bond with her older sister is threatened by a growing awareness of their step-relationship. And at the end of *Relationship*, the focus is on Mangat Rai's divorce and the tax problems that prohibit Sahgal's re-marriage, rather than on the union of the two lovers. Furthermore, the final section of *Relationship* comprises political essays by Mangat Rai which act as the afterword, delegating both the personal and the female to the background. The afterword reminds the reader of the dominant framework, the public forum of the literary marketplace that continues to be defined by patriarchal nationalist discourses. The feminist project in these two texts then, is, if anything, a journey, an exploration rather than a fixed agenda to be achieved within the well-defined parameters of the nation-state.

NOTES AND REFERENCES

1. Gayatri Chakravorty Spivak, "The Political Economy of Women as Seen by a Literary Critic", in *Coming to Terms: Feminism, Theory, Politics*, ed. Elizabeth Weed, (New York: Routledge, 1989), pp. 218-29, here p. 224.
2. Partha Chatterjee, *The Nation and Its Fragments: Colonial and Postcolonial Histories*, (Delhi: Oxford University Press, 1995), p. 138.
3. Ibid.
4. Ibid., p. 139.
5. Ibid.
6. Tanika Sarkar, "A Book of Her Own. A Life of Her Own: Autobiography of a Nineteenth-Century Woman", in *From Myths to Markets: Essays on Gender*, ed. Kumkum Sangari and Uma Chakravarti, (New Delhi: Manohar Publishers, 1999), pp. 85-124, here p. 116.
7. Ibid., pp. 116-17.
8. Meera Kosambi, "Realities and Reflection: Personal Narratives of Two Women from Nineteenth-Century Maharashtra", in *From Myths to Markets: Essays on Gender*, ed. Kumkum Sangari and Uma Chakravarti, (New Delhi: Manohar Publishers, 1999), pp. 125-60, here p. 156.
9. Ibid.
10. Ranjana Harish, *Indian Women's Autobiographies*, (London: Arnold Publishers, 1993).
11. Though histories of women's movements in India and / or Indian feminism do not usually talk about distinct phases, they do focus on three time periods that are characterized by significant differences in their approach to the women's question: the nineteenth-century reform movement, the early twentieth-century nationalist Gandhian feminism, and the 1970s engagement specifically with

gender inequality and violence against women. Detailed analyses of this history are found in books like Nandita Gandhi and Nandita Shah's *The Issues at Stake: Theory and Practice in Contemporary Women's Movement in India*, (Columbia, MO: South Asia Books, 1992) and Radha Kumar's *The History of Doing: An Illustrated Account of Movements for Women's Rights and Feminism in India 1800-1990*, (New York: Verso, 1993). Taking these three divisions as the first three phases of Indian feminism, I am calling the latest shift (starting in the late 1980s), wherein the focus is on divisions caused by caste and community affiliations within women, and the strategies to deal with the rise of Hindu fundamentalism, the fourth phase of the Indian women's movement.

12. Nayantara Sahgal, *Prison and Chocolate Cake*, (New York: Knopf, 1954), and *From Fear Set Free*, (London: Gollancz, 1962).
13. Mrinal Pande, *Daughter's Daughter*, (New Delhi: Penguin Books, 1993), pp. 11-12.
14. Ibid., p. 13.
15. Nayantara Sahgal and E.N. Mangat Rai, *Relationship: Extracts from a Correspondence*, (New Delhi: Kali for Women, 1994), p. ix.
16. Mary E. John, *Discrepant Dislocations: Feminism, Theory, and Postcolonial Histories*, (Berkeley: University of California Press, 1996).
17. Pande, p. 25.
18. Ibid., p. 48.
19. Ibid., p. 11.
20. Sahgal, p. 97.
21. Ibid., pp. 209-10.
22. Ibid., p. 210.

SHARMISHTA LAHIRI

Family Lexicon of Natalia Ginzburg: Re-living Life in Words

When *Lessico famigliare* (*Family Sayings*) was published in 1963, its author Natalia Ginzburg (1916-1991) already had several works of fiction to her credit. After *Lessico* she continued with her literary career, experimenting with other narrative forms and brought out volumes of plays, essays, short stories and novels, as well as a historical biography, establishing her reputation as one of the most widely read contemporary writers of Italy.

On the plane of autobiographical narration, *Lessico famigliare* is about identity and family memory, about identification with roots and retrospective cognition. Natalia Ginzburg writes in the Author's Note in *Lessico famigliare* that she did not have a great desire to talk about herself: "This, in fact, is not my story, but with all its gaps, it is the story of my family."[1] Yet, in a distinctive way, she narrativizes personal identity in *Lessico* through the story of her family, re-visits the past, confers a temporal dimension to the self (adding history to the sedimentation of habit, as Paul Ricoeur would say),[2] and thematizes character. As the title suggests, the writer here recreates in memory the world of her past, tracing the itinerary of *family sayings*, and evokes in the concreteness of 'words' a complex network of values, customs and situations that represented life in the family, and created a particular semantic universe inhabited by everyone who participated in its constitution. By bringing back voices of the past through verbatim quotations and recapturing them in the moment of 'utterance', the author relives time in retrospective, in the warmth, directness and immediacy of conversation, and attempts to reconstruct family identity, threatened and dispersed under the shadow of Holocaust. Mentioning that they were five brothers and sisters in the family and explaining the significance of the particular words and phrases, which constituted their family vocabulary, Ginzburg writes:

> When we meet we might be indifferent or unmindful towards each other. But just the mention of one word of those family sayings is enough for us (. . .) to get back at once our old connection, and with it our childhood and youth, bound indissolubly to those phrases, words (. . .) Any one of those phrases would have us recognize each other even inside a dark cave, among millions of persons.[3]

Words and expressions thus confer identity to a group in the same way as they give names to things. As a memory account of a formative phase, the text presents a choral narrative, where the author's life can be read in fragmentary sketches, almost incidental, lying entwined with the life histories of others. In a singular iterative style of narration, the writer illustrates in these phrases the traces of a continuous testimony or, as Francesca San Vitale puts it, the 'archaeological certainty'[4] of family identity. Ginzburg writes:

> These phrases are our Latin, the dictionary of the days gone by (. . .) like the hieroglyphs of the Egyptians or Assyrian-Babylonians, the testimony of a vital nucleus that ceased to exist, but survived in texts, saved from the (. . .) ravages of time.[5]

My paper proposes to offer a reading of the text to consider the elements in which *Lessico* emerges as a variant category within the autobiographical genre, using the representational mode of fiction. It uses a narrative strategy in which the autobiographical subject does not merge into the three concurrent roles of author, narrator and character in the autodiegetic mode, but distances the narrator from the character in the manner of a homodiegetic narrator. Nor does the text adhere to conditions of the *autobiographical pact* as envisaged by Philippe Lejeune, who refers to an implicit understanding between the writer and the reader on the expected rendering of 'personal' experiences in autobiography.[6] Here the writer, in effect, denies that the book represents *her* story.

I begin with the Author's Note (*Avvertenza*) which explains the author's rationale behind the text and helps us formulate the premises of our study: "I never had a great desire to talk about myself,"[7] Ginzburg writes in the same note, and elsewhere, "I had a horror of writing autobiography." The paratextual elements here provide a key to the analysis of the textual ordering and strategy. She continues in the note: "Places, facts and persons, in this book are real. I have not invented anything (. . .) even the names are real (. . .), to me they are indissoluble from the persons in reality."[8] Having thus affirmed the authenticity of the facts and faces named in the text, Ginzburg hastens to add a cautionary note that her book should be read more as a novel than a chronicle, making allowances for the inevitable lapses in memory: "I have written only what I remembered, and if one read the book as a chronicle one would object that it contained infinite lacunae." Accordingly, she suggests that the book, "even though taken from reality, should be read as if it were a novel".[9] Facts then would be presented in the manner of fiction, creating a memory narrative, to be read 'as a novel', but denied all the same of the inventive element, given the veracity of the events recounted within. The author's note ends with a statement of intention: that of her long-standing project of writing a book on the family, but this again not without reminding the reader about the invariably fickle nature of memory:

> In my childhood and adolescence I always thought of writing a book that would tell the story of the people who then were living around me. This is, partly, that book: but only partly, because memory is fleeting and books drawn from reality can often present only but the tenuous glimpses and splinters of what we have seen and heard.[10]

These repeated disclaimers on the part of the author as to the documentary import or the chronicle-like testimony of the text, in short, as to its wholeness or the completeness of portrayal, are significant not because they express any doubt on the authenticity of what has been said, but because they direct our attention to what has *not* been said, to what has been excluded or left *unsaid*, that is, to the element of omission implicit in the selection process of memory. It can be read in the almost total absence of the author's voice from the choral repertory of *family sayings*, apart from some of rather marginal nature, for example, an instance of infant chatter about her doll 'Olga', remembered from their Palermo days, of which she "pretended to be nostalgic", but had no recollection herself.[11] Most importantly, exclusion lies in her omitting to narrate consciousness, thought processes or inner reflections of the self in her account, which, to quote Franco Moretti, expresses "a discontinuity between the hero and his world."[12] This conscious removal of the self from the level of narration is verified also in the subject's silence on reporting personal emotion, while recounting tragic events of the past. Discontinuity with the world is equally evident in the omission of chronology in terms of calendar dates, months and years, or in the order of the events narrated. While the data pertaining to the world of referential realities find mention in *Lessico* in absolute generic terms, to be gleaned more in the way of inferences drawn from the account of related events in the domestic sphere, temporal indications are given at most as a passing mention of the season or the hour of the day. Express references to historical moments and events are banished from the text unless they enter to form part of the perspective on the family or its ambit, which extended to include a wide circle of friends, relations, and acquaintances. At a personal level, the 'discontinuities' coincide with an unsettling phase in her life marked by isolation, war, and death of her husband. As it stands, Ginzburg would publish a text in the diary form only in 1970 (*Mai devi domandarmi*), with annotations dated and sequenced in chronological order, referring to moments from a later period of life, but was evidently not prepared to talk in a similar spirit about the earlier phase, which unfolds in *Lessico famigliare*. She resolves the *hiatus* by writing a memorial narrative in the form of fiction, which leaves her with the freedom of selection and exclusions, and in choosing to say little about herself she says a lot. We can identify accordingly an ordered employment of the narrative technique of fiction in *Lessico famigliare*, which distances it from the standard autobiographical text. The discontinuities in terms of narrated time and time of narration, with the condensation of certain episodes into the length of one sentence and the blocked out zones that appear in between disjointed references to different phases of life – all point to the conscious strategy of occultation, if not abolition, in the process of narration, the 'acts of will', in Freudian term, which are revelatory in relation to the authorial voice. A reading of the text in view of these considerations would render explicit its insertion in the dimension of fiction.

The domestic scene dominates in Ginzburg's account. Born in an Italian Jewish family in 1916, Natalia Levi grew up in the liberal and anti-Fascist intellectual ambience in Turin, where her father Giuseppe Levi was professor of comparative anatomy at the university. We are told that he belonged to a Jewish family of bankers from Trieste, and notwithstanding that, was notoriously lacking in any kind of "money-managing skill", whereas her mother came from a Roman Catholic family background in the same city. The parents offer character studies in contrast: her academic father, who is outwardly stern and gruff in manner, has a diametrically opposite temperament in relation to the chirpy and sunny disposition of her mother, Lidia. The narrative is woven around their life, bringing up children, taking annual vacations in the hills, their social life with different groups of friends and family, their moving houses, and living in Florence, Palermo and Sardinia in the initial years before settling down finally at Turin where her father joined the faculty in the university. Related episodes concerning individual members of the family are grouped as subplots around this central narrative nucleus. Having lived in the period of Fascist ascendancy from the days of early childhood right through the years of her youth, Ginzburg was witness to traumatic events of history, which, however, can be gleaned in her account only as glimpses appearing from under the flow of the quotidian life of the family. On these occasions her narration, in Genette's term, gets 'focalized',[13] and the gaze is mediated intermittently through a child's eye, which builds an alternative dimension of reality-fantasy in the text. Second, following this inner logic of fiction in the text, the writer relates external events only to the extent they impinged on the life and destiny of the family, and not from the documentary standpoint of History. Domestic themes prevail in her narrative and she quotes the *sayings* of homely figures such as grandmothers and aunts with as much alacrity as those of the public figures whom the family knew or who frequented the house, for example, the underground revolutionary Filippo Turati, his companion Anna Kuliscioff (her narration is *focalized*, for example, on this occasion when she reports her perplexity about Anna's status, not able to determine whether Anna was a friend or the wife of Turati), progressive industrialists like the Olivetti family, publisher Giulio Einaudi, not least intellectual figures and activists like Leone Ginzburg, Vittorio Foa, Cesare Pavese, Felice Balbo – an impressive presence of well known personalities, indicating the rich interaction of cultural influences that shaped her formative phase.

If in relation to the self, personal feelings were left unuttered, there was no high drama or sentimental effusion that ever finds its way in the narration. The author lived through turbulent times in the prime of her youth, saw anti-Semitic waves and state-sponsored violence that percolated down the levels of state and society marked by sharp divisions on racial lines, circumstances in which it was normal that the distinction between the public and the private would blur. Her Jewish identity, however, does not dominate the narrative, and ideological references do not surface, if not by way of reporting the tenor of routine family conversation. Her parents admired the 'conspirers' against Fascism, like Turati, the historian Salvatorelli, or Bissolati. After their arrests, her father grew increasingly skeptic that Fascism shall ever end, but she keeps ideology half hidden under a patina of comic irony:

> My mother was an optimist by nature and waited for a sudden change (. . .) She would go out in the morning, saying: 'Let me go out and see if Fascism is still there. I am going to find out if Mussolini has been thrown out' (. . .) At lunch she would tell father: 'There is so much of discontent brewing around. People cannot stand it any more.' My father yelled: 'who told you?' And my mother: 'the vegetable seller'.[14]

The narration finds its fulcrum in these *family sayings*, reported in direct speech, in which regional dialects and sub-dialects freely intermingle with standard Italian to create the plurilinguistic universe of Bakhtin's modern dialogical novel. An element of drama is added to the quotidian family chronicle by creating a tension of contrasts. Inimitable expressions of the father form the leitmotif in her account, as his *thundering voice* reverberates in the house: for example, his onomatopoeic expressions for all manners of slovenly eating (whether it was slurping or dipping bread in soup) and lack of etiquette were *potacci* and *sbrodeghezzi*, whereas every mode of inappropriate behaviour was infallibly *negrigure*, a term he used mostly to describe the inelegant and careless ways of his children.[15] On the other hand, her mother's pet phrase for describing the rigorous mountaineering trips, which their father organized meticulously for them, was: "the entertainment that the devil offers to his children."[16] The carefree image of the mother was of one "who found things to love in every situation and was loved in return." Writing about her parents, Ginzburg states that apart from socialism and anti-Fascism, the "things which my father appreciated and held in esteem were: England, Zola's novels, Rockefeller Foundation, mountains and the guidebooks of Val d'Aosta. The things that my mother loved were socialism, poetry of Paul Verlaine, music, particularly *Lohengrin*, which she used to sing for us every evening."[17] As a counter-point, she adds, "my father hated music", whatever might be the instrument. While the antithetical constructions emphasize the individual contours of characters, the contrasting predilections of the family members are expressed through a collection of emblematic phrases, which are then organized synchronically as the varying episodes of a sub-plot. Further, a line of romantic interest is opportunely built into the narrative in the manner of a novel. The open household of the Levis was the meeting ground of friends for free discussions and articulation of dissent. It was frequented by her father's friends as well as those of her brothers, progressive men and women, many of whom were destined to become noted intellectual and public figures in future. One among them was the future industrialist Adriano Olivetti, her brother Gino's friend, who would later marry her sister Paola. Another was Leone Ginzburg, intellectual activist, the future husband of Natalia. As the romantic involvement between Paola and Adriano unfolds in the story, proceeding through courtship, resolution of doubts, years of marriage and eventual break-up, it utilizes a manner of emplotment, typical of novel. Similar sub-plots are created around the life pattern, marriage and family lives of her three brothers, Mario, Gino, and Alberto. The oppositional role of the father who invariably offered an initial resistance to the marriage plans of his children is a common thread, which introduces an element of contrariness, as the ingredient of drama in these stories.

There is a thread of adventure too to nuance the narration in the pace and style of fiction. Ginzburg reports the events related to the clandestine group in which her brother Mario and friends were actively involved, and among others, narrates the episode in which her brother Mario and others were intercepted carrying anti-fascist publications and material across the border and caught, with Mario finally managing a daring boat escape to cross over to Switzerland.[18] Another brother Alberto was arrested and put in prison because of his association with the noted figure Vittorio Foa, both charged as anti-fascist conspirators.[19] Another episode narrated in the tone of adventure story relates to the days the revolutionary leader Filippo Turati, hunted by the police, stayed in hiding in the Levi household where the plans for his clandestine escape to France were organized.

While she recounts with some details the life choices and experiences of her siblings, Ginzburg, as mentioned earlier, is totally silent on her own inclinations and vulnerabilities, on the individual phases related to her personal growth, from a child to a young woman, or the story of her love and marriage. Apart from an abrupt one line information that "Leone and I got married and lived in our house at Via Pallamaglio,"[20] there is no other mention of their meeting, marriage, relationship or domestic life in her account. The fracture with the world manifests in the fragmentary nature of narration. The task of piecing together the broken ends of life and giving coherence and pattern to the past brings out personal memory, which the past self had guarded in the innermost being. As a solution, the 'narrating self' reduces them in the emotive content and renders only a skeletal account of these moments of scarred memory. Her father, brothers and friends were members of an association called *Giustizia e libertà* (Justice and liberty), for which they became the target of attack quite early in the Fascist regime. The family suffered racial persecution after the passage of anti-Semitic laws in Mussolini's regime, leading most of them to leave home and the country for prolonged spells (her brother Mario, for example, chose to marry and live in France; another brother Gino went away, taking up a job in Latin America). Her father was relieved of his chair in the university and left the country, with a teaching assignment at Liege, in Belgium. He had to flee that city at the time of German invasion, but was apprehended at Boulogne by the Germans who later sent him back to Liege. After a year he moved back to Italy but shuttled between different cities, under a different name, trying to hide his identity from the Nazi occupational army. The days of forced internment of Leone along with Natalia and children in the Abruzzi, their privations and the difficulties, the arrest of her father and imprisonment of the brothers, are all facts narrated without a harsh line, and shorn of brutality or sentimentalism. Holding back on emotive expressions and sentiments is evidently another element of exclusion built into the narrative, in which the gravest of situations finds a matter-of-fact mention, especially those which concerned the immediate family. Her husband Leone Ginzburg, an expatriate of Russian origin, was a writer and an active participant in the underground resistance movement. He was arrested and tortured to death in the Nazi prison cell in Rome in 1944, only a few days before the Liberation. Natalia was left homeless with three orphaned children. After having mentioned that her husband was arrested and taken away from home at Rome, Natalia reports his death in only one poignant line: "I never saw him again."[21] She returned home to Turin, and while her parents took care of the children, she joined the Einaudi publishing house, then a fledgling concern. Here Ginzburg worked with distinguished writers and critics like Cesare Pavese, Vittorio Foa, Felice Balbo, colleagues with whom she bonded with lasting friendship. Their voices appear frequently in her narration, reflecting their impact in her life. She deeply mourned the suicide of Cesare Pavese at Turin in 1950, but mentions the event in her typically measured tone, trying to analyse and interpret:

> Pavese committed suicide in summer, when none of us [his friends] were there. He planned his death with the same precision and calculation with which one planned one's daily walk or an evening programme (. . .) He was always meticulous about everything to the last detail, leaving nothing to chance (. . .). After the war ended we were all scared that there would be war again, but he was terrified more than any of us. He loathed to be drawn into the vortex of the unforeseeable and the unintelligible, anathema to his lucid intellect (. . .) appearing like the dark whirlpool of menacing waves, threatening to submerge the bare dunes of his life.[22]

In the workplace, she remembers Felice Balbo's enthusiastic projects as against Pavese's spirit of irony, which she missed reading in his books; above all his dry sense of humour which used to come out in his carefree moments with his friends.[23] The story thus continues to proceed across different episodes of varying intensity, involving friends, family and acquaintances, and constructs a choral narrative, sketching cameo profiles of diverse characters that had thronged her universe. *Lessico* turns out an open-ended narrative, without a specific beginning of any phase in the story and ends the narration around the 34th year of her life. The book covers the traces of her life till her second marriage, to literary critic Gabriele Bandini, and transfer of residence to Rome in 1950. There is definitely a moment of conversion in the end in *Lessico*, when the narrator emerges from under the protective wings of parental support and family home in Turin and moves to Rome, beginning a new, independent chapter in her life, with her own home and family. Significantly, it initiated the phase which saw the actualization of her potential as writer, fulfilling thereby a promise noted early in childhood. Natalia's second husband died in 1969. She eventually engaged herself totally in writing and came to represent one of the significant voices among the women writers of her time, leading interventions on various political and social issues, and was elected to parliament in 1983. Natalia Ginzburg died in Rome in 1991. She continued with the surname of her first husband till the end. Ginzburg attempts to go over the past in a retrospective narration, which would offer a more unitary reading on life, offering a possibility that the fractures might heal through narration. Autobiography in this case purports to be a transformative experience, which by elucidating the past, gives a meaning of one's life, in which even the discontinuities, fragmentariness and incoherence find a placing of significance. The narrative unity of the text helps the writing subject find, among brief actions, its identity on the scale of an entire period of life. It reminds us of Dilthey's concept of the '*connectedness of life*' in autobiography, to which Ricoeur refers in his theoretical reflections in *Oneself as Another*.[24] Ginzburg's presentation of the book "as a novel" is indicative in this context, for, in the very decision to tell it as a story, the author exercises her 'will' to restructure and elaborate the past, and recompose it. For the subject, it is a deliberate and *self*-conscious move to connect with the past self, elucidating and interpreting 'experiences' in the light of the present. Ginzburg arrives at a narrative configuration in *Lessico* through what Ricoeur calls 'discordant concordances', meaning the changes from the point of beginning, which are narrated as in a story to give a fictive movement to the account, in the manner of emplotment.[25] Ricoeur's model provides us a key to the narrative strategy. The upsets, sudden events that change the course of life, disappointments, etc. constitute elements of discordance in memorial narrations. In Ginzburg's *Lessico*, fluctuations in the fortune and rhythm of life of the family, her father's expectations in his children not fulfilled and his spirit of conflict with his sons – specifically in case of the life choices of Mario and Alberto, the traumatic events of the war, the arrests, forced internment, her husband's imprisonment, torture and death, her homeless situation, financial insecurity – are all elements that signify dramatic changes in relation to the initial situation in the author's life and give a twist to the storyline as in fiction. In fact, the consonances and dissonances between the past self and the present self, between the "experiencing self" and the "narrating self" – terms introduced by Leo Spitzer – constitute different modes of self-narration in autobiographical texts.[26] A 'lucid narrator', turning back on the track of memory, is able to intellectualize and clarify the ignorance and confusion of the past self, and shed light on things which were hazy and incomprehensible before. Dorrit Cohn, in her analysis of narrative modes of presenting consciousness in fiction, cites Proust's *A La Recherche* as "an inexhaustible source-book for the type of self-narration in which the benighted past self is 'lit up' by a sovereignly cognizant narrator".[27] Since in dissonance, a distance is established between the 'narrating self' and the 'experiencing self', retrospective narration becomes a cognitive experience for the self as it was for Marcel in Proust's text: "True life, life at last discovered and illuminated, the only life therefore really lived, that life is literature."[28] No doubt, in *Lessico* Ginzburg follows a variant line, distancing the self from being the subject of her story, but her subject cannot help lapsing occasionally into a dissonant narration – fluctuating between the 'moments of remembrance' and the 'moments remembered', when the ignorant past self is lit up by the cognizant present self. Two episodes stand out in this context. Recounting the days when she had to be hospitalized, Ginzburg remembers her mother telling her that the hospital was the house of the doctor and the patients roaming around were his children and family. "I believed obediently, though I knew all along that it was a hospital; and then as it was in other times, truth and falsehood mingled in me."[29] The episode of Turati is another case in point:

> One evening I heard my mother talking to someone in the next room; and I heard her opening the linen closet. I saw shadows on the glass door. (. . .) Sig. Paolo Ferrari was in the dining room, drinking tea. As I saw him I immediately recognized him as Turati, for he had come once to our house in Via Pastrenga. But since I was told he was Paolo Ferrari, I obediently believed, and thought that he was both, Turati and Ferrari; again truth and falsehood mingled in me.[30]

She describes Turati as Ferrari observed with a child's eye: "Ferrari was heavy, big as a bear (. . .)." She remembers that Turati presented to her mother a book dedicated to the memory of Anna Kuliscioff and signed it as 'from Anna and Filippo':

> My ideas were always confused; I could not understand how he was Anna and also Filippo, if he was instead, as they said, Paolo Ferrari.[31]

In another instance, the author describes Adriano Olivetti, then in military service, sitting at dinner at their place:

> He had a sad air, perhaps owing to his dislike of military service, and was timid and silent, but when he talked, he talked at length and at a very low voice. His little blue eyes were cold but dreamy, and stared into the vacant space, while he would keep talking, at once confused and obscure. Adriano then seemed to be the living incarnation of the type my father called '*impiastro*' (odd, painfully shy, fumbling bloke), but he never referred to him as '*impiastro*', or '*salame*' (inept) (. . .): he never used his typical epithets on him. I wonder why: and I think may be my father had a much deeper psychological insight than we credited him for, and he could see through the vests of that shy boy the man he would become in future.[32]

Thus, here we have situations, in which elements of discordance are verified as retrospective cognition of the past self. The writer expressly mentions in these instances how things which were unclear and confused at the time of their occurrence in the past became clear and comprehensible with the experience of the present. As we redirect our gaze, to use the light and shade imagery of Proust – like a lamp throwing light on our life on reverse, just as a photo negative held against light, the past is "illuminated" and understood: "Only then, when one has thrown light upon it and intellectualized it can one distinguish (. . .) the shape of what one has felt."[33] It is interesting to note that Natalia Ginzburg was among the first translators of *A La Recherche* in Italian, and her translation of the first part of the book was published by the Einaudi. Intertextual links to Proust's *Recherche*, especially to *Côté du Chez Swann* (*Swann's Way*) recur in *Lessico*, and are explicit, for example, in the episodes in which the narrator detects resemblances between M. Swann of *Recherche* and her father's friend and colleague in the faculty Prof. Terni, who was a frequent visitor to the Levi home. To the author, Terni seemed to be "consciously resembling Swann", especially noticeable in his habit of keeping a caramel in the mouth or his penchant for discovering similarities between their faces and those in the famous paintings. The connections compound as it is Terni again who brings into their home a copy of *Recherche*, thus introducing them to Proust's work, which the family grew to love, especially her mother, Mario, and sister, Paola. Ginzburg does not forget to mention either the keen interest with which her mother would later follow the progress of her work of translation of *Recherche*.[34] Thus, Proust's text is present in Ginzburg's *Lessico* not only in the concept of retrospective cognition of the past through the memorial process, but is further intertexted through these recurring references and constructions of parodic correspondences, which combine a sort of postmodern *pastiche*. In the frequent transtextual addressing to the assumed 'model', in the correspondences traced between Swann and Terni, highlighting the latter's mannerisms and his anxious intellectual air (*un poseur*, as her father was fond of saying), the original image in Proust is reinvented with irony, recast in comic lines and lowered into the 'banal'. In terms of textual category, Ginzburg's narration fundamentally deviates from Proust's work in her near obliteration of the self from the text. Unlike Marcel she does not narrate *her* past consciousness, but relives it in the silence of her heart, listening to the words voiced by others. That she views the period covered in this book as a single phase or a unique chapter in her existence is revealed in the organization of the text. The book is not divided into chapters as other novels, but continues in a series of paragraphs, with only a line of blank space left in between. Here we might allow us a little digression, for this feature also brings up in *Lessico famigliare* a structural similarity with the Family Books (*Libri di famiglia*) of the past, in which we might be tempted to trace the antecedents of the structure of Ginzburg's text.[35] To our interest, these family books were written in an unbroken series of paragraphs, without any demarcating line or chapterization, keeping only a single blank space before each new annotation. In these texts, written mostly between fourteenth and sixteenth centuries (spreading in the period of Humanism and Renaissance, as a popular practice mostly among the mercantile class in Tuscany and the regions of northern Italy), apart from business or professional advices, important family events especially the registration of birth, death and marriages were reported with religious regularity, without any significant affective input. External events were reported only as a part of necessary information to draw lessons and counsel for the family, and the book continued through generations, regularly updated with new entries, aimed at preserving the record of family identity. Though the *family book* was not typically included as a category in literary genres, an evolution can be traced in the successive changes of its thematic physiognomy. From its initial stage limited only to the reporting of family data and business records, family books extended in later phases to incorporate anecdotes of important events and occurrences of interest to the family, graduating from the purely informative and prescriptive to a proto-narrative text. It was a system through which the *family* sought to continue as an independent organism in which the individual found his identity, institutionalizing the models and norms to be passed in heredity. Ginzburg's text shares two elements of the medieval family book: its narration in quality of reportage, shorn of any affective input, and the formal organization of the text as a *continuum*, without division into separate chapters. Needless to mention, *Lessico* varies from this genre of writing in the storyline, in its narrative structure similar to the novel. We are tempted to hazard an opinion that in Ginzburg's text one can detect a tenuous strain of the genre of family books, which had carried within its fold latent possibilities of extension into a literary category, attempting to compose in narrative mode the data of family chronicle. In the final analysis, *Lessico famigliare*, notwithstanding the author's stated intention to the contrary, reads as a variant category within the autobiographical genre, locating the self in the formative stages of its identity. As Ricoeur writes on the question of self and narrative identity: "The person, understood as character in a story, is not an entity distinct from his own "experiences" (. . .) The narrative constructs the identity of the character, what can be called his or her narrative identity, in constructing that of the story told."[36] Lasting dispositions are formed within the family tradition. While the family has a significant role to play towards character formation through inculcation of habit and identification with a system of values (which, to say it with Ricoeur, makes us place a "cause" above our own survival, defining the moral aspect of character[37]), it represents a collective identity in its history and experiences with which the self is related and inextricably bound. Thus, in constructing the story of her family, the author of *Lessico* constructs her own identity recognized in each habit acquired, in each value identified and internalized, in each experience confronted, adding structure to character in a relational sense. In *Lessico famigliare*, the author constructs an image of the family as a super individual entity, which has its own history, its typical virtues, its models, its 'myths', in which the self recognizes and re-identifies itself.

NOTES AND REFERENCES

1. Natalia Ginzburg, *Lessico famigliare*, (Turin: Einaudi, 1963), p. 5. (Eng. trans. mine).
2. Cf. Paul Ricoeur, *Oneself As Another*, trans. Cathleen Blamey, (Chicago: University of Chicago Press, 1992), pp. 121-22.
3. Ginzburg, p. 28. (Eng. trans. mine).
4. Francesca San Vitale, in AA.VV., *Natalia Ginzburg. La narrativa e I suoi testi*, (Rome: La Nuova Italia Scientifica, 1986), p. 33.
5. Ginzburg, p. 28. (Eng. trans. mine).
6. Cf. Philippe Lejeune, *Le pacte autobiographique*, (Paris: Éd. du Seuil, 1975, 1996), pp. 26-36.
7. Ginzburg, p. 5 (Eng. trans. mine).
8. Ibid. (Eng. trans. mine).
9. Ibid. (Eng. trans. mine).
10. Ibid. (Eng. trans. mine).
11. Ibid., p. 31. (Eng. trans. mine).
12. Cf. Franco Moretti, *The Way of the World*, (London: Verso, 1987, 2000, 2nd ed.), p. 147.
13. Cf. Gérard Genette, *Figures III*, (Paris: Seule, 1972), pp. 198, 216-17. Genette uses the term 'focalized' when the 'narrating self' expresses the view-point of the 'experiencing self'.
14. Ginzburg, pp. 94-95. (Eng. trans. mine).
15. Ibid., p. 9. (Eng. trans. mine).
16. Ibid., p.11. (Eng. trans. mine).
17. Ibid., pp. 21-22. (Eng. trans. mine).
18. Ibid., pp. 101-02. (Eng. trans. mine).
19. Ibid., pp.110-12. (Eng. trans. mine).
20. Ibid., p. 133. (Eng. trans. mine).
21. Ibid., p. 167. (Eng. trans. mine).
22. Ibid., p. 205. (Eng. trans. mine).
23. Ibid., p. 203. (Eng. trans. mine).
24. Ricoeur, *Oneself as Another*, p. 115.
25. Ibid., p. 141.
26. Cf. Leo Spitzer, *Stilstudien* II, (1922, rpt. Munich: 1961), p. 478, cited by Dorrit Cohn, *Transparent Minds*, (Princeton: Princeton University Press, 1978).

27. Cf. Dorrit Cohn, pp. 145-153.
28. Marcel Proust, *A la recherche du temps perdu*, (Paris: Gallimard, 1954), p. 895. ("*La vraie vie, la vie enfin découverte et éclaircie, la seule vie par conséquent réellement vécue, c'est la littérature;. . .*"). Eng. trans. by C.K. Scott Moncrieff and Frederick A. Blossom, *Remembrance of Things Past* II, (New York: Random House, 1932), p. 1014.
29. Ginzburg, p. 81. (Eng. trans. mine).
30. Ibid., pp. 81-82. (Eng. trans. mine).
31. Ibid.
32. Ginzburg, p. 72. (Eng. trans. mine).
33. Proust, p. 896. Eng. trans. Moncrieff, cit.
34. Ginzburg, pp. 21, 59, 60, 66, 67, 123, 214.
35. Maintenance of 'family books' was an established tradition in Italian society in the period of Humanism and Renaissance. It was prevalent initially among the mercantile class but spread gradually to other classes in the society, as a mode of preservation of family history, carrying forward through generations the record of useful information, data and advice. While the published texts have been found mostly in Tuscany and some areas of Northern Italy, they have been traced in unpublished form in almost all the regions of Italy. While the practice began around 14th century, it peaked during the 15th century and lasted in its usual form till 16th century. However, chronological extensions of the genre can be traced till the beginning of the 19th century. Cf. Angelo Cicchetti, Raul Mordenti, *La scrittura dei libri di famiglia*, in Alberto Asor Rosa (ed), *Letteratura italiana*, Vol. III, (Turin: Einaudi, 1984), pp. 1117-59.
36. Ricoeur, pp. 147-48.
37. Ibid., p. 122.

REMO CESARANI

Autobiographies of Contemporary Intellectuals: What to Make of Them

Some time ago, a colleague and friend from the University of Rio de Janeiro in Brazil, by the name of João Cezar de Castro Rocha, young and of a vehement character, wrote a polemical article for the prestigious German daily "Die Frankfurter Allgemeine Zeitung", entitled *Exil als Metapher des Behagens* (Exile as Metaphor of Well-Being).[1] In this article he condemns without much ado the recent fashion, among quite a number of university Professors, and especially Professors of literature, to write, once they have reached a mature age, their own autobiography. He specifically aims at two prominent targets: the Palestinian-American Professor of English and Comparative literature at Columbia, Edward Said, who four years before his death in 2003, had written a memoir entitled *Out of Place*,[2] and the Oxbridgian Professor of English Literature, Terry Eagleton, who has recently moved from his ill-accepted Oxford college to a less prestigious academic institution, but in a familiar surrounding with a higher salary and good fringe benefits. Eagleton also published in 2001 a Memoir entitled *The Gamekeeper*.[3] In both cases we have to do with more than just ordinary academics: they are, or were, prominent intellectuals, with a political, or at least an ideological militancy. In the case of Said, there has been a steadfast support and promotion of the Palestinian cause, which brought on him a storm of criticism when he was elected the President of the Modern Language Association, from American Professors who were siding with Israel in the dispute between the two peoples. Eagleton, of course, is well known for his anti-capitalist stance.

De Castro Rocha mentions other autobiographical writings, for instance *Colored People. A Memoir* (1994) by the Harvard Professor Henry Louis Gates and *The Edge of Night. A Confession* (1994) by the Duke Professor Frank Lentricchia. He seems to think that it is probably due to them, and to the success of their books, that this kind of writing has become fashionable. In actual terms, the phenomenon is a much larger and persistent one, and I can give you a very long list of examples, especially from Europe. De Castro Rocha compares these various attempts with two different models supplied by the historical tradition of autobiographies by men of learning – in the first model the life of the protagonist is presented as practically eventless and is treated cursorily, soon giving way to a description of the man's intellectual work. It is, we could say, a biography of his writings. This is the case, for instance, of David Hume's *My Own Life* (1776), which starts with this phrase: "It is difficult for a man to speak long of himself without vanity; therefore I shall be short."[4] In conformity to this view, the narrative of Hume's life takes no more than twenty to twenty-five pages. It resembles one of our modern CVs, and can also remind us of the well-known tradition, in Christian literature, of the lives of the saints, in which what was important were not their private experiences or feelings, but their acts in public and the miracles performed. A typical example of this kind of autobiography, which was written even earlier than that of Hume, is represented, says De Castro Rocha, by Giambattista Vico, whose autobiography (*Vita*, 1725) is written in the third person, is completely devoid of any private detail and concentrates on showing how its author came to form the ideas that are expressed in his masterwork *La scienza nuova* (1725). De Castro Rocha does not mention it, but there was, in the humanistic age, an important earlier example of a third person autobiography, and those were the *Commentarii* (1464) by Pope Pius the 2nd, Enea Silvio Piccolomini.[5] In this case the author recounts in the first book his life, from childhood to the election to the papacy (travels and adventures, but especially his diplomatic career, his intellectual encounters and his numerous writings), and in the following eleven books he describes in vivid, often subjective and partisan details, his political activity, his many travels (with numerous geographic and historical descriptions), his programmes for strengthening the papacy and changing the balance of powers in Italy and Europe. The book, with all its anecdotic liveliness, its perceptive portraits of many historical figure of the time, its flippant, typically Tuscan comments on the pope's many enemies, has even an allegorical, or a mythical superstructure: the books are twelve (plus an unfinished thirteenth one), as in Virgil's *Aeneid*, and the author often alludes to his Virgilian names Aeneas and Sylvius. He presents himself as Sylvius, the Latin mythological figure, and as a newly-born pious Aeneas, who has come again to save the city of Rome.

As to the second model that, according to De Castro Rocha, stands behind many autobiographies by men of letters, it is characterized by the presence of a common theme, that of exile. According to De Castro Rocha, the condition of exile under which these autobiographies are written, gives shape and significance to their narratives. From Ovid to Dante Alighieri, the exile has become an existential "topos" in many autobiographies, especially by thinkers, poets, artists, professors and even by those who did not really go into exile (or in prison) for political reasons. The intellectuals of the Romantic age made a point of representing themselves as exiled from a world in which they could not find a place or feel at home. According to De Castro Rocha, the memoirs of Said and Eagleton are clearly connected with this tradition. They not only show an excess of vanity and indulge too easily in narrating the most private and intimate experiences of their life or in representing with a critical attitude, in the case of Eagleton even a satirical vein, the world of their family of origin, and the world from which they received their education, but they represent themselves as exiles, divided between two worlds, two languages, two cultures. Said says that he never knew which was the first language he spoke, Arabic or English, or which one was without any doubt his true language.[6] Terry Eagleton represents himself as profoundly divided, not between two languages, but between two social classes:

> Literacy was not the strongest point of my childhood community. It was a world which would no more have understood how you could make a living by writing books than how you could make one by picking wax from your ears.[7]

Both authors represent themselves as people banned to an unfriendly land and sent to live far from their real world, marginalized. But is this their real situation, asks De Castro Rocha. After all they are popular authors. They sell their books at home and abroad in great number, and teach in prestigious universities. Their condition is certainly very different from that of Ovid, who was sent by emperor Augustus to the desolate and backward shores of Pontus. Their exile is supported and made comfortable by strong and rich academic institutions. Their autobiographies, thinks De Castro Rocha, use the theme of exile simply as a literary topos, to express a melancholic and a paradoxical view of the world, to look with nostalgia or with an ironic, at times sarcastic detachment, on the totally different world from which they come and to express strong political opinions that have very little connection with the actual social and economic situation in which they now live.

In the case of Eagleton the sentiment of nostalgia is mixed with a much stronger sentiment of sarcastic detachment from the world of his youth: a rigid, absurd, doctrinarian and spectacular religion, a family that struggles to free itself from proletarian values only to embrace the values of the petit-bourgeoisie, etc. The intellectual career is played down while many details from the private life are given to the surprised reader, who feels amused and entertained. Said tells how his strong mother forbade him to marry his first love. Eagleton makes fun, in a very witty and entertaining way, of his family, of his teachers at Cambridge, of his fellow students, of his colleagues and of his scholarly discipline: Theory of Literature. He says of the religion which he was raised in:

> Catholicism was a world which combined rigorous thought with sensuous symbolism, the analytic with the aesthetic, so it was probably no accident that I was later to become a literary theorist. You did not see reason and mystery as incompatible. There was no danger that you could murder God, or a poem, by dissection. If the universalism of your faith encouraged you to ride roughshod over the particular, all those garish icons recalled you to what could be seen and handled, to the material world as signifier or sacrament.[8]

De Castro Rocha writes:

> Perhaps Said and Eagleton using the topos of exile try not to be there where their professional career has required them to be. This curious behaviour, on the other hand, is a clear negation of the self-critical attitude that they teach and recommend to their students.[9]

De Castro Rocha's reaction is probably exaggerated, but it is also understandable. In its hostility to the autobiographies of Said and Eagleton, one can recognize the awareness of two great transformations in our intellectual life: 1) on one hand the figure of the intellectual, as critical conscience of a nation, the "great intellectual" like Lev Tolstoj, Mohandas Karamchand Gandhi, Theodor Adorno, Jean-Paul Sartre, or Susan Sontag has almost entirely disappeared from our world and is being substituted with media and TV figures like Francis Fukuyama, Camille Paglia, Jean Baudrillard, Samuel Huntington and Oriana Fallaci. Rather than speaking of the death of the author – a formula that I believe lost any value even before the death of the critic that gave birth to it, Roland Barthes – I would speak of the minimization and reduction of stature of the intellectual as author, and at the same time of the multiplication of their public images, all dazzling and superficial and flat like the TV screen on which they appear in the talk shows; 2) on the other hand the contribution of the contemporary intellectuals to the modernization of the sexual and social habits of the common people, the models of transgression and experimentation offered by, for instance, the avant-garde intellectuals in the Bloosmbury or the Schwabing of the early twentieth century, or in the New York and Paris of the *entre-les-guerres* and the post-war times – the times of Sartre and Simone de Beauvoir – are not necessary any more, for transgression and experimentations are much more widespread and generalized. The private habits of the intellectuals or the professors have successfully been made fun of, and for good, by David

Lodge. In the general culture they have been substituted by new models coming from the film and musical industry, the world of fashion, that of the yuppies etcetera.

Two features seem to me problematic in the contemporary practice of autobiographical writings. The first one is the age-old problem of justification. In most of the autobiographies that I have read, there is a moment, usually in the preface or in some concluding remarks, in which their authors try to explain the reason why they have felt the necessity of writing an autobiography and why their readers should be interested in reading it. I have one here with me that has not only two different printed justifications, one at the beginning and one at the end of the book, but carries a personal, hand-written dedicatory note to me that says: "To Remo, who has witnessed some of the events of this book, in a gesture of friendship, and with the request of forgiving this senile sin." So to write an autobiography can be considered a sin, an act of vanity as Hume would have said. What can prompt an old Professor to recount his life and what can the reading public find interesting in it? Most of them try to find a strong motivation, which at times sounds convincing, at times not too much. Said would say that, by telling his own life, he tries to inspire in the reader some sympathy for the Palestinian people and to explain the historical reasons of the Israel-Palestinian conflict. Cesare Segre has two reasons that can justify his recounting the life of a Professor who has never been a prominent public figure and has had a rather uneventful private life.

> To write one's autobiography is an action of responsibility. Those who can present themselves as exemplary characters, as models for others, are in a fortunate position. They have a programme, which helps them to choose and accordingly treat their material. Others may write their autobiography because they have participated in some memorable events in their life: they invite their readers to share with them the exceptional experiences they have lived.
>
> It is rather difficult to apply these situations to me. I have no reason to present myself as a model, neither have I lived such an interesting life that justifies the effort of preserving its memory. Then why write it? It is the horrible times in which I lived; it is the perspective that those times have endowed me with against my own will, which perhaps deserve to be known by those who are younger. Later in life, my activity as literary critic and theoretician of literature allowed me to take part in important cultural events and to know scholars and critics who in those events have played a significant role. These reasons can perhaps justify this endeavour.[10]

"The horrible times" in which Segre lived refer to his childhood and youth when he had been, together with his family, the victim of the persecution of the Jews under Italian Fascism and German occupation of North Italy, a persecution which he fortunately survived, while many of his relatives were sent to die in the concentration camps. The second reason, i.e., "the important cultural events" he participated in, refer to his discipline. At the peak of his intellectual career Segre was a leading figure in founding, together with Roman Jakobson, Thomas Sebeok, Nicolas Ruwet, Umberto Eco and some others, the International Society of Semiotic Studies and in bringing to Italy the linguistic and critical school of Structuralism. He gives many interesting details on the way in which in a few years an enthusiastic intellectual network was built in many countries of Europe and America, and also on the way in which the movement gradually lost its momentum and entered into a period of crisis. He further argues:

> Some might think that I am driven by a hidden tendency to exhibitionism, as Vittorio Alfieri has intelligently confessed in his Life ("in writing my own life I was driven by many reasons, among which the strongest one was the love of myself"). If I denied this reason, a mischievous reader could raise the objection that mine was a Freudian negation. Alfieri adds that he feels justified by the fact that "every day one sees many other authors, many of whom are of minimal value, but of voluminous production, who write, read, or, at least, sell their own life". I could say, on my part, that every day one sees that people write, read, or, at least, sell the life of football heroes, of film stars, of adventurers, and of crownless kings: why not write, then, the life of an old philologist?[11]

Less convincing is probably the motivation of others, for instance of Romano Luperini, author of an autobiography full of interesting insights into his coming of age in the Tuscany of small cities and traditional farming villages and then of his travels and visiting professorships, in the multicultural cities of Canada.[12] But when he tries to connect his sentimental and intellectual experiences with the great political events of his country – the students movement, the assassination of Moro, the advent of postmodernism – we follow him with some effort.

The other problematic feature of contemporary autobiographical writings is properly connected with the passage from modernity to post-modernity and with a relevant change in our view of the human subject and the construction of his individuality. While, for instance, Terry Eagleton or Alberto Asor Rosa can still consider the experiences that they extract from their memory as a linear, compact one, as made up of successive stages in their personal *Bildungsroman*, others seem less sure of the inner coherence of the events of their life. Asor Rosa, for instance, who recounts in *L'alba di un mondo nuovo (The dawn of a new world)* only the first twenty so years of his life, creates a strong parallelism between his coming of age in Rome in the hardest years of the war and Italy's liberation from Fascism and the start of a new phase in its history. He goes so far as putting on the same level the memory of mankind, in its long history, and that of his own short life. He underlines with a certain pride the fact that the coming of age of Alberto Asor Rosa, in 1945, symbolically coincided with the new coming of age of the Italian people, after the dark period of Fascism:

> The memory of lost civilizations, of the great cities that once existed and now are no more, of men, things, objects, paths that originate from the darkest corners of the past and then spread out in an infinity of directions, the whole gigantic assembly of figures and events that can be included in such a small space [as that of our brain] and can be read, sorted, arranged and endlessly rearranged in every moment of our life (. . .) Genghis Khan, Tamerlane, Julius Caesar, the paladin Roland, Napoleon and Suvarov: all present, all contemporary in this sort of unlimited dark-room that is my mind, when I put together ages, historical periods, lifestyles, ways of being, traditions, continents and different geographical spaces. But all this is nothing when compared to what the human mind can conceive when one passes from the wide screen to the microscope and endeavours to analyze, or better to re-analyze, that great small personal universe that each one of us carries within himself, wherever he goes, wherever he is, whatever he might be doing, either good or bad, pleasant or unpleasant, and whatever might happen around him. (. . .)
>
> Remembering "my" past, I am at the same time my "I" of then and my "I" of today: that bodiless, impalpable image that dangles among the fog of past years and decades, and this concrete and active "I", this intellectually and physically self-perceptible person, a lump of lived experience that is still acting out, who is the only subject who can recall that image from the fog and give it back its life that otherwise it could never recapture. There is an immense power, which could hardly be compressed, in the human faculty of personal memory that is strictly bound to my individual "I", from which it can neither be cut off nor, more importantly, rejected. If I were not here, now, nobody else could manage the resurrection of the "I" of that time, of the bandaged and sleepy Lazarus who is in me.[13]

Many of the postmodern autobiographies are fragmentary. They are variously selective in choosing the episodes worth telling and do not try to find a general plot and a superior significance to all the narrated events. They often resort to different narrative strategies, shifting from a first person to a third person narration, including pieces of diaries, letters, general reflections, quotations of poems, imaginary dialogues or interviews.

An interesting example is offered by the autobiography of a French Professor of Hungarian origin, André Lorant, titled *Le Perroquet de Budapest – Une enfance revisitée* (*Budapest's Parrot – A Childhood Revisited*).[14] Born in 1930 in a rich Jewish family in Budapest, converted to Catholicism and perfectly integrated in the Hungarian society, Lorant witnessed with horror the Nazi persecution of the people of his race, the downfall of his family, the arrival of the Communist regime until he abandoned, like many others, in 1956, his country and went to live in Paris, where he became a Professor and a specialist of Balzac. What is particularly interesting in Lorant's autobiography is the way in which the narrator addresses his material: he is hesitant, not totally confident in his memory, aware of the psychoanalytical implications of the mechanism of remembrance and oblivion and not ready to find a significance in all the fragmentary memories of his childhood and youth. When he finally goes back to Budapest in 1997, and is given a room at the Hotel Peregrinus, meanwhile transformed into a residence for the guests of the University, he finds himself at less than a hundred meter from the house, in Fejér György Street, where he spent a great part of his adolescence and youth, from 1940 to 1956. Those hundred meters are for him an enormous distance, he walks around and around in the streets of the centre of Budapest without daring to go up to his former house. These peregrinations are accompanied by long hesitations and wanderings within his mind and the space of his memory. The transformations in his character and individuality, the formation of a new subject, in a new life, make it very difficult for him to recover that other self. Thus the actual writing of an autobiography becomes in this case an occasion for reasoning about the conditions and difficulties encountered in writing an autobiography.

NOTES AND REFERENCES

1. Joao Cezar De Castro Rocha, "Exil als Metapher des Behagens", in FAZ - *Frankfurter Allgemeine Zeitung*, September 4, 2002.
2. Edward Said, *Out of Place, A Memoir*, (London: Granta, 1999).
3. Terry Eagleton, *The Gatekeeper. A Memoir*, (London: Lane, 2001).
4. David Hume, *My own Life* (1776), electronic edition by James Freser, 1995, p. 1.
5. Enea Silvio Piccolomini. Papa Pio II, *I commentarii*, Latin text and Italian translation; trans. and ed. Luigi Totaro, (Milan: Adelphi, 1984).
6. Said, pp. XIII-XIV.
7. Eagleton, p. 51.
8. Eagleton, p. 33. A somewhat different position that Eagleton has taken in the essay "The Meaning of Life", (Oxford: Oxford University Press, 2007), in which he confesses that the Catholic education has given him important philosophical and logical tools.

9. De Castro Rocha, *FAZ*. In original: "Im Vergleich dazu ist das Exil von Said oder Eagleton eher ein literarischer Topos, der Kritik abwehren soll. Während beide Autoren über marginalisierte Kulturen oder Gesellschaftsklassen schreiben, haben sie in dem von ihnen immer wieder kritisierten Zentrum eine akademische Karriere gemacht. Die Ironie liegt auf der Hand. So konnte ein Buch wie Saids *Orientalism* kaum außerhalb des westlichen Universitätssystems geschrieben und rezipiert werden, ebensowenig wie Eagletons radikale Kapitalismuskritik. Vielleicht machen Said und Eagleton mit dem Topos des Exils den Versuch, nicht dort zu sein, wo sie ihr berufliches Lebens verbracht haben. Dieses Vorgehen negiert allerdings die selbstkritische Haltung, die sie ihre Studenten gelehrt haben."
10. Cesare Segre, *Per curiosità*, (Turin: Einaudi, 1999), pp. 3-4. (English trans. mine)
11. See Cesare Segre, *Notizie dalla crisi*, (Turin: Einaudi,1993).
12. Romano Luperini, *I salici sono piante acquatiche*, (Lecce: Manni, 2002).
13. Alberto Asor Rosa, *L'alba di un mondo nuovo*, (Turin: Einaudi, 2002), pp. 7-8. (English trans. mine)
14. André Lorant, *Le perroquet de Budapest – Une enfance revisitée*, (Paris: Hamy, 2002).

MANFRED STASSEN

The "Stasi" as Eckermann: Reflections on Christa Wolf's Post-Wall Autobiography *What's Left*

This slim volume allegedly written, but not published, around the 30th anniversary of the former (communist) German Democratic Republic (GDR), and the 50th anniversary of the author, in the summer of 1979, and then re-worked, to an extent unknown, ten years later, in November of 1989 – i.e., immediately after the fall of the Berlin wall of November 09 – and published shortly 'b e f o r e' the official German unification in October of 1990 only, was the object of a major literary and political controversy in the early days of United Germany. The detractors of its nationally respected and internationally acclaimed author, Christa Wolf, charged her with cowardice for not having published the book – in the West – at the time it was written, and with political expediency and white-washing of her past allegiances, for having published it 'a f t e r' the end of the regime that is meant to be the villain of the piece.

Both the official English translation of *Was bleibt*, "What remains", and a British Germanist and specialist of the works of GDR writers, Keith Bullivant's proposal, "What will remain", forego the opportunity (which English provides!) of referring to the at once nostalgic and utopian elements of a "left" alternative – as a "third way" for Germany – that is very much part of Christa Wolf's agenda in this book.

What's left (my translation!) is primarily a chronicle of only one day in the privileged life of an author in a dictatorship – compare A. Solshenytsin's *Один День Йвана Денисовица (One Day in the Life of Ivan Denissovitch)* – whom the regime used as a show-case on the international stock exchange of cultural competition between the two blocs on either side of the Iron Curtain. By her own assessment, it is an "accountant's account" (*ein krämerischer Bericht*) of, not at all an investigation into, (her) life in a society where many have lived the lives of "Stasi-amese twins", i.e., where perpetrators and victims could not then, and cannot easily today, be told apart. To be able to tell them apart better, the United German government has created the largest "literary" research agency in the world, the *Amt der/s Bundesbeauftragten für die Unterlagen des Staatssicherheitsdienstes der ehemaligen Deutschen Demokratischen Republik (BStU)* or *Gauck-Behörde* (after its first director, the pastor Joachim Gauck), where 3100 civil servants study 180 kilometres of "denunciation literature": it consists of Stasi files which assemble the "intelligence" gathered by some 500,000 ordinary citizens, engaged as "informal (government) informants" (*Informelle Mitarbeiter* - IM), on the rest of the GDR population of 20 million in the 40 years of its existence. Unwittingly, United Germany thus gave the world a new literary genre which is perhaps the GDR's largest cultural legacy. While the romantic infatuation of the German intellectuals with India in the 19th century was institutionalized in 19 chairs of Indology at Germany universities (which persist to this day), the postmodern infatuation, by victims and voyeurs alike, with denunciation literature (pieces in which they frequently play the leading role!), led to a monstrous research institution the size of all Max-Planck Institutes put together, whose lease on life is as yet anybody's guess.

I. THE CONTEXT

The account is a condensation (*Ver-Dichtung*) of three years of being the object of intense observation by the ubiquitous, anonymous, yet easily identifiable minions of the "authorities", into one single day, which affords the author – much like the protagonists in Joyce's *Dubliners* – a myriad of epiphanies about herself and life in this strange and increasingly estranged habitat which was the capital of the GDR, East Berlin.

The account thus becomes a novel of recognition and its genesis. The recognition is that in a state such as the GDR, perpetrators and victims are largely identical: being part of its "officialdom" is as much a sign of complicity as accepting one's victimization is a form of strengthening the regime.

The three years in which Christa Wolf recognizes that she is being "observed", are three significant years in the short history of the GDR: the years 1976 through 1979. The integration of the GDR as a second, separate German state into the system of the United Nations in 1973 and the cultural thaw that occurred after the further cooptation of the GDR by the Conference on Security and Cooperation in Europe (CSCE) in Helsinki in 1975, had sufficiently threatened the regime. The ensuing collective paranoia of its leadership led to the expulsion of the dissident song writer Wolf Biermann after his globally televised concert in Cologne in 1976: the first case of a forced German-German exile. Biermann who had deliberately left West Germany in 1953 in order to join the state which he thought had emerged as the better German alternative out of the Nazi dictatorship, had received an iconic status in the GDR, even though – or perhaps because – he was not allowed to perform publicly anymore ever since 1964. The records of the twelve years between 1964 and 1976 – produced by West German specialists in his "Chausseestrasse 131" refuge and then smuggled out of East Germany – with his guitar fighting the noise of the street car traffic outside, became cult objects for the left on either side of the Wall. His tremendous popularity prevented the East German regime from "eliminating" him. When they revoked his citizenship and visa after the Cologne concert and did not allow him to go back to East Berlin, Heinrich Böll, the German Nobel Laureate for Literature, said to him: *Jetzt bist Du ein In-die-Heimat-Vertriebener!* (Now they have "displaced" you into your home-country!). Simultaneously, in his elective "home-country", the GDR, the largest protest of (otherwise GDR-loyal) artists and intellectuals known in its history was mounted against this decision. They immediately became the prime target group for observation by the State Security, the Stasi. Implicitly, Christa Wolf, despite her being the decorated show-piece of the regime's cultural politics, was one of them. Many observers of these events today would agree that 1976 and its immediate aftermath was the beginning of the end of the GDR.

It is hard to imagine for citizens of the free world what it meant to be a writer in the GDR (and the other satellite states of the former Soviet Union). With the "normal" truth-telling institutions – the Press, Historiography, the Churches, etc. being eliminated or *gleichgeschaltet* (brought in line with the official ideology of the State), the writers had to assume their erstwhile function. In order to fulfil it adequately, they had to be overtly loyal to the regime and its proclaimed socialist and anti-fascist principles of the "better" state on German soil, and they had to deal judiciously with the ensuing "privileges" accruing to them. They had to develop special writing skills, in order to write around the censor and still reach their readers and win their trust. This required duplicity turned the more sensitive among them into near-schizophrenic existences or drove them into "exile" (where the quality of their writing invariably declined so that, after a few years in the lime-light of ideological exploitation by the West, they disappeared into total oblivion). Those who remained walked a tight-rope between responsibility and a bad conscience.

II. THE TEXT

The 1979 version of *Was bleibt* – so Christa Wolf tells us – had a question mark at the end: *Was bleibt?* As we have seen, writers in the context of a censorship-driven literary culture have "to make a mark" (*Zeichen setzen*). Punctuation, therefore, such as an added or omitted question mark, is more than a mere convention: it becomes part of the message. In 1979, the question mark clearly pointed the account into the direction of an accountant's account (*krämerischer Bericht*) that could easily have degenerated into an enumeration of the 'p a s t' legacies and achievements of the GDR (*das anti-faschistische Erbe, die sozialistischen Errungenschaften*). In 1989, however, the omitted question mark clearly points the text into the direction of the 'f u t u r e', especially the future of socialism, i.e., of the "Left", in Germany. A number of writers had gotten together and formed a group working on a "third way" for Germany: a new Democratic East Germany, not communist and not capitalist, existing alongside West Germany, at least for the time necessary to work out a new Constitution for a United Germany. And in the good old German tradition, it was the writers who worked on this project. The title of Christa Wolf's text – without the question mark – recalls Hölderlin's dictum: *Was bleibet aber, stiften die Dichter* (it is the poets who create the legacy for posterity).[1]

On closer inspection, the account reveals itself as a classical autobiography. For this genre, and for Christa Wolf's text, St. Augustine's *Confessiones* is the model. A *con-fessio* is, first and foremost, a self-incrimination. Here, the writer incriminates herself for not having lived up to the responsibility of a writer vis-à-vis the masses in a dictatorship. She pleads guilty of intellectual pride and of shirking away from translating her privilege into saying what can normally not be said: the writer's imperative is *das Unsagbare sagen*. A socialist *confessio* contains, of course, no *mea culpa*, since a *mea culpa* makes sense only where there is the prospect of an absolution. Her autobiography is, therefore, an *apologia pro vita sua*, much like Socrates'. A *confessio* is, second, a *pro-fessio*, a profession of faith in true socialism over against the perverted one (*der real existierende Sozialismus*) in the Soviet bloc. It takes tremendous courage to pro-fess, to give testimony (*Zeugnis ablegen*) to one's faith, in the face of a hostile state religion. *Zeugnis ablegen* is the business of the *martyros*, the martyr: Wolf (Biermann) and Christa (Wolf) – her very name signals the identity of the political program between her and Biermann! – become thus the legitimate heirs of the socialist martyrs Karl (Liebknecht) and Rosa (Luxemburg). It is true that Wolf and Christa were never in danger of being assassinated – as Karl and Rosa actually were assassinated only 60 years earlier (in 1919), when true socialism was repressed in Germany, but then from the political "right" and not, as now in the GDR, from the so-called political "left". Wolf and Christa were "killed" through forced "exile" and silenced through their forced practice of applying "scissors in the head" (anticipated, internalized repression, auto-censorship), the *Schere im Kopf* tactics of Meister Neunmalklug,[2] the wizard of dissimulation. However, the situation deprived the new martyrs both of the life of the City (*bios politicos*) and the life of the Language (*bios logos*).

The internalization of surveillance leads to the surveillance of the self by itself. Both subjects of surveillance, the *Ministerium für Staatssicherheit* (The Ministry for State Security)[3] through its *Hauptabteilung* (Main Division), and the writer with the awareness of being both a subject and an object of surveillance, ultimately serve the same goal: *Aufklärung* (enlightenment): the one by providing intelligence on every possible subversive aspect of the public and private lives of its citizens, and the writer, dancing on a tight rope, by attempting to say the unsayable. The forces of surveillance thus become a testing board for the writers, against which they bounce off verbal experiments like balls in squash, in order to try out their "compatibility" (Christa Wolf, e.g., used to write *Als ob-Briefe* – letters written "as if" the author did not suspect that they were read by the intelligence services). The Stasi becomes the writers' Eckermann.[4]

The day of recognition that prompted the *confessio/professio* is a day in Spring season, in the month of March, on Easter (cf. Faust who gave the Bible a new language and was saved from suicide when the Easter bells rang), when the dialectic between the death of the Old and the birth of the New is suggested by nature. Of course, here the "Old" is the old language of writing about "really existing" socialism, and the "New" is the new, "free" language of testifying to the unperverted, pure socialism, the unsayable.

> Sie standen wieder da. Es war neun Uhr fünf. Seit drei Minuten standen sie wieder da, ich hatte es sofort gemerkt. Ich hatte einen Ruck gespürt, den Ausschlag eines Zeigers in mir, der nachzitterte. Ein Blick, beinahe überflüssig, bestätigte es. Die Farbe des Autos war heute ein gedecktes Grün, seine Besatzung bestand aus drei jungen Herren. Ob diese Herren ausgewechselt wurden wie die Autos? (. . .) Sie waren nicht meinesgleichen. Sie waren Abgesandte des anderen. Lange schon war es mir nicht mehr in den Sinn gekommen, dicht an jenen Autos vorbeizustreichen und grimmigen Gesichts hineinzustarren, um den gläsernen Blicken der Insassen zu begegnen, deren Auftrag es doch sein musste, als das, was sie waren, ausgemacht zu werden und dadurch Wut, besser: Angst zu erzeugen, die bekanntlich manche Menschen zum Einlenken treibt, andere zu unüberlegten Handlungen, welche ihrerseits wieder als Indizienbeweis dienen konnten für die Notwendigkeit der Observation. Irgend jemand, das fühlte ich stark, musste versuchen, diesen Teufelskreis zu durchbrechen.[5]

The story of this recognition is told through four extended epiphanies:

(i) Jürgen M. and the "Elfi Story" (a friend having turned into her "intelligence officer" at the Stasi, and a sales woman's Jewish friend, first "observed" in 1936/37, and later, in 1942, deported to the death camps by the Nazis);

\ (ii) the man with the Manchester jacket in the supermarket (emotional reminiscence of true socialism in the early days of the 19th century);

(iii) the young female writer whose "work" she reads (compare the all-decisive *tolle lege!* episode in Augustine's *Confessiones*, which both occur at 3 p.m.) – the hour of the death of Christ and the beginning of the New Awakening and Resurrection;

(iv) the writer's evening at the *Kulturhaus*, *Club der Volkssolidarität*, and the electrifying question by a nurse about what kind of future might emerge from this present ("What will be left?"!), which leads to a spontaneous expression of Volkssolidarität against the State (later, during the GDR's velvet revolution, articulated as *Wir sind das Volk!* (We are the people !)) in the streets of Leipzig.

And the four epiphanies are garnished and reinforced by four songs that follow the significant stages of the genesis of her recognition, from childhood innocence through political commitment, to near-resignation and, finally, the awareness that, no matter how estranged your state has become, you can never really leave it (just like St. Augustine's recognition account is punctuated by his prayers following the stages of his conversion):

(i) *Auf einem Baum ein Kuckuck saß, simsadimbam. . .*
(A cuckoo sat upon a tree . . .);

(ii) *Dem Karl Liebknecht haben wir's geschworen, der Rosa Luxemburg reichen wir die Hand*
(We've sworn allegiance to Karl Liebknecht, and we hold out our hands to Rosa Luxemburg);

(iii) *Geht nicht, sagen kluge Leute, zweimal zwei ist niemals drei*
(No way, the smart people say, two time two will never be three);

(iv) *Fremd bin ich eingezogen, fremd zieh' ich wieder aus.*
(As a stranger I moved in, as a stranger I shall leave again.)

III. OLD VS. NEW LANGUAGE

When writers diagnose a dichotomy in their language, i.e., stipulate two divergent languages in and for their writing, it is worth looking at the distinction a little closer. We already know that Christa Wolf's old language is a language in chains, it will never be able to say the unsayable. Writing in the old language means writing in words that are accurate, but that do not hit the mark (*die Wörter treffen zu, aber sie treffen nicht*). They select and describe facts (Wittgenstein's *Tatsachen*: *Die Welt ist alles, was der Fall ist*), but they do so only to camouflage reality (*das Tatsächliche*). Her new language, of which we already know that it will be free, is a language the sounds of which she already has in her ear, but not yet on her tongue. But aural language must become oral language, before it can be communicated. In a dictatorship, the otherwise obsolete oral tradition of cultural communication celebrates an important revival. The publicly unsayable is either literally "said" or written through the "samizdat" (a distribution network for clandestine copies of hand-written or dactylographic texts). The new language has to learn to sacrifice the visible to the invisible (cf. Ralph Ellisons's *Invisible Man* which gives a voice to the allegedly non-existence of race discrimination in the United States). And, the new language will articulate the author's inner unrest (compare St. Augustine's *cor inquietum* (restless heart) with which he opens his *Confessiones*) of someone who has not been able to come into his own under the old regime. The new language will be a genuine expression of the author's new-found life, only once she has realized that the visceral fear of the State's surveillance apparatus will not have disappeared when there are no real cars left outside her window, but only their phantom pictures on her retina. That genuine language will finally be able to talk about "what's left": what the author's City is founded on (*was ihr zugrundeliegt*), and what will eventually "un-found" it (*woran sie zugrundegeht*).

IV. THE AFTERMATH

The "City", the former GDR, was un-founded before Christa Wolf had fully found her new language. It is anybody's guess whether events in Germany would have taken a different turn if Christa Wolf and her colleagues in East Germany had found that new language earlier, i.e., sometime between 1979 and 1989. As it is, it was not the poets who were able to guarantee what might have been worth preserving, what should have/could have been "left" in the United Germany. For all those who had wished for a different outcome, Hölderlin's optimism finally died in the unification process: there are no (more) private, poetic solutions to public, political problems. Christa Wolf's *con-fessio* of a romantic poet's bad conscience of having recognized, but not materialized a new language in time, and her *pro-fessio* in favour of a German future with many shades of grey, came too late. From Martin Luther's heartland, she had rejected his dictum *Deine Rede sei: Ja, Ja, Nein, nein!* (Thou shalt opt for either Yes or No!) in favour of a "third way". The events of the politically accelerated unification, the "Kohl-onisation"[6] of the GDR by the FRG, have proven that the people who believed that *zweimal zwei* could sometimes be *drei*, are simple not *kluge Leute.*

The West German more and more *angepaßtes Feuilleton* (streamlined cultural press) has drawn two reprehensible, slanderous conclusions from this *con/pro-fessio*: Christa Wolf's late publishing of her autobiography shows the moral deficiency of an author who had deliberately stayed with the old regime and, for the most part, supported it. And, we were wrong in West Germany, together with the majority of the Germanists abroad, in praising East German literature as the better German literature for the 40 years of the GDR's existence: as one can allegedly see now – when no more bonuses need to be given to potentially dissident GDR writers for political reasons – a cool analysis will reveal their limitations as writers and, because of the high moral status that they enjoyed, but ultimately betrayed, their hypocrisy. To the *Besserwessis*, Western Germany was, and a reformed East, on the exact blueprint of the West, certainly is the better Germany - *quod erat demonstrandum*.[7]

NOTES AND REFERENCES

1. Friedrich Hölderlin, "Andenken". Die vaterländischen Gesänge in *Werke und Briefe*, 3. Bände, hrsg. V. Friedrich Beissner und Jochen Schmidt, (Frankfurt a. M.: Insel, 1969), pp. 194-96.
2. A figure from German folktales, one who is, "nine times smarter than all others"; in the GDR a "master of dissimulation" to outsmart the "authorities"; later after the *Wende* (unification), a "Besserwessi" – one of the many West-German experts who swarmed into the territory of the former GDR to teach the population the ropes of capitalism.
3. *Stasi* – short for *Staatssicherheit* (State Security Administration in the GDR in the rank of a ministry).
4. Goethe's private "secretary" with whom he discussed issues of the day and of his writings, and to whom he dictated most of his literary works. The reference is to Wolf Biermann's satirical song "Die Stasi ist mein Eckermann".
5. Christa Wolf, *Was bleibt*. Erzählung, (Berlin/Weimar/Frankfurt a.M.: Luchterhandverlag, 1990), pp. 15-21.
6. A pun on the charge that the Federal Republic of Germany "kohl-onized / colonized" the former GDR, under the leadership of the architect of German unification, Chancellor Helmut Kohl.
7. "what was to be proven" (by the streamlined Western feuilleton press).

MARGIT KÖVES

"As if I were in a Novel . . .": Péter Esterházy's *Corrected Version*

The diary requires a stable, persistent "I" and here exactly this will become the mysterious subject of doubt. In the formal sense too, because next to the "I" presented as "I" emerges a writer (ha-ha!) named: I(mre) K(ertész). It seems one should take the motto seriously: one can be at best the co-author of the "I", this fiction.

Péter Esterházy about Imre Kertész's *Another One*

This paper deals with *Corrected Version*,[1] which is the "epilogue" of Péter Esterházy's novel *Celestial Harmonies*. The motto of the paper, taken from Esterházy's review of Imre Kertész's work, refers to the construction of the "I", the narrator of the autobiography with emphasis on the blending of fact and fiction. In *Corrected Version*, which is presented in the form of the writer's diary, Esterházy establishes his individuality in a specific context, in relationship to his father. My paper shows the manner in which Esterházy's diary presents a constructed "I" in this autobiographical space and adopts the features of the genre.

Christa Wolf's autobiography[2] *Was bleibt* (*What remains*), written in 1979-1989 and recent autobiographical writing from East Germany and the Eastern part of Europe invoke the role of the Stasi, i.e., police supervision in Eastern Europe till the fall of Berlin wall. In this paper I am going to give details about the involvement of Péter Esterházy's father, Mátyás Esterházy, with the Hungarian secret police. In the first part of the paper, I give information about the role of the secret police in Hungary in order to place Esterházy's book in its political-historical surrounding. The location of the book in the contemporary network of power is important because of the illusions of innocence, resistance and purity that surround the position of the poet and the writer in Hungary. In the second part of the paper I examine *Corrected Version* in the framework of its genre, language, the subject and the reader.

Corrected Version is defined as an additional third part of a trilogy. The first two parts, Book One *Numbered Sentences from the Lives of the Esterházy Family* and Book Two *Confessions of an Esterházy Family* were published in *Celestial Harmonies*[3] (2000). *Corrected Version* appeared in 2002 with the subtitle: *Supplement to Celestial Harmonies.* The title relates to Errata, the list of errors attached to a publication. It is the disclosure of Esterházy's father's secret past as a police informer, with the code name, Csanádi.

I

In 1999 after the death of his father, while Esterházy was correcting the proofs of his novel *Celestial Harmonies* he made a shocking discovery. On a hint from K., a friend, he went to the Historical Archive in Budapest; he saw his father's handwriting and his involvement with the police became evident. Esterházy immersed himself in the files to find out about the circumstances and depth of his father's participation. He describes *Corrected Version* to his publisher as a "quasi-detective story" and re-reads his father's files and *Celestial Harmonies* in a diary. The narrator takes on four roles, which overlap the narrative voices: transcriber-copyist-the voice of his father, Mátyás Esterházy as Csanádi reporting to the police, with the remarks of the police officers. The other voice is the voice of the diarist – the essay-writer, the third is the witness and the fourth, the historian who re-reads his notes and interprets them at different points of time, between 1999 and 2002. To use Esterházy's comment on Kertész's *Another One*, these voices are the "co-authors" of the diarist – narrator in *Corrected Version.*

The book builds on the personal involvement of the readers. As an observer, the narrator shows in his diary how Csanádi becomes entangled in the reporting and how his initial resistance gradually changes into submission and later cooperation, offering voluntary information. The first reviews of *Corrected Version* responded to this aspect, recalling personal memories and family history.

Ferenc Szijj[4] describes in a review how he found incriminating documents in his elder brother's desk; Sándor Radnóti[5] writes about the great Central- and East European secret police, denunciation, the everyday life of the informer and the role of the Secret Police. Criticism also deals with the aesthetic aspects of *Corrected Version* and Esterházy's turning point from a postmodernist to a realist writer. Beáta Thomka[6] stresses that Esterházy's diary is a fictional and historical re-reading of his life and his earlier work. The form of the diary creates the autobiographical space for self-understanding and a new interpretation.[7] This space provides the author the opportunity for the re-reading of his earlier novel *Celestial Harmonies* and links confession and autobiography. This also implies the change in the poetics in the three books *Numbered Sentences from the Lives of the Esterházy Family, Confessions of an Esterházy Family* and *Corrected Version* in terms of the constitution of the subject and space and time.

Secret Police

The enthusiasm over the political changes in Eastern Europe was supplemented by the discovery of the pervasive presence of the police in the everyday life of citizens in the earlier system, the fact that individuals connected with the secret service informed on their colleagues, their network of friends and their families. The information about this involvement was explosive, as in the case of the well-known "Stasi-scandal" even though the proportions were different in each country. The secret police seemed to be the most sinister feature of the system. In Hungary, the first democratically elected Parliament (1990-94) made it possible for every individual to look into reports written on him or her, but the issue of police informers was not dealt with thoroughly. Suspicion and new information about internal spying stirred up emotions several times. A scandal erupted in 2002 involving the newly elected Socialist Prime Minister, Péter Medgyessi when it was discovered that he worked for the Hungarian security. He had to answer charges in a public interview lasting 90 minutes where he argued that as an expert in international finance, he belonged to the III/2 category, and at this post he protected Hungarian national interests against Soviet positions.

The publication of *Corrected Version* followed soon after this upheaval. The coalition Government of Socialists and Free Democrats made the archive of police files more accessible since 2002. This can be connected with the internal developments in the Hungarian Socialist Party. Since 2003, any individual can have the name of persons who reported about him. A new bill in Parliament suggests that information about the identity of agents should be available to everybody. The issue of police reporting remains an effective political weapon in Hungary and in other countries of Eastern Europe. On 1st March 2005 a new list of 218 agents was released on the Internet in Hungary by an independent organization. The list consists of the names of selected persons only which leaves ample scope for manipulation. Such lists were published in Romania,[8] in Poland in 2005,[9] in Bulgaria,[10] in the Czech Republic,[11] in Slovenia[12] and in Slovakia.[13] These lists without the details of collaboration are open to political manipulation.

In the period 1956-1980 when Mátyás Esterházy worked for the secret police, the state was trying to protect itself against the "class enemy", "foreign interference and possible spying" from abroad. The aristocratic Esterházy family, which was categorized as class enemy could easily establish contact with individuals who belonged to similar social groups. Mátyás Esterházy, under the pseudonym, Csanádi reported about bridge partners and family members in Hungary and abroad.

There is legal[14] and historical research dealing with the police reports. János Kenedi's *Small Reader for State Security*[15] shows the complex system of collaboration between the police and the party apparatus: the mechanisms of misinformation, exaggeration and trivialization. In my paper I would like to show how these features of the system, the object of Esterházy's research in the State Archives, repeat themselves and are re-enacted in the form of absolutism and relativism in *Corrected Version*. Dominique LaCapra[16] calls them parallel processes, when past events, which you study in your research, resurface in your behaviour and action.

The subtitle of Kenedi's book *23rd October, 15th March, 16th June* refers to the fact that police phobia centred around dates symbolizing political events or national independence: 15th March, the 1848 revolution against the Habsburgs, 16th of June, the execution of Imre Nagy in 1962, and 23rd October, the beginning of the 1956 Uprising. The attempt of the state and the Communist Party to protect itself from ideological enemies created a double system, a double discourse at several levels. The III/III department of the police, which engaged Mátyás Esterházy focused on the Church, on oppositional figures, the alternative Marxist left, cultural institutions, music ensembles and football fans. Informers were instructed to visit frequently these institutions and establish contacts.

Double System

Kádár's reforms relied on this double system in many ways. In economic terms — on the one hand they adopted socialist planning and subordinated themselves to the division of market in COMECON, and on the other hand they introduced reforms and through delays and manipulation increased the production and the flexibility of the system. This created a higher quality of life and living standard than what existed in other socialist countries and Hungarians appreciated this difference.

In September 1957 after the failure of the 1956 Revolution and the occupation of Hungary by the Soviet Army, Hungarian writers and scientists, many of them supporters of the 1956 Revolution, signed a joint statement condemning the same Revolution, thus ratifying the official position of the Kádár Government. This was the price which was paid for the relative peace of the next three decades. The statement was addressed to the UNO and it lent legitimacy to Kádár Government. When events connected with '56 are discussed, silence envelops this particular document in the same way as with other, similar events in the past when writers and poets were in complicity with the establishment. The image of the poet and writer who offers resistance to the evil in history persists. István Eörsi (1931-2005) calls it in psychoanalytical terms the "suppression of suppression",[17] the unwillingness on the part of Hungarian writers and scientists to acknowledge their participation in the compromise. István Margócsy[18] refers to a line of historical events and to writers like Mór Jókai (1825-1904), Petõfi's friend who tried to ingratiate himself with Francis Joseph (1830-1916), the Habsburg ruler (1848-1916) or the contribution of the Hungarian populist writers to the Lillafüred meeting in 1942 during World War II. Esterházy calls this feature in *Corrected Version* self-deception, the refusal to see our own role in our calamities. The writers who agreed to the terms and conditions that they would not directly participate in politics or denounce "official" Hungary were released from prison after 1961. Imre Kertész's novel *Fiasco*[19] depicts the atmosphere of insincerity and suspicion in the context of the obstacles in the publication of his Nobel-prize winning novel *Fateless*.

II

Esterházy (1950) brought "ontological happiness" (7) in the atmosphere of suspicion. This is how Miklós Mészöly (1921-2001) described his state of mind, after the publication of his initial books *Fancsiko and Pinta* (1976) and *Do not Sail on the Waters of Papistry* (1977). In 1979 Esterházy published the *Novel of Production,* an ironical imitation of Soviet novels of production in the 1930s. The 'Novels of Production' were representing industrialization and nationalization in a stylised, unproblematic way. Esterházy poked fun of the genre of the novel of production; his *Novel of Production* transformed the factory and its surroundings into grammatical space with linguistic games and this book created a literary sensation. In 1986 *Introduction into Literature* established a place for the postmodern novel in Hungary. In it he referred to the well-known aristocratic position and mythology of his family. The information about his father's betrayal transformed, however, his relationship to the world and cast a shadow on the "ontological happiness" that had become part of his identity as he looked straight in the face his father's double life.

> I didn't know this was the last second of my life when I could be happy the way I can, because I can, such is my constitution, I am gifted in this, this is what I received from the Sky (. . .) I didn't know it will end soon and such a shadow will settle into me. Well not so big: only as big, as I am, I didn't know that my heart was light for the last time. (7)

The development of the subject in the novel as the evolution of inner and outer events is part of the realist and modernist novel. Esterházy developed different methods of the formation of the subject. In *Corrected Version* the author suggests in the beginning of the novel:

> This realist prose does not suit me. I should write down what happens without adding, deducting anything; I am fifty years old, but I have not done so far such a thing. I would like to have continuously a cassette-recorder and a video-recorder around, with me. I used to measure my sentences to sentences, not to »reality«, this is why I see how deformed they are. (27)

Realism

The narrator raises the problem of interpretation in *Corrected Version.* He provides the parameters and the framework in which his book needs to be read. He emphasizes the "hide and-seek" between the fictive and non-fictive elements of his earlier work. He is not satisfied with the realist character of his work; he calls it a "shitpulp" (16) and gives it the title "The whining of a poor little realist guy".

A section of critics (Péter Balassa and Gergely Angyalosi) ask whether *Corrected Version* is not a step back from Esterházy's earlier prose. The realism of *Corrected Version,* where the reports are unchangeable, replaces the attitude of the first two books of *Celestial Harmonies.* In *Numbered Sentences* the sentences, the units of the novel build on a situation, on a condition or on a feature of character. In *Confessions of an Esterházy Family* the narrator introduces the members of the Esterházy family in reported speech, the "confessions" of the "sceptical" and "authoritarian" grandfather, Móric Esterházy and other family members. *Corrected Version* claims that it has chosen a different rhetoric, the greatest possible objectivity. The police reports cannot be changed, because their existence and evidence are primary. In the diary, he interprets the reports and counters his past and present. The commentary relies on the authenticity of the original text. Esterházy asserts that his book is a record: "This is not a confession: it is a record." (23)

The narrator refers to "realism" as part of his work; he has to go through his father's files and takes them down faithfully. Realism indicates "civil sincerity" in *Corrected Version,* which is established by a series of autobiographical and historical references. Realism additionally means that the narrator has to go through a struggle of self-understanding within reality, and time and surrounding are factors in these changes.

The voices of Mátyás Esterházy as Csanádi, the remarks of the police-officers, the diarist, the witness and the essayist emerge as the author re-reads his transcriptions at various points of time between. To emphasize the multiplicity of voices Esterházy uses the tools of postmodern fiction:

insertion, supplement and overwriting. He emphasizes the fissures of reports: The informer's files (his father's reports) are copied in brown and the reports written by his father and his superiors at the internal security are separated. He distances the earlier texts, his own commentary by marking and using different types of brackets. The poetics of *Corrected Version* evolves along the contrast of the police reports and the personal language of the narrator, loaded with shame, responsibility, occasional irony and fun.

Language: Language in Esterházy's novels reflects the statement of Wittgenstein that there is only language usage and no inherent meaning in words. Esterházy constructs situations with great spontaneity where his sense of linguistic invention can unfold. *Celestial Harmonies* unfolds this trend further. But the narrator clarifies in *Corrected Version* that his linguistic facility is in jeopardy: "I imagined: I was losing my language. I lost my language together with my father."

In *Corrected Version* he breaks up language into fragmented parts. In the first place this means a revision of the mode of the script. He uses letters to signify the automatic responses of the body: 1. ö – *önsajnálat* [S- self-pity]; 2. k – *könnyek* [T- tears]; 3. j.e. – *jut eszembe* [R- remember]; 4. "e" – *elképzeltem* [I- I imagined]. Esterházy shortens the names of friends, relations and acquaintances his father reported about, using their initials. Apart from the practical function of hiding the names from publicity, this method guarantees the documentary nature of evidence and distances the text.

In the diary, Esterházy scrutinises the reports and the remarks made by his father's superiors. He comments on how his father is "slipping into his role" as an agent "step-by-step", first taking care "to say only what they [his superiors] already know" (68), to make one more step offering small pieces of information, which he considers harmless; to emerge as a skilful, creative agent and pass into the category of voluntary collaborator.

In *Corrected Version* two levels meet, the documentary style of the reports and the personal. The colour of the font (brown and black) and the style (various forms of brackets) emphasize the temporal fault lines. The contrast of the two: the mechanical language of the reports, their vacant official references at one level and the narrator's personal language of memory, confession and self-analysis, form the autobiography. Uncovering and clarity replace the double discourse of hiding, secrecy, coercion, intimidation, forgetting and insinuation. Interpretation and critical language of self-perception in Esterházy's case create self-irony, like in his other novels.

Subject – Identity

In *Celestial Harmonies* Esterházy undercuts the constitution of personality. The narrative "I", the writing subject is transformed by exploring the "I-We" relationship. This also means that Esterházy extends the notion of "I" to his father. In an interview[20] Esterházy pointed out that the main problem of twentieth century is who to address, whether what is said would reach or not, whether it would be considered "ideological small talk", or "one mumbles to oneself". "The stake is whether it reaches from the 'I' to the 'We' in some way".

The plural subject of *Celestial Harmonies* changes in *Corrected Version* to the single subject of the author. He emphasizes it in the beginning of the novel: "Here Péter Esterházy is speaking, born on 14th April, 1950, mother's name is Lili Mányoky". (19) He also stresses that he has come to an end of the narrator's game with masks: "the face as a mask, role-playing and quotations".(19)

Psychoanalytical theory underlines the father-principle as an essential part of identity, the history of the self and family as a background. The father-principle has been an important element of Esterházy's work even before *Celestial Harmonies*[21] and *Celestial Harmonies* was based on the symbolic coherence of the father and family. The autobiography in *Corrected Version* evolves in the transformation of the son, Péter. In his commentary Esterházy interprets the details of his father's betrayal: who was his father reporting about, to what extent he satisfied the demands of his employers, what was his relationship to them, and his own relationship to his father at each stage. He identifies the dates of reports relating to his life like the birthday when his father arrived late. He recognizes his father's reports about football fans at matches which they visited together. He is upset when he sees the appreciating note of a superior of the secret police. The view of his own life becomes more complete when he sees his father's report from 1977 just when he completed *The Novel of Production* and the memory of his happiness at finishing his novel mixes with the sorrow of his father's situation at that time.

Esterházy spent a year in the Archive and his intensity of work was connected with his fear, described in detail, that somebody will find out about his father's past and make it public before his novel is published. He watches and analyses his own reactions when he sees Gy., a colleague he has always condemned as "a traitor", because of Gy.'s proximity to the establishment in the age of Kádár. But then thinking about his father's past as a police informer, Esterházy makes the connection with his own "topsy-turvy hatred" that "oozes from" his "unarranged I". He watches an interview with Sasha Anderson (the GDR poet and the former Stasi agent) and Martin Lüdke and understands how the feelings of "disgust, compassion, love, and contempt" lie close to each other.

We see how Esterházy in the course of reading his father's reports confronts his own self-portrait, the past and faces the present. On 11th September, 2001:

While I copy here my copy the two towers in New York collapsed. 11/9 took place. Everybody says the world has changed because of this. It hasn't changed, only we cannot pretend that we don't see the face of the world any more. Of course this is a great change. [The story] of my father blends smoothly into the brutality of creation. (231)

The father's portrait also changes while he reads the reports: "How much this is my father's voice, this gentle, dry and real humour." (163) He can see that even in his position as an informer his father can be compassionate, rationalistic and sincere.

III

The father's story merges with the son's confession in the notes: the son attempts to exculpate the sin of his father. The proposition of moral absolutes brings the diary close to confession. Confession, as an act of sincerity and un-dressing, moves in the direction of fiction as Esterházy interprets the facts. Self-understanding and the transformation of value system form *Corrected Version* as autobiography: avowal of sin and repentance (*contritio*) that brings a sin from darkness to the light.[22] The text is close to confession also because of the intensity of self-chastisement. The guilt exposed and magnified, made almost absolute at its first examination is to be brought later to more realistic proportions. The "I", the subject of the narrator in the course of confession, expands his consciousness.

Péter Balassa[23] approaches the text from the point of view of confession as secularized history of liberation and rectification of life-story. In his opinion, Esterházy overstretches the identification with the historic name. Balassa claims that though Esterházy puts himself in his father's place by taking on the moral weight of police reporting and the public remission of sins, he is not using his imagination to put himself in his father's place.

Reader: Mátyás Esterházy's double life as an agent was unknown to all but two persons. Only Esterházy's wife, Gitta and M., the Director of the Archives were aware of it. The true, verifiable elements and the gravity of facts transform Esterházy's earlier playful, intimate relationship to the reader. From 'The Preface' to *Corrected Version* that spells out the conditions of the completion of *Celestial Harmonies* we find out that *Corrected version* was typed by Gizella who is presented as crucial to his text. Gizella is an understanding but a reserved reader. To her the author "cedes" authority in the Barthean sense. The narrator establishes his relationship to the reader through his remarks about Gizella, whose compassion, understanding, approval or enthusiasm is pivotal for the writer. In *The Pleasure of the Text,* where the author directly speaks to the body of the reader, Esterházy plans to hold

Gizella's hand while he breaks to her the news of his father's betrayal. The plan of Gizella's initiation into the secret applies to other readers.

> I was ready on the 8th of January. I again wrote *READY* on Saturday morning (I didn't take down the minute) I took the copybooks to Gizella, the typist. I understand Dostoyevsky very well, who fell in love with his secretary. He dictated, until (. . .). Gizella is the first stranger who reads my novels; her position is very delicate, similarly to mine. A gentle, cultured lady, and though she is a strict spirit (because she does not lie), in my defenceless situation (the text is still warm, it still steams, freshly made), she behaves perfectly, for which I am always grateful.[24] (9)

History

In the last pages of *Corrected Version* Esterházy suggests that in the two earlier books of *Celestial Harmonies*, he failed to deal with the history of Hungary and he suggests postmodern ways of reading as the reason of this shortcoming.

> The book [*Celestial Harmonies*] narrates not only the history of the family, but that of the whole country. (. . .) The personal story of the family does not contain that, what is in the historical story. (. . .) Here is an absence. (35)

The postmodern novel creates for the reader various possibilities how he chooses to read. "*Celestial Harmonies* has possibilities of soft reading, which I think contributes to its success." (35)

Esterházy seeks to know what motivated his father to become a police agent. First he looks for the factual circumstances of his involvement and the exact history of his entanglement. Esterházy wants to reconstruct the exact event of betrayal that is, however, inaccessible and he transfers the elusive mechanism of the functioning of the system in the 1960s to his father's problem.

Corrected Version is the presentation of specific details. The reader is exposed to the double reality of the system, the murky underside of the increasing liberty in the sixties and seventies and the hidden ways of complicity that guaranteed special position to Hungary as the "happy barrack" in the socialist camp. In *Corrected Version* Esterházy re-enacts the tension between relativism and the moral absolutism of purity, two modes of political-pragmatic thought which were present in the historical reality in the age of Kádár. The image of "ontological happiness" Esterházy had identified with embodies purity and innocence that can be retained if the author remains outside politics. This he transcends by examining historical details, with lists of court cases, punishments and executions.

In connection with the age of Kádár many critics speak in generational terms: those who were born in the fifties (Esterházy's generation) and the younger critics who were born in the end of the sixties and the seventies. The younger generation underlines and analyses moral absolutism as the key feature of *Corrected Version.* The moral absolutism of Esterházy comes from his university years when police reporting was a crucial issue and a betrayal at the personal level. In his earlier novel *The Book of Hrabal,*[25] Esterházy emphasizes the extreme nature of collaboration, the lawyer who asks for capital punishment for minor or no offences.

Corrected Version struggles with the idea of how the two value systems, the father's (how he could convey "calm, the ability to resist provocation") and the police informer's could be coordinated. Esterházy depicts a situation which relativizes morale in various ways and connects this with more differentiated systems of collaboration.

Part of moral absolutism is sincerity. Esterházy's sincerity is complete. Lists of judgements and names of the executed in 1957-1961 supplement the reports of the father in the first years. Yet he sees this also as problematic and comes to the understanding of vulnerability.

> Sincerity is an unusable category. [One could see this already in the case of Hrabal] The story is already inextricable and the wish to survive ties new knots. One thing that becomes clear is the vulnerability of man. I think anybody can become an informer. Reading the reports of these poor people [Sasha Anderson and "Karin Lenz"], I see that this possibility is there in all of us, because of human vulnerability and fragility. (252)

The reader finds out from *Corrected Version* what he tells in this diary, in his least fictionalized work that Mátyás Esterházy had a family with four children, just like his son, Péter. Mátyás provided the minimum that was necessary for bringing up his family. As class enemies they were resettled in the country-side. Later in the fifties the father worked as an unskilled parquetry inlayer and made extra earnings as a part-time translator. Only in the 1960s could he put to use his degrees and his knowledge of languages as a journalist in *Budapester Rundschau,* a German language newspaper in Hungary. As a police informer he asked for favours twice: that his eldest son, Péter, be admitted to the university in case he has sufficient marks and that Péter be permitted to go abroad, to Vienna in Austria. In the course of time Mátyás Esterházy might have identified with many elements of his actual position.

Esterházy deals with the history of his father's compromise: how the father acquires the phraseology of the police and state; how operatively useful information gets into the reports; how from a phase of crisis, he emerges as a more creative agent and starts giving information about possible new recruits and identifies with the tasks. Esterházy concludes that "observation changes the observer". (163)

Esterházy's autobiography breaks a deadlock and engages seriously with the age of Kádár, an important time period from the point of view of contemporary Hungary. The autobiography develops from despair and rejection to the assertion of human fragility. The responses to the father's secret are moral absolutism and relativism, re-enactments of past positions which are no longer valid. Esterházy first expresses shock over the enormity of crime, but as the autobiography develops, he changes his position and arrives at the painful, but compassionate acceptance of his father's actions.

NOTES AND REFERENCES

1. Péter Esterházy, *Javított kiadás* (*Corrected Version*), (Budapest: Magvetõ, 2002). The page numbers in the paper in brackets refer to this edition. Translations of the excerpts are mine.
2. Roswitha Skare's article discusses *Was bleibt* in the context of political changes and Genette-ian paratexts. Roswitha Skare (Tromsø), Christa Wolf's *What remains* – One document or a Document Unit?, http://209.85.175.104/search?q=cache:XJfPHB7i4IcJ: www.ub.uit.no/munin/bitstream/10037/1092/1/paper.pdf+Christa+Wolf%E2%80%99s+autobiography&hl=en&ct=clnk&cd=6&gl=in.
3. Péter Esterházy, *Harmonia Caelestis,* (Budapest: Magvetõ, 2000). English translation: *Celestial Harmonies,* trans. Judith Sollosy, (London: Flamingo, 2004).
4. Ferenc Szijj, "Kiadás és visszafogadás" (Release and Acceptance), in *Élet és Irodalom,* [Hungarian weekly], Budapest, 24 May, 2002. http://www.rev.hu/html/hu/tanulmanyok/esterhazy/szijj.html, downloaded on 1.12.07.
5. Sándor Radnóti, "Kelet-európai diszharmónia, Esterházy Péter: Javított kiadás – melléklet a Harmonia Caelestishez" (East-European Disharmony, Péter Esterházy – Supplement to Celestial Harmonies), in *Népszabadság* [Hungarian daily], Budapest, 25 May, 2002. http://www.rev.hu/html/hu/tanulmanyok/esterhazy/radnoti.html, downloaded on 3.12.07.
6. Beáta Thomka, Újraélt, újraírt önértés (Rewritten, re-lived Self-Understanding), in Gábor Böhm, ed., *Másodfokon, Esterházy Péter Harmonia Caelestis és Javított kiadás címû mûveirõl* (Judgment of the Appeal Court, on Péter Esterházy's Celestial Harmonies and Corrected Version), (Budapest: Kijárat Kiadó, 2003), pp. 201-14.
7. Philippe Lejeune, *Önéletírás, élettörténet, napló (On Autobiography),* trans. Zoltán Z.Varga, (Budapest: L'Harmattan, 2003), pp. 17-105.
8. Romanian Daily Publishes List of Securitate Agents Working in Intelligence. http://cryptome.org/ro-spy-list.htm

9. MTI [Press Information of Hungary] Data of the Polish Secret Service on the Internet, in *Népszabadság Online,* 3 February, 2005.
10. MTI [Press Information of Hungary], Bulgária megnyitja a kommunista titkosszolgálatok levéltárát [Bulgaria opens up communist archives], *Origo* 5 June, 2006. http://origo.hu/nagyvilag/20060605bulgaria.html
11. MTI, [Press Information of Hungary] Ügynöküg yek Prágában is [Informers in Prague also], in *Magyar Figyelõ (Hungarian Observer).* http://www.fn.hu/index.php?action=nyomtat&id=4&cid=134176&layout=no&id=4
12. Szlovénia – ügynöklista – odahamisították az államfõ nevét. [Solvenia- list of agents - the name of the president was faked]. http://cseke.atw.hu/milos/milos0304.shtml
13. Tagadó-botrány, Vezetõ magyar politikus a szlovákiai ügynöklistán, [Scandal. Leading Hungarian politician on the list of agents in Slovakia]. http://cseke.atw.hu/milos/milos0304.shtml
14. Gábor Halmai, Ügynöktörvény és alkotmány, [Informer -bill and Constitution] *Élet és Irodalom,*[Hungarian literary weekly *Life and Literature*] Vol. 49, No. 5. http://www.es.hu/pd/display.asp?channel=PUBLICISZTIKA0505&article=2005-0206-2157-42JCES
15. János Kenedi, *Kis állambiztonsági olvasókönyv., október 23.-március 15.-június 16 a Kádár-korszakban (Small Reader for State Security in the age of Kádár – 23rd October, 15th March, 16th June),* (Budapest: Magvetõ, 1996), I-II.
16. Dominick LaCapra, *History, Politics, and the Novel,* (Ithaca and London: Cornell University Press, 1987).
17. István Eörsi, "Az elfojtás és elfojtása" (Suppression and its Suppression), in *Kritika* [monthly], (Budapest, 1990), No. 10, pp. 30-34.
18. István Margócsy, "Dávidházi Péter *Per passivam resistentiam,* Változatok, hatalomra, írásra,(Péter Dávidházi *Per passivam resistentiam,* Variations on Power and Writing) in *Hajóvonták találkozása, Tanulmányok, kritikák a mai magyar irodalomról, (The Meeting of Towing Ships, Studies, Criticism about contemporary Hungarian Literature),* (Budapest: Palatinus, 2003), pp. 389-402.
19. Imre Kertész, *Kudarc,* (Budapest: Szépirodalmi, 1988).
20. "Én egy kiegyensúlyozott magyar úr vagyok" Esterházy Péterrel beszélget Vickó Árpád (I am a balanced Hungarian gentleman", Péter Esterházy in conversation with Árpád Vickó). http://www.zetna.org/zek/folyoiratok/51/esterhazy.html, downloaded on 10.12.07.
21. Gergely Angyalosi, "A kritikus õszintesége" (The Sincerity of the Critic), in Gábor Böhm, ed., *Másodfokon, Esterházy Péter Harmonia Caelestis és Javított kiadás címû mûveirõl, (Judgment of the Appeal Court, On Péter Esterházy's Celestial Harmonies and Corrected Version),* (Budapest: Kijárat, 2003).
22. Péter Balassa, "A név nevében, editioról és emendatioról" (On behalf of the name, about Editio and Emendatio), in Gábor Böhm, ed., *ibid.*, pp. 187-200.
23. Ibid.
24. Ellipsis is a stylistic technique often used by Esterházy. "He dictated, until . . ." implies that Dostoevsky dictated and dictated to his secretary till he ended up falling in love with her.
25. Péter Esterházy, *Hrabal könyve,* (Budapest: Magvetõ, 1990).

CARMEN ULRICH

Mended Holes of Memory: The Meaning of Pictures in Elias Canetti's Autobiography – *The Tongue Set Free*, *The Torch in My Ear*, *The Play of the Eyes*

> "Delayed encounters have played an extraordinary role in my life," the narrative person confesses in Elias Canetti's *Play of the Eyes.* These have been with places, people or pictures as well as books. There are cities I yearn for as if I had been predestined to spend my whole life there. I resort to all kinds of subterfuges to avoid visiting them, and every new opportunity I neglect to take advantage of increases their importance for me enough to make it appear that I lived for them alone and would have perished long ago if no such places existed. There are persons I so much enjoy hearing about that I seem to know more about them than they do themselves, yet I avoid looking at pictures of them and make no attempt to find out what they look like.[1]

We are not talking about memories here, but about "elaborate preparations for things to come."[2] The ability to fantasize seems to be the greatest fortune. The fear that imaginations could be replaced by reality implies a romantic longing for infinity, which goes beyond ordinary life. From this perspective, real experiences become insignificant. A remarkable approach in case of an autobiography! The crucial point is not to describe somebody's (one's own) lifetime, but to enjoy to the full the future life-to-be by refusing to take into consideration pictures from the past. However, this paragraph raises some doubts about the credibility of this written life and about the conception of authenticity.

Admittedly, the word *Bild* or 'picture' – the narrator tries to flee from – creates some problems because the singular form implies the unification of much differing details. Indeed, only a tiny part of perceived reality is enough to construct a picture, which – separated from its environment and time – represents another wholeness. According to Martin Heidegger, the difficulty concerning pictures lies in the proximity to portrayal, which alludes to a complete philosophy of life represented in it.[3]

The intention of producing a 'realistic image' bears the risk of being only a reproduction, which results in a generalized abstraction. A world without differences would arise, because in the form of an image, things would lose their material reality.[4] However, in Canetti's three-volume autobiography there is a tension as the reception of the past in the form of pictures results in a living past. How is that possible?

Three types of pictures exist: 1) material pictures, which approach in the medial way, 2) mental representations, that means pictures, which are complex products of acts of perception, and 3) pictures of imagination. We distinguish between the exterior picture visible in public and the interior picture of memory[5] as well as between a picture as reproduction and as imagination[6] – which Canetti prefers – that comes into existence whenever we speak, hear or read.[7] Canetti's refusal of pictures assumes at the same time a production of pictures by imagination. It is often noticed that Canetti gives lively descriptions. His way of writing enables visualizations. How does it work?

To take an example: "My earliest memory is dipped in red. I come out of a door on the arm of a maid; the floor in front of me is red, and to the left a staircase goes down, equally red." In the following scene a smiling young man commands him to show his tongue.

> He says: 'Now we'll cut off his tongue.' (. . .) Every morning we step out of the door and into the red hallway, the door opens, and the smiling man appears. I know what he's going to say and I wait for the command to show my tongue. I know he's going to cut it off, and I get more and more scared each time. That's how the day starts, and it happens very often.[8]

The journey into the past starts with a sensual and a symbolic experience at the same time. The red interior is associated with the blood, which would flow from his cut tongue; it indicates also the secret eroticism, the tête-à-tête between the maid and the foreign man, in which the child plays his first role with a thrill of fun. This long past and mysterious event becomes actuality through the present tense, but not only that; prior and later episodes, rhetorical and stylistic devices and terms which announce the repetition of the scene, do not permit a precisely temporal identification. Only later, and by this the scene gains authenticity, the secret of place and time becomes clear for him, when he asks his mother "much later." By the red colour she recognizes the hotel in Karlsbad, where they had spent the summer of 1907. For the two-year-old boy they had brought along a young nanny from Bulgaria. Her acquaintance with the young man living opposite was to be kept secret. "The threat with the knife worked, the child quite literally held his tongue for ten years."[9]

The recommended reading of 'autobiography' provokes the question what is real and unreal, what are facts and fictions. This is a considerable cultural distinction, because it refers to prevailing ideas of identity and authenticity. Descriptions, which seem to be genuine, assume social values, which do not have much to do with the individual. Rather, the points are key experiences, steps of development, first-contact-scenes, dealing with taboos and agreements about symbols and their meanings, which are parts of social and cultural life.

The incorporated memoirs are linked so artificially that all accidental, heterogeneous and inconsistent parts are banished; by this the identity of the narrator seems to be most constructed. One can see it, for example, in the free arrangement of the experiences and reflections. In the second chapter the narrator starts earlier, namely, with his birth:

> Ruschuk, on the lower Danube, where I came into the world, was a marvellous city for a child (. . .) for people of the most varied backgrounds lived there (. . .). As a child, I had no real grasp of this variety, but I never stopped feeling its effects. (. . .) It would be hard to give a full picture of the colourful time of those early years in Ruschuk, the passions and the terrors. Anything I subsequently experienced had already happened in Ruschuk.[10]

As it is predicted by the future tense, it is practically impossible to describe adequately the colourfulness of the early years. The pace of the flashback – with all the past tenses – of the childhood and its tremendous impact, is dizzy. On a few pages Canetti arouses particular expectations: The marvellous native town gives hope for unusual, exotic, even magical experiences. However, there are obviously not sufficient words to describe his early years.

Besides the chronological sequence of events, announced by the subtitles of the three-volume autobiography (*Remembrance of a European Childhood*, *Life Story 1921-31*, *Life Story 1931-37*), there are flashbacks, hints, explanations and interpretations as well, written in different temporal spaces. Past moments are illuminated; the fog of the past is cleared for a while, only to thicken again. The narrator seems to be unable to reconstruct the chronology of the remembered moments. The subtle alternations of tenses and the games with flashbacks and flash forwards signify liveliness and inexhaustibility. Canetti's narrative technique takes not only the past into the present, as it is usually observed; rather, present and younger past, like parasites, grow rich on the earlier periods; they have to refer back to the old times to gain significance at all.

Vice versa: the past needs an interpretation, an endowment of life with meaning afterwards, because the abundance of meaning is not recognizable at the moment of experience. There are no questions about the demand of the autobiography, even if singular details are slightly changed. However, it becomes another point of view, because the subsequent meaning provokes an interpretation as it is demanded by a novel – the search for structures embedded in a specific semiotic system.[11] The question, therefore, is not which details of the description are realistic, rather, what is worth mentioning. By renunciation of all accidental and insignificant facts, one's life becomes a story.

The above-mentioned 'delayed encounters' hint at a time lag between former and later times and between imagination and reality. How about the remembered encounters? In *The Human Province* Canetti praises the memory as it increases what is recognizable, without abandoning the terrible. "In reminiscences, the terrible past appears perhaps differently, but not less cruel, not more bearable, not less senseless, bitter, and not satisfied because it is over, nothing is over. The real sense of reminiscences consists in the understanding that nothing is over."[12]

Childhood experiences become his nourishment for the future.[13] The abundance of fears including hidden fears makes him wish for an endless life.[14] Interestingly enough, the counterpart is missing, namely, the lamentation about the transient existence, which – as an expression of disillusionment – is nothing other than an understanding of the facts. How is eternity – as an undeniable option of being – comprehensible? Life transformed into language gains a new rhythm, a new structure by a different tense. This is constituted of the structural elements of repetition or recognition: The authentic incident is realized in an aesthetic way.[15]

Memories – the real subject of autobiography – stand in contrast to the reality of the immediate experience, which becomes an interpreted experience only as soon as it is recognized. As it is written in *The Torch in My Ear:* "Something you recognize and know becomes *real* only if you have experienced it previously."[16] Therefore, reality develops only by reflection, by drawing the attention back to oneself or one's thinking. According to Immanuel Kant, logical reflection means to define the relations of ideas to one another.[17] But the arrangement of facts and ideas is also a creative performance. From a distance, the narrator has to interpret the ciphers of the past. Several impressions, which intensely reproduce the past, gain – combined with later associations – power and liveliness. Even so, they still remain in their original context. In the process of remembering, the narrator reflects on the past from his current perspective; at the same time the ambiguous pictures of memory, in addition to the respect for the hidden mechanisms of memory, put him in the position of an enquiring observer of his own life.[18]

In retrospect, the perceptions and feelings of the child will be analysed to find out the motives for his way of thinking and behaviour at that time and their relevance for today.[19] The narrator realizes that memory is not the same as memorized past.[20] Here begins the aesthetic reconstruction of the historical material, which does not allow an exact distinction between facts and fiction. The text includes realities which cannot be identified as real, but are nevertheless not fictional. In the reproduction of the past, something imaginative appears insofar as the recurrent reality becomes a sign.[21] Therefore, the text avoids a distinction between chronological and creative details; not the strictly fixed experiences, but accumulated, often unconscious incidents that coagulate to a picture in mind,[22] which represents something generalised. In *The Torch in My Ear*, Canetti writes:

> For one road to reality is by way of *pictures*. I don't believe there's any better road. You adhere to something that doesn't change, thus exhausting the everchanging. (. . .) However, it's important that these pictures exist *outside* a person, too; inside the human being, even they are subject to change. There has to be a place where he can find them intact, not he alone, a place where everyone who feels uncertain can find them. Whenever a man feels the precariousness of his experience, he turns to a picture. Here, experience holds still, he can look into its face. He thus calms down by knowing reality, which is his own, although merely depicted here. Apparently, it would be there even without him; but these appearances are deceiving: the pictures need *his* experience in order to awake.[23]

These pictures or paintings protect the narrator in the flux of life, because they show the end of transformation, the unchangeable.[24] The subjective power of imagination makes sense only if it is made public, as vice versa, the public needs to be given a personal meaning as otherwise it would be only accidental. By the reception of paintings, the experiences are recognized and digested. Referring to Rembrandt's painting *The Blinding of Samson* (*Die Blendung Simsons*), the narrator explains the meaning of hatred. He had already felt it when he was five years old, when he had tried to kill his cousin with an axe. "But you don't know what you have felt: you have to see it in front of you, in others, in order to recognize it and know it. Something you recognize and know becomes *real* only if you have experienced it previously."[25]

The beholder awakens the painting to new life, through his own experience, and brings it into his presence. Thus, the past remains alive while the present is changed. The peasants revolt at the Wenceslas Square (Prague) moves the narrator deeply as he recognizes the dancing peasants in Brueghel. He comments as follows: "Paintings mould our experience. They become an essential part of us, a kind of native soil. According to the pictures we consist of, we embark on different kinds of life."[26] What does this mean? Paintings determine the perspective. The trained onlooker takes the view of the artist. He gains distance towards everyday life and its banalities. The revolt of peasants seems to be a festival: he perceives them dancing. Through this vision, political actions lose their controversial nature.

In *The Play of the Eyes* the narrator confesses: "I was as fond as ever of Brueghel, I loved his richness and scope, and always will."[27] Paintings, such as those of Rembrandt or Brueghel, show a different reality, which is wider than the dull and pragmatic life of everyday.[28] Interpreted occurrences become experiences and contain, as such, a general meaning, which inspired the famous painters. He criticises the full from this immense general views to the small, banal excerpts. Their attenuation and fragmentation of reality strike him as fraudulent.[29] According to this view of reality, the current ideas of fact and fiction are shifted. Aesthetic totality is therefore truer than concrete details – which has a revealing character. As in Dante's *divine visibility* where the eternity turns to a moment, the temporally scattered is gathered in one space, where you can see everything at the same time.

An autobiography is not only interesting because of the selection of some events but also because of that "which fills the empty places".[30] Every text has empty places and needs the reader who fills them with his knowledge. Nevertheless, there is a demand made for subsequent illustrations, exaggerations and enlargements. Thus, the question is not whether the reminiscences are really true, but rather how they are integrated in his life story.[31] This method of writing should become clear through the following short analysis. The narrator describes an "illumination" which remains present to him walking down a street in Vienna at night. The following episode, which illustrates one of many tensions in the text between personal experience and historical situation, is introduced by the repeated idea that there exists a "crowd instinct" which is always in conflict with the "personality instinct"; the struggle between them can explain the course of human history.[32]

> These tendencies seemed so strong and so blind that I regarded them as an instinct, and labelled them one. However, I didn't know what the crowd itself really was. This was an enigma I now planned to solve; it seemed like the most crucial enigma, or at least the most important enigma, in our world. But how stale, how drained, how anaemic my description now

> sounds. I said, 'tremendous force', and that's exactly what it was. For the energy I was suddenly imbued with made me walk faster, almost run. I dashed along the Alserstrasse, all the way to the Gürtel; I felt as if I'd gotten here in the twinkling of an eye. My ears were buzzing; the sky was still red (. . .), I was still stumbling, but never falling; my stumbles were an integral part of my overall movement. I have never again experienced motion in this way; nor can I say that I would care to do so – it was too peculiar, too exotic, a lot swifter than is appropriate for me, an alien thing that came out of me, but that I didn't control.[33]

The search for an explanation for the crowd instinct becomes the narrator's (and the author's) life task. The narrator founds his philosophy of life on this unique mysterious occurrence. But, what exactly happened ? In the Alserstrasse, the full length of which he runs in a very short time or rather in one moment of ecstasy without any notion of time, he is suddenly overcome by a "tremendous force". It seems to meet his need for a "state of intoxication, an intensification of possibilities for experience, an increase of the person"; he frees himself from limitations and "comes to other persons leaving their confines, and forms a higher unity with them".[34] The focus is meanwhile on his own self. His own exercise, the immediate physical reaction is important. At the same time, the adventure exceeds all previous experience; it appears to him almost unreal and gives him a sense of the difference between reality and sensation. Under the illuminated red sky a feeling of strangeness attacks him, which is part of himself and yet inexplicable. He becomes aware of the limits of language – on the one hand, because the description of the experience is inadequate, on the other hand, because language is bound to the self-conscious individual, who dissolves within the crowd. He describes what is inexplicable for himself and in that there is something frank, like a confession, which insists upon the reader's goodwill. As in no other genre, here is a peculiar intimacy between reader and author.

Immediately after this episode, a peculiar description of a woman follows: Veza, his wife-to-be. She reminds him of a fictional figure and conveys at the same time a definite conception of herself – "her image never melted, it never dissolved; it retained its sharp outline and its radiance."[35] Veza's strangeness is part of reality, even if this reality is invented. However, he conceives his own strangeness in such a radical way that he cannot compare it to anything. It is not representative and that is why it is believable. As the idea of representation includes – in philosophical aspects – always the assumption of a difference between reality and its 'doubling'.[36] To say it in other words: the representation includes the difference between inner meaning and outward appearances, between essence and idea. Canetti's memoirs contain real, fictive and imaginary parts, including the illustrative comparison. If the imaginary takes a concrete shape, it crosses the border between fantasy and reality. By transfer of the diffuse imaginary into concrete ideas the imaginary becomes real.[37] The reality of a literary text means not the illustration of a concrete actuality, but the offering of an understanding of it.[38] The fiction becomes conclusive in its own logic and acts.

Nevertheless, Canetti's scene by night remains mysterious and surreal. What does that mean in terms of autobiographical writing? As the experience of crowd instinct cannot really be described, it seems to be particularly authentic, even a documentary. The narrator does not turn into a figure, because he becomes one with the first person who remembers – the first person at that time and the author, who dedicates his life to the exploration of the crowd instinct.

Veza, however, awakens his interest, because she reminds him of earlier pictures and first reading experiences; she becomes a parameter for him: "You had encountered her in *The Arabian Nights*, the very first time you'd read any of the tales."[39] Her picture keeps its clear contours, and for him this steadiness represents happiness.

Even as a child, he clings to that which seems to be durable to him. After he had taken a ride on the Tunnel of Fun at the *Wurstelprater*, an amusement park, he thought that everything would be destroyed. He staggered to the giant chestnut trees beyond. "I grabbed the trunk of a tree and tried to calm down. I punched it, feeling its resistance. It couldn't be moved, the tree stood fast, nothing had changed, I was happy. It must have been back then that I put my hope in trees."[40] The tree is, in this context, a metaphor for hope of something that will endure through time. His own existence seems to be changeable and unpredictable, but Veza's fabulous beauty shifts him in its clear contours to an artificial world and gives him the continuity he needs to arrange a coherent picture of himself.[41]

At this point, the reader may probably ask, why does the autobiographical way of writing in the 20th century still need to follow this idealistic construction of first-person-speaker. Did not the experiences of the First World War lead to an estrangement and isolation through which the idea of a self-confident and homogeneous self became doubtful?[42] "I am, but I don't have (or own) myself"; Helmuth Plessner refers to the difference between the immediate experience and a higher sense of life.[43] To have myself means to understand humanity in its abundance und significance.[44] The historical process in the first half of the 20th century turned out to be a path of disaster; it put every attempt of giving sense to the individual on trial. The single person threatens to become irrelevant compared to the global danger.[45] To accept these would mean to give way to the crowd instinct. This crowd instinct made possible the war and what is more that we are still kept prisoner to its consequences.[46]

His occupation with the mystery of the crowd allows the narrator to see history from a distance. And although he does not exclude himself from the seduction of crowd instinct he maintains certain independence. You may call it the cultivation of a personality instinct, embedded in the aesthetic construction of autobiography. This guarantees a structure of double sense. According to Wolfgang Iser, the structure of double sense consists of a manifest sense, which refers permanently to a hidden sense; it means one thing and at the same time another one (without ceasing to mean the former thing).[47]

Here the point is not to interpret a subjective form of writing history, but rather to discover an ecstatic condition, which makes it possible to liberate oneself from limits, that means to overcome one's personal identity. The writer takes himself as if he were someone else, or more precisely, the protagonist is himself and at the same time out of himself.[48] This tension is a result of the distinction and also a result of the relationship between author and narrator. Where the reader expects to find a contemporary witness, he also meets a potential fantasist.

The literary methods aim for a precise perception and enlarge, with a new arrangement of structures, our ideas of truth and reality. The autobiography does not refer only to the past; it puts also something on stage. It is not only a transcription of reality but rather a product of imagination, a new creation of the considered past; insofar as the narrated time, which is clear in memories, yet contains for the narrator a hidden sense which he would like to track down. Interpreted experiences generally contain something which also inspire the painters.

Among paintings and pictures of personal reminiscences, death masks also concern the topic of picture in Canetti's autobiography – death masks, which seem to preserve the bating of breath.[49] The picture of a stifled breath seems to abolish death. Pascal's death mask confronts him with dying beyond lament: "A gradually acquired nearness to death, in ineffably tiny, minute steps, borne by the wish to cross the threshold of death, in order to gain unknown things beyond it."[50] The mask, hiding and revealing what is no further accessible, keeps quiet about that what it shows. We cannot understand a picture as long as we don't grasp how it shows what is not seen.[51] According to the old testamentary idea of creation – "Let us make man in our image, after our likeness"[52] – a picture is not only a material illustration, it conveys also an idea, established by the onlooker.

The death mask demonstrates a fluid boundary between individuals and types; this is, as the narrator in *The Tongue Set Free* says, "a true concern of the real writer".[53] The death mask combines living people with the dead person; so to speak, it gives a face to death and absorbs the nameless emptiness. Like a photo, a death mask reminds of the past life. In trying to see something lively in it or to lose the discomfort towards death, it appears to be related to archaic theatre, a sort of 'living picture' as Roland Barthes describes: The new actors cut themselves off from the community by playing the role of dead people. Make-up means to mark oneself as a living and dead body at the same time.[54] The death mask shows a print of life between authenticity and deception, because the stifled breath is at the same time the last sign of life and the first sign of death. The metaphor of theatre lends an aesthetic dimension to impermanence; the person who remembers makes use of it in a creative way.

The mask which preserves the lively breath stands in analogy to autobiographical literature, because it keeps the remembrance and puts the death – even the death of the author – in its place.

The question is: What is left? A portrait of himself? The challenge for the reader is to wriggle out of the close-meshed fabric of the text and avoid looking at pictures. Anyway, we will not see the countenance of the writer, we will not meet him. The text is a game with changing parts, disguises, productions, but not according to the postmodern game of references. Rather, there is still a claim to authenticity, identity and the search for one's own roots, which makes the autobiography problematic. To resist the seduction we have to take the first commandment literally – without any "attempt to find out what they look like"[55] – and should not make any graven image of the person who tells his life story.

NOTES AND REFERENCES

1. Elias Canetti, *The Play of the Eyes*, trans. from German by Ralph Manheim, in *The Memoirs of Elias Canetti*, (New York: Farrar, Straus and Giroux, 1999), pp. 585-834, here p. 592f.
2. Ibid., p. 593.
3. "Bei dem Wort Bild denkt man zunächst an das Abbild von etwas." Martin Heidegger, "Zeit des Weltbildes", in *Holzwege*, (Frankfurt a.M.: Klostermann, 1977), pp. 75-113, here p. 89.
4. "In the picture all dimensions of the object as weight, premises, smell, depth, time and sense are put out. We are used to seeing the world in an abstract manner, through pictures. In the form of picture, we lose the reality because our perception gets abstract." Dietmar Kamper, "Bildzwang. Im Gefängnis der Freiheit", in Hans Belting, Dietmar Kamper ed., *Der zweite Blick. Bildgeschichte und Bildreflexion*, (München: Fink, 2000), pp. 13-21, here p. 20.

Cf. also Roland Barthes, *Die helle Kammer. Bemerkungen zur Photographie*, trans. from French by Dietrich Leube, (Frankfurt a.M.: Suhrkamp, 1985), p. 129f.

5. As a reminiscence the picture gets part of the own life story. The incorporated past is still living as a picture, vice versa the picture remains only lively, if it is incorporated. See Hans Belting, "Zu einer Anthropologie des Bildes" (preface), in Belting, Kamper ed., *Der zweite Blick*, pp. 7-10, here p. 7.
6. In German the etymologic origin of picture betrays its ambiguous meaning: The old german word 'bilidi' means "Nachbildung, Abbild, Muster oder Gestalt, Gebilde"; the German base form bil- is translatable with "Wunderkraft, Wunderzeichen". *Das Herkunftswörterbuch. Etymologie der deutschen Sprache*, ed. Günther Drosdowski, (Mannheim: Duden, Vol. 7, 1989), p. 82, headword *Bild.*
7. Hartmut Böhme, "Der Wettstreit der Medien im Andenken der Toten", in Belting, Kamper (ed.), *Der zweite Blick*, pp. 23-42, here p. 38.
8. Elias Canetti, *The Tongue set Free. Remembrance of a European Childhood*, trans. from German by Joachim Neugroschel, in *The Memoirs of Elias Canetti*, pp. 1-285, here p. 5.
9. Canetti, *The Tongue set Free*, p. 6.
10. Ibid., p. 6f. Probably he means above all sensual impressions like odours, sounds, colours, moods and visualized parts of reality, but also sentiments as fear, rage or joy that have been kept in mind – until they reappear in other contexts later. This contains doubtless a big treasure of childhood experiences; at the same time it is the attempt to make the new and foreign familiar as the moon cousin in Canetti's *Ohrenzeuge* says: "Instead of travelling in the distance to feel foreign, you should travel to feel at home." Elias Canetti, *Der Ohrenzeuge. Fünfzig Charaktere*, (Frankfurt a.M.: Fischer, 1983), p. 60. (my translation)
11. Cf. Umberto Eco, *Im Wald der Fiktionen. Sechs Streifzüge durch die Literatur*, trans. from Ital. by Burkhart Kroeber, (München, Wien: Hanser, 1994), p. 51.
12. Elias Canetti, *Die Provinz des Menschen. Aufzeichnungen 1942-1972*, (München: Hanser, 1973), p. 348. (my translation)
13. Canetti, *Die gerettete Zunge*, p. 19f.
14. Ibid., p. 81. According to that, writing has not the function to overcome fears; reminiscences rather help to memorize astonishment about the world and to realize its greatness.
15. Ibid., p. 171.
16. Elias Canetti, *The Torch in My Ear*, trans. from German by Joachim Neugroschel, in *The Memoirs of Elias Canetti*, pp. 287-584, here p. 383.
17. *Dtv-Lexikon in 20 Bänden*, (Mannheim: Dtv-Verlag, 1997) headword *Reflexion.*
18. Oliver Sill, *Zerbrochene Spiegel. Studien zur Theorie und Praxis modernen autobiographischen Erzählens*, (Berlin, New York: Walter de Gruyter, 1991), pp. 177, 182.
19. Ibid., p. 183f.
20. Ibid., p. 191.
21. Cf. Wolfgang Iser, *Das Fiktive und das Imaginäre. Perspektiven literarischer Anthropologie*, (Frankfurt a.M.: Suhrkamp, 1991), pp. 18-51, here p. 20.
22. Sill, p. 176.

23. Canetti, *The Torch in My Ear*, p. 379f.
24. Cf. Kristina Michaelis, *Dimensionen einer europäischen Identität. Studien zu Elias Canetti*, (Frankfurt a.M.: Europäischer Verlag der Wissenschaften, 2003), p. 125.
25. Canetti, *The Torch in My Ear*, p. 383.
26. Canetti, *The Play of the Eyes*, p. 824.
27. Ibid., p. 795.
28. The narrator describes it as a big joy to have found these pictures in Vienna, when he was threatened with false reality, "the reality of soberness, rigidness, usefulness, narrowness; and to counteract this false reality, I needed to find the other reality, which was vast enough to take command of those harshnesses and not knuckle under to them." Canetti, *The Torch in My Ear*, p. 380.
29. Canetti, *The Play of the Eyes*, p. 796.
30. Cf. Canetti, *Die Fliegenpein. Aufzeichnungen*, (München, Wien: Hanser, 1992), p. 122.
31. "While it is impossible (and irrelevant) to dispute whether or not this is Canetti's first memory, the fact that the tongue and the capacity for language come to dominate the first volume suggests that the text is constructed around the principle of symbolic selection rather than historical truth." Michael Jopling: "Elias Canetti: Verwandlung and Self-Sufficiency," in *Re-placing the self. Fictional and autobiographical interplay in modern German narrative (Elias Canetti, Thomas Bernhard, Peter Weiss, Christa Wolf)*, (Stuttgart: Akademischer Verlag, 2001), pp. 14-83, here p. 47.
32. Canetti, *The Torch in My Ear*, p. 387.
33. Ibid., p. 388.
34. Ibid., p. 353.
35. Ibid., p. 388.
36. Johannes Fabian, "Präsenz und Repräsentation. Die Anderen und das anthropologische Schreiben", in Eberhard Berg, Martin Fuchs ed.: *Kultur, soziale Praxis, Text. Die Krise der ethnographischen Repräsentation*, (Frankfurt a.M.: Suhrkamp, 1993), pp. 335-64, here p. 335f.
37. Wolfgang Iser, *Das Fiktive und das Imaginäre. Perspektiven literarischer Anthropologie*, (Frankfurt a.M.: Suhrkamp, 1991), p. 22.
38. Wolfgang Iser, *Die Appellstruktur der Texte. Konstanzer Universitätsreden*, ed. Gerhard Hess. (Antrittsvorlesung vom 9.6.1969 an der Universität Konstanz).
39. Canetti, *The Torch in My Ear*, p. 388.
40. Canetti, *The Tongue set Free*, p. 86.
41. There is a conspicuous parallel between the trees and the woman, between nature and Veza's fabulous beauty. According to Oliver Sill this is the important ability of autobiographical writing, more important that its documentary character. Sill, p. 13.
42. Sill, p. 70ff.
43. Helmuth Plessner, *Die anthropologische Dimension der Geschichtlichkeit. Sozialer Wandel. Zivilisation und Fortschritt als Kategorien der soziologischen Theorie*, ed. Hans Peter Dreitzel, (Neuwied, 1972), p. 160. (my translation)

44. Cf. Wolfgang Iser, *Fingieren als anthropologische Dimension der Literatur. Konstanzer Universitätsreden*, (Konstanz: Universitätsverlag, 1990), p. 25.
45. Cf. Sill, p. 85f.
46. "The young people I associated with hadn't been to war. But (. . .) it thus constantly remained before their eyes; and since they didn't wish to forget, since they hadn't been forced to escape the war, in haunted them incessantly. They did not investigate the dynamics of human beings as a crowd, in which people had devotedly and willingly gone into the war, remaining trapped in it – albeit in a different way – years after it was lost." Canetti, *The Torch in my Ear*, p. 386.
47. Iser, *Fingieren als anthropologische Dimension der Literatur*, p. 13.
48. Ibid., p. 16.
49. Canetti, *The Torch in my Ear*, p. 483.
50. Ibid., p. 483.
51. W. J. T. Mitchell: "Was ist ein Bild?", in Volker Bohn ed.: *Bildlichkeit. Internationale Beiträge zu Poetik*, (Frankfurt a. M.: Suhrkamp, 1990), pp. 17-68, here pp. 43, 50, 55.
52. *Bible*, Genesis 1, 26.
53. He learned from many of his teachers. "They were the first representatives of what I later took in as the intrinsic factor of the world, its population. They are non-interchangeable, one of the supreme qualities in the hierarchy; their having become figures as well takes nothing away from their personalities." Canetti, *The Tongue set Free*, p. 161f.
54. Barthes, *Die helle Kammer*, pp. 23, 41.
55. Canetti, *The Play of the Eyes*, p. 593.

DORETHEA JECHT

At the Border of Autobiographical Writing: Peter Handke's *Report of a Consciousness*

The title does not tell which text of Handke I am going to focus on. It is *Das Gewicht der Welt* (*GdW*),[1] translated literally as *The Weight of the World*, for which Handke, however, himself chooses the name "Report of a Consciousness". Before I discuss this text, allow me a few remarks regarding the structure of the essay. First I would like to reveal my motives for choosing this topic. Second I give a short overview on the autobiographical works of Handke. In the third place I analyse the text *Das Gewicht der Welt* and identify its autobiographical features. Finally I introduce a catalogue of features, worked out with the example of *GdW*, for the text type "Protocol of consciousness".

My approach to *GdW* is from a broad point of view. In other words, I am not so much interested in a *textimmanente Untersuchung* (text-immanent analysis) of *GdW*. As the readers of this book belong to various disciplines such as Italian, Spanish and French Studies, history of arts, philosophy and many more, it is probably better to consider *GdW* in a wide frame in order to generate the interest also of those readers who are not particularly familiar with the German language, and more precisely Austrian literature. Only towards the end do I address the question of the "death of the author", but only briefly. I feel one can refrain from this discussion, since Peter Handke is still very much alive.

I. MOTIVES

Why would one want to discuss Handke, an Austrian author, who is hiding in a suburb of Paris most of the time and hardly visible on the international stage of authors? And why would I want to confront you with a text which is rather unknown even among the literary canon of Handke? The aim is to show that *GdW* can without doubt be considered an autobiographical text by situating the text in the repertoire of autobiographical literature both systematically and historically. *GdW* is used as an example for the thesis that specifically texts created at the border of autobiographical writing are most likely to be innovative and formally interesting in the history of autobiographical literature. I shall take a closer look at the text type "Protocol of Consciousness" with the intention of clarifying this often used but seldom well analysed concept. According to the German literary scholar, Michaela Holdenried,[2] the protocol of consciousness is one of the open text forms which still lack fixed patterns.

II. ON THE AUTOBIOGRAPHICAL WORKS OF HANDKE

Looking at the autobiographical work of Peter Handke means looking at a paradox: On the one hand Handke is known in literary studies as a "routine narcissist", on the other hand Handke has not yet written any book comparable to an autobiography, autobiography meaning the description of one's own life. Neither has he ever published a text which could be considered as an autobiographical novel. Spitefully one could say: No surprise! Whatever Handke writes, it is only about himself anyway. And one could, according to the German literary scholar, Wolfgang Paulsen,[3] add: He not only writes *about*, he even writes only *for* himself. Although many texts of Handke with titles like *Afternoon of a Writer* or *I Live in the Ivory Tower* do indeed evoke a close relation between the author and the text, there are some texts which can be clearly considered as his autobiographical works. Besides *GdW* there is his prose text *Wunschloses Unglück* (*Perfectly Unhappy*), published in 1972, actually a biography of his mother, his notes *Die Geschichte des Bleistifts* (*The Story of the Pencil*) from 1976-1980 and his monumental book *Mein Jahr in der Niemandsbucht* (*My Year in No Man's Bay*), published in 1998, which he calls a "fairy tale". I am afraid I cannot give you details on these three texts. I move on to the results of the comparison of these texts. The autobiographical text types used by Handke are (in chronological order): Biography, Protocol of Consciousness, Notes and Novel-like Fairy Tale.

For these four texts we can identify two classes of autobiographical literature: *Perfectly Unhappy* and *My Year in No Man's Bay* belong to the class of *Handlungsautobiographie* (action-related autobiography), *GdW* and *Story of Pencil* belong to the class of *Reflexionsautobiographie* (reflection-related autobiography). Among these four texts I understand *GdW* as the most interesting and innovative book in terms of both form and content.

III. THE WEIGHT OF THE WORLD

3.1 The genesis of GdW

The collection of notes (*GdW*) was written without any autobiographical intentions. The text is 282 pages long, an unusual length for Handke who is mostly known for short texts. The notes are structured like a diary: Initially information about year and month is given, later also the day, starting from November 1975 until March 1977. There is a foreword of two pages before the chronological notes. Within the entries the text is structured through paragraphs, mostly miniatures up to five lines, the longest paragraph is only half a page.

Reading the foreword, it becomes clear that *GdW* was started as a work and study book for a story or a silent play.

> Diese Aufzeichnungen sind in der Form, wie sie hier erscheinen, nicht von vornherein geplant gewesen. Es wurde mit ihnen in der Absicht begonnen, sie in einen Zusammenhang zu bringen, etwa einer Geschichte oder, wie noch an der häufigen Beschreibung bloßer Gesten am Anfang zu erkennen, eines (stummen) Theaterstücks.
>
> To start with I did not intend to write these notes in the form in which they are published now. My intention was to put them in a context, for example of a story or as the frequent description of mere gestures show, a (silent) play.

The notes are mostly report perceptions, in the beginning recorded sporadically, then daily. Handke selects only those perceptions which are directly useful for his literary aim (as for example the gestures for the silent play), but as the notes progress he starts doubting that aim and the entries break free.

> Die täglichen Wahrnehmungen wurden also im Kopf zunächst übersetzt in das System, für das sie gebraucht werden sollten (. . .). Erlebnismomente, bei denen es nicht gelang, sie auf den gemeinsamen Bezugspunkt der im voraus gewählten literarischen Form einzustellen, wurden dabei vernachlässigt. (. . .) Es erschien mir sehr bald als ein Versäumnis, und so fing ich an, auch die nicht-projektdienlichen Bewußtseins-Ereignisse sofort festzuhalten.
>
> The daily perceptions were translated in my head into the system, for which they should be used (. . .). Moments of experience which could not be related to this system were ignored. (. . .) Soon I found this an omission, and so I started to note down also those events of consciousness irrelevant to the project.

Handke's break up with the original aim of the notes is also documented through the development of the entries in *GdW* which continuously become more frequent and detailed. Handke describes this change during writing as *Befreiung von gegebenen literarischen Formen* (liberation from existing literary forms). The idea of a workbook is now replaced by the idea of *einer bis dahin unbekannten literarischen Möglichkeit* (a literary possibility unknown until now), by an open and immediate documentation of the daily perceptions. I quote from the entry of 27th October 1976:

> Ich beschloß, das Ziel [eines Theaterstücks oder einer Geschichte] aufzugeben, das mich nur noch funktionieren ließ, und fühlte mich endlich, zum ersten Mal an diesem Tag existieren; eine wie herzliche Phantasie fing an, mich auf der Stelle zu beflügeln (. . .); ich hatte meine Stimme wiedergefunden, in der Dämmerung, in der Menge, „Phantasie durch Ziellosigkeit", dachte ich.
>
> I decided to drop the aim [of a story or a silent play] which let me only function and for the first time this day I finally felt myself existing; a warm fantasy starting to inspire me (. . .); I had found my voice again, in the dawn, in the crowd, "fantasy through aimlessness", that was my thought.

It is this liberation of the notes from any literary aim which enables Handke to find a new form for his notes, which he names "report of a consciousness".

3.2 Structure and Content of GdW

So far I have mostly talked about the author's opinion on his own text. It is obvious that the author is not always the best source for interpreting his or her own text. Therefore, it is best to have a look at the text itself. By doing this the following questions have to be kept in mind:

- Is Handke's definition "report of a consciousness" really appropriate for *GdW*?
- Where is the difference between *GdW* and a diary?
- Are his notes not only a new version of the method of inner monologue or stream of consciousness?
- Where is the difference between *GdW* and aphorism or think books?
- And finally: Which features allow us to consider *GdW* as an autobiographical text?

Before we look at the text let me clarify a concept with respect to the first question. In order to decide whether *GdW* is a report of a consciousness, first of all we have to know what a report is. (On that we may be able to agree easily), and secondly: what does consciousness mean? Philosophers are trying to figure out this concept since the antiquity, even if the word *Bewußtsein* was introduced to German language only in the 18th century by the philosopher Leibniz. This concept involves a lot of intricate problems. Nevertheless I would like to continue using this word with a heuristical intention. In this context I offer a definition of consciousness, not complete, but sufficient for our literary aims: I want to understand consciousness here as the medium of inner and outer perception, perception taken as thoughts and feelings including receptive as well as productive process. We could then understand a report of a consciousness as documentation of (ideally) all perceptions of an individual consciousness without interpreting or commenting on them.

Now I analyse some aspects of the text. The quotations are already structured after the four main perspectives which can be found in the text: First Person Singular or Plural (I / We); Third Person Singular or Plural (He / She / It / They); Impressions; and Neutral direct speech (Dialogue or Monologue)

Erste Person Singular / First Person Singular

Example 1: Entry 17.10.1976

"Ich bemerkte beim Schachspielen, dass ich von der Stelle, die ich bedrohte, extra woandershin schaute."
"While playing chess I realized that I purposefully looked away from the piece I was planning to attack."

Example 2: Entry March 1977

"Ich merkte, daß etwas, was ich zu sagen vorhatte, dumm war; dann sagte ich es doch, wie unter Zwang, und ausgesprochen wurde es noch dümmer; aber jedenfalls hatte ich eine Art Pflicht erfüllt."
"I noticed that I was about to say something silly; nevertheless, as if forced by someone, I said it, with the result that it became even more silly; but after all I had fulfilled some kind of duty."

Example 3: Entry 22.10.1976

"Angebettelt, schaute ich in Verlegenheit auf andre Leute; in noch größerer Verlegenheit, dass ich mich zu anderen geflüchtet hatte, schaute ich auf die Uhr; usw."
"Confronted with a beggar I looked embarrassed at other people; even more embarrassed that I had looked at them I started looking at my watch; and so on."

Dritte Person (Third Person) Singular / Plural

Example 4: Entry 22. Mai 1976

"Eine Frau, die vor jeder (für sie) besonderen Tätigkeit alle ihre Ringe von den Fingern zieht und auf den Tisch legt."
"A woman who takes off her rings and puts them on the table before every (for her) special activity."

Example 5: Entry November 1975

"Sie sitzen stierend nachmittags in den Cafes, als ob sie schon fernsehen"
"In the afternoon they sit in the cafes, staring, as if they were already watching TV"

Eindrücke und Gedanken / Impressions and Thoughts

Example 6: Entry 19.10. 1976

"Momente der Frechheit gegen den Tod"
"Moments of cheek against death"

Example 7: Entry November 1975

"Etwas auspacken und statt das Papier den Inhalt in den Abfall werfen"
"To unwrap something and throw the content away instead of the paper"

Example 8: Entry November 1976

"Eine Stimme wie eine vollendete Tatsache"
"A voice like a perfect fact"

Wörtliche Rede / Direct Speech

Example 9: Dialogue, Entry 10.03.1976

"Was machst du gerade?" – "Ich schaue vor mich hin und lasse mich treiben ins Universum."
"What are you doing?" – "I look in front of me and let myself drift into the universe."

Example 10: Entry 30.10.1976

"Ich will erst wieder ein Gedicht schreiben, wenn ich eine neue Lebensauffassung habe"
"I will only write a new poem, when I found a new world view"

These entries make an interesting comparison with the notebook entries of G.C. Lichtenberg's *Sudelbücher*[4] (rendered in English as *Waste books*) published posthumously. The book contains reflections and observations about life that Lichtenberg, the German scientist (1742-1799), found worth recording from his student days until the end of his life.

Example A: Sudelbücher 1 (D 481) with similarity to GdW:

"Er hatte sich ein gewisses System gemacht, das nunmehr einen solchen Einfluß auf seine Denkungsform hatte, daß die Zuschauer sein Urteil immer ein paar Schritte vor der Empfindung vorangehen sahen, ob er selbst glaubte es hielte sich hinten."
"He had created a certain system which had such an influence on his way of thinking that his audience would know his judgement a few steps before his sensations, whereas he himself thought it would stay in the background."

Example B: Sudelbücher *2 (F 32) with difference to GdW:*

"Ich bin überzeugt, daß, wenn Gott einmal einen solchen Menschen schaffen würde, wie ihn sich die Magistri und Professoren der Philosophie vorstellen, er müßte den ersten Tag ins Tollhaus gebracht werden."
"I am convinced that if God is to create a human being according to the ideas of the Masters and Professors of philosophy, this human being would have to be brought into the mental asylum the very first day."

I point out some important aspects of *GdW*:

1. The notes have the shape of fragments or miniatures. There is an open end.
2. The topic is the description of observations, impressions, associations and thoughts, but always in interaction with a perception. In example 10: *Ich will erst wieder* the direct speech is indicating that the phrase was expressed in reality (if during a dialogue and where we do not know). It is a characteristic of Handke's writing that he refrains from any kind of general comment on the relation between writing and worldview. The focus is on this particular situation only.
3. The text is a report. All criteria for a reporting text type are fulfilled, following the German literary scholar Jürgen Lehmann, that is:
    - no profile of the reporter (he remains more or less anonymous)
    - absolute sincerity (the reporter documents only what he really perceives or has perceived)
    - focus on results (not the relation to the person and individual memory of the reporter is important, but the actual perception itself)
    - lack of interpretation or evaluating comments

Concerning this last point there is a very interesting entry which throws light on the general attitude of Handke as a writer in his note book *GdW* which I would like to quote: "All you have done is interpreting and changing the world; but the important thing is to describe it."

4. The observations are reported immediately as they are perceived. The common retrospective method of autobiographical texts is changed into a perception of the mere presence. Best examples are the impression-like entries (6-8). We can also have a look at the examples 9 and 10, the examples of direct speech. The words are recorded immediately and remain without any revision or contextualisation. Handke himself comments on this method of writing in his foreword:

   > [Die Aufzeichnungen wurden] in allen Lebenslagen gemacht, nur nicht am Schreibtisch; bis in den Schlaf hinein zwang ich mich. sofort zu reagieren.
   >
   > [The notes were] taken down in all kind of situations, not only at the writing desk; into the sleep I forced myself to react immediately.

5. Most of the perceptions can be or at least could be checked, if at that time a camera or a tape recorder would have been installed. Example No. 3 and 5 show that very clearly. At least the moment in which the reporter is writing down the notes, could be theoretically traced back.
6. There is a double perspective in the report: personal on the one hand, neutral on the other hand. Never does the perspective become omniscient. The reporter cannot know and therefore cannot describe anything beyond his own perceptions.

These six characteristics of the text already enable us to answer three out of the five questions raised earlier, that is: the questions of difference to diary, stream of consciousness and aphorisms. There is a significant difference to all these three forms. The difference to diary is mainly that *GdW* is only by chance structured as a diary. The chronological order does not play a role at all, what is dominant is the simultaneousness. The difference to Stream of Consciousness is that there is not at all a stream of perceptions, but isolated fragments. And so far as aphorism is concerned there are neither general reflections in *GdW* nor "surprising subjective opinions", the major point of an aphorism.

Now the question remains whether *GdW* can be considered as an autobiographical text.

IV. AUTOBIOGRAPHICAL FEATURES OF GDW

There are two kinds of perspectives: the systematic and the historical perspective. I explain the systematic perspective (six are named out of which three are explained in detail):

1) There is an identity of author and reporter in *GdW*. 2) The dominant speech act in *GdW* is reporting. 3) There is a foreword (*Vornotiz*) in *GdW*. 4) There is a strong interaction between fact and fiction 5) Reference is dominant against performance. 6) The end of *GdW* is open.

To No 2) The reporting mode is without doubt one of the three speech acts typical for autobiographical texts. I refer mainly to Jürgen Lehmann's book "Confess-Narrate-Report", published in 1988.[5] Lehmann shows that all speech acts in autobiographical texts are first of all assertive, and then confessional, narrative or reporting. So the text type 'report' is not at all in opposition to autobiographical writing, it is on the contrary the first feature for autobiographies noticed by the scholars of autobiography.

To No 5) An important feature of autobiographical texts is the dominance of reference (relation to world outside the text) instead of performance (relations on text level). As already pointed out, the single fragments of *GdW* are not so much connected with each other, but with the world outside the text. This character of reference is in *GdW* not only simple, but double. On the one hand the fragments refer to the situation in which they were written; secondly, as they all describe human perceptions of mostly everyday life, they refer even more to the experience of the reader. The typical question of the reader of an autobiographical text: "Is that true?" acquires here a different meaning: In an autobiography the question is asked in the sense of: "Has that really happened?" In *GdW* the reader is more likely to ask "is it true" in the sense of "Have I ever experienced that myself?" So reading *GdW* means permanently overstepping the text towards the own experience.

To No 6) Open-ended: Autobiographical texts are by definition incomplete. The author does not normally die in the very moment he is putting down his pencil or switching off his laptop (although many authors might dream of a situation like that). His life goes on, and therefore whatever he wrote about himself, is to remain incomplete.

Besides these systematic features one can draw many similarities to autobiographical texts in the history of literature. *GdW* shows a similarity to mystic and visionary autobiographical literature of the middle ages, anthropological autobiographical literature of the enlightenment and contemporary autobiographical writings, that is in the 1970s, which is known as *Neue Innerlichkeit* (new sensitivity or new introspection).

V. CONCLUSION

Handke's text is one of the rare documents of a very interesting text type of autobiographical writing which I would like to call "Protocol of Consciousness". Personally I feel sorry that Handke did not continue with this very challenging project of noting down his perceptions. It would be enlightening to have such a protocol for the period of ten or even twenty years. The most interesting aspect of this text is that as a reader one can follow the creation of a new text form. In that context *GdW* is an important document for the issue of genesis of new literary forms.

I now want to present, so to say as final conclusion, a list of features which I have developed only with reference to *GdW*. The next step now would of course be to compare this catalogue with the structure of other similar texts. To name a few of them, one could mention *Rom, Blicke (Rome, Views)* of Rolf Dieter Brinkmann, 1979, in which documents of the real life like photos, postcards, bills, etc. are included. Of course one could also think of Wolf-Dietrich Schnurre's *Schattenfotografen* (*Shadow Photographs*) and some texts of Friederike Mayröcker, for example *Brütt,* 1998, and there is the recent example *Really Ground Zero* by Kathrin Röggla who describes September 11 by documenting her walks through New York, again framed by photos and other real life documents. There is also the young Russian author, Wiktor Pelewin. Comparing these texts would be an interesting task for further research. For the time being I can only summarize the features for the text type "Protocol of Consciousness" (PoC) developed with *GdW*:

- The PoC is an autobiographical text type.
- I suggest the term „auto-perception", in order to situate the PoC in the repertoire of autobiographical literature.
- The PoC is focussed on inner and outer perception.
- The PoC does not narrate, it reports.
- There is no narrator in the PoC, there is only a reporter.
- Reporter and author are identical.
- There are no major and minor characters, only persons more or less thoroughly described.
- There can be no omniscient perspective in the PoC. The main perspective is neutral and, in order to describe the inner perceptions, personal.
- Reference, not performance, is dominant in the PoC, and reference is very strongly reader-related.
- The PoC is necessarily fragmentary.
- The PoC critizises the culture of perception, memory and identity of the society.
- There is always a reflection on language as medium of perception.

The last point leads to the end of my essay, to the remark on the "death of the author". So far I have not said much about the meaning of language in Handke's text. But what actually happens in *GdW* is an *Engführung von Schreiben und Wahrnehmen*, i.e., a strong interaction between writing and perceiving. It is not just a matter of chance that Handke describe the moments of perception in his foreword as "moments of language" (*Augenblicke der Sprache*). His concept of intense awareness also affects the language which becomes, in the moment of perceiving and writing down the perception, a new character free from conventions and fixed patterns of the everyday language. That means that the experience itself is a construction of language and perception. In these moments of experience the concept of "author" is so to say constantly reborn. Because all our acts of perception are mediated through language, we are on the basis of the definition of our mechanism of perception, natural authors. Every single perception can be considered a text – invisibly written in our brain and body while interpreting the world through language. Therefore it may be possible to read *GdW* as a veiled objection to the simultaneous published thesis of the death of the author.

NOTES AND REFERENCES

1. Peter Handke, *Das Gewicht der Welt*, (Salzburg: Suhrkamp, 1979). All quotations in the article are from this edition. The text is abbreviated as *GdW*. The English translations are mine.
2. Michaela Holdenried, *Autobiographie*, (Stuttgart: Reclam, 2000).
3. Wolfgang Paulsen, *Das Ich im Spiegel der Sprache. Autobiographisches Schreiben in der deutschen Literatur des 20. Jahrhunderts*, (Tübingen: Niemeyer, 1991). (Untersuchungen zur deutschen Literaturgeschichte, Bd. 58)
4. G.C. Lichtenberg, *Sudelbücher*, (Hrsg.) Franz H. Mautner, (Frankfurt a.M. u Leipzig: Insel, 1984).
5. Jürgen Lehmann, *Bekennen-Erzählen-Berichten. Studien zu Theorie und Geschichte der Autobiographie*, (Tübingen: Niemeyer, 1988). (Studien zur deutschen Literatur, Bd. 98)

DIRK WIEMANN

"It Ain't Me, Babe": Bob Dylan's *Chronicles* between Concealment and Disclosure

"It's Halloween and I got my Bob Dylan mask on." This playful aside, documented on a by-now canonised 1964 concert bootleg,[1] testifies to the conspicuous evasiveness that Bob Dylan has been creating around himself right from the earliest phases of his long-standing career that spans more than four decades. This exceptionally long life in the limelight appears as one continuous series of embarrassingly public experimentations with identities: from the young Woody Guthrie revenant to the transgender minstrel to the evangelical preacher and beyond. Excessive identities thus obviously unsettle the sense of one stable coherent self. It is not a coincidence that Dylan's highly unrevealing 1970 record, comprising nothing but cover versions of other artists' songs, should absurdly be titled *Self Portrait.* For the still substantial Dylan fan community around the globe, this aura of an enigmatically evasive personality that refuses to settle in one identity gives rise to as many inconclusive hermeneutic speculations as the rich lyrics and poems themselves. Between Dylan and his constituency, then, a special contract seems to prevail that ensures the invisibility of the star's 'real self' while, simultaneously, this mysterious 'self' becomes the cherished grail of every Dylanologist's quest. What happens when such an institutionalised protean figure decides to succumb to the obligations of the autobiographical pact which, as Philippe Lejeune points out, engenders an 'intimate literature' rife with expectations of confession and self-revelation? This paper will argue that Dylan as autobiographer keeps his enigmatic 'self' in hiding while producing a text that utilises the fundamental contradiction built into the genre of autobiography: namely, that autobiography can never fully relate the story of the life that is its subject matter.

I

"The nature of the character in a novel cannot be presented any better than is done in this statement, which says that the 'meaning' of his life is revealed only in his death."[2] This observation by Walter Benjamin allows for a determination of the difficulty any autobiography, in contradistinction from a novel, has to face: A well-emplotted, fully conclusive autobiography would have to be written posthumously. Autobiography is, in Lejeune's definition, a "retrospective prose narrative written by a real person concerning his own existence, where the focus is his individual life, in particular the history of his personality".[3] The subject matter of the autobiography is, then, the very life of the selfsame person who writes the text; hence the raw material that the autobiographic author has the task to process is not exhausted at the moment of writing. Therefore, the identity of author, narrator, and protagonist that Philippe Lejeune places at the centre of the autobiographical pact makes it impossible for autobiography to ever arrive at that emphatic moment of closure, resolution and quietude, if not death, that narratologists from Walter Benjamin to Frank Kermode, from Roland Barthes to Peter Brooks have defined as the ultimate object of narrative desire. According to Kermode, "[a]ll plotting presupposes and requires that an end will bestow upon the whole duration and meaning".[4] It is, as Brooks insists, this expectation that motivates "the active quest of the reader for those shaping ends that, terminating the dynamic process of reading, promise to bestow meaning and significance on the beginning and the middle".[5]

Different from other forms of narrative, autobiography has to withhold this sense of an ending simply because the protagonist, whose development we are made to witness, is at the same time the narrator who recounts this protagonist's development *and* the author, that empirical person, who continues to exist outside the text. It is due to this last point that all autobiography is necessarily incomplete: It can never relate the full course of the protagonist-narrator-author's life because the author's life will go on even after the writing process. At any subsequent point in his/her lifetime, the writer of an autobiography could theoretically produce a sequel. Any autobiography, however comprehensive in design, comes with an implied mark that declares "to be continued".

In narratological terms, autobiography tends towards the genre of the chronicle which, as Hayden White points out, "starts out to tell a story but breaks off in *medias res*, in the chronicler's own present".[6] The chronicle provides inconclusive accounts of accumulating data along the linear axis of chronological time. It does not *emplot* these data into narrative events but simply states that this or that happened. Since it cannot have an end (in both the sense of a terminating ending *and* the sense of a goal), it is not teleological.

Bound to the actual and as yet unresolved presence of its author, the chronicler's account is history before the invention of history.

Walter Benjamin makes a distinction between modern historiography and the novel on the one hand, and traditional storytelling and chronicles on the other. While the former two impose narrative coherence onto the contingent, the latter do not (have to) do so because they implicitly assume a non-contingent world that is essentially impregnated with significance. According to Benjamin, the form of the chronicle is grounded in the medieval metahistory of divine salvation, the narrative genre of the story in the immanence of natural history. By contrast, both modern historiography and the novel bespeak a worldview that no longer relies on an already given meaning of the "course of the world"; they focus on the individual and have to *explain or construe motivations*, whereas chronicles have to produce neither coherence nor motivation because both are taken for granted as always already there, *outside* and independent of the narrative in the theocratic world view of the Middle Ages:

> [it] will take no effort to gauge the difference between the writer of history, the historian, and the teller of it, the chronicler. The historian is bound to explain in one way or another the happenings with which he deals; under no circumstances can he content himself with displaying them as models of the course of the world. But this is precisely what the chronicler does, especially in his classical representatives, the chroniclers of the Middle Ages, the precursors of the historians of today. By basing their historical tales on a divine plan of salvation – an inscrutable one – they have from the very start lifted the burden of explanation from their own shoulders.[7]

Chronicles, therefore, require that a given picture of the world be generally shared, accepted and taken for granted. For the modern reader, the medieval chroniclers seem to simply enumerate events and state that these events took place without endowing them with any significance whatsoever: On April 25th, the Emperor went to Cologne; on May 3rd, the Archduke of the Palatine met the Emperor at Trier; on May 6th, a heavy storm set in; and so on and so forth. It is easy to see that this sort of account resembles the example that E.M. Forster, in his *Aspects of the Novel*, gives in order to explain the difference between emplotted and non-emplotted narratives: Forster's first example – "The king died and then the queen died" – is clearly a chronicle, a "narrative of events arranged in their time-sequence"; his second example – "The king died and then the queen died of grief" – is already an emplotted narrative: "The time-sequence is preserved, but the sense of causality overshadows it".[8] Since this second narrative constructs a cause-and-effect relation between two distinct happenings, it no longer relies on what Benjamin has called the assumption of the givenness of a significant 'course of the world'. The teller of that second account – "The king died and then the queen died of grief" – has already begun to shoulder the burden of explanation himself.

Of course no modern autobiography can revert to the radical mode of the chronicle; the writing of one's own life will be heavily burdened with explanation, motivation and causalities. And yet the autobiographer will have to work out these plot structures in a genre that categorically forbids the full closure that, according to Benjamin, only death can provide.

Bob Dylan's autobiography, published in 2004, has this constitutive paradox of the genre inscribed into its second-most prominent paratext, the title: It is called *Chronicles*, and as if that were not enough, *Chronicles: Volume One*. Every reader gets thus alerted to the inevitable inconclusiveness and open-endedness of whatever the covers of this book may bracket. While this is readable as a disclaimer, a gesture of withholding, or concealment, that cautions us, even before we open the book, that we are not going to get 'the whole picture', this very same paratext functions simultaneously as an acknowledgment, a reflexive disclosure of the ineluctable limitations of the autobiographical form. It is between these two poles of concealment and disclosure that Dylan's book seems to waver, and in that respect it can certainly be read as one more piece in the inconclusive jigsaw puzzle that is Dylan.

II

Looking at the cover of Dylan's autobiography, one cannot but be struck by the conspicuous dominance of the author's name – a name that is firmly entrenched in the cultural lexicon of the Western world. This name, 'Bob Dylan', operates in the modality of the generic cultural figure of the star, even though the heyday of Dylan's stardom belongs to a period that appears further remote than it chronologically is. Dylan is canonised as a cultural hero of the 1960s, that period that according to Fredric Jameson, "now stands as the high-modernist moment" of pop/rock music.[9] Dylan, established as a central figure of that heroic phase in which pop appeared coterminous with counterculture, holds a star status not only for those who formed his real-time constituency back then; he also figures prominently as 'heritage' in current pop music which is increasingly preoccupied with its own history – a preoccupation verging at times on auto-cannibalism. For both target groups, one can assume, Dylan as autobiographical author implies the promise of a nostalgic return to, or critical revision of, that formative period in which Dylan played such a central part as one of its definite superstars (matched only by the Beatles).

A star, according to film critic John Ellis, functions as a "narrative image", an abbreviated narrative encapsulated in the aura of the star persona.

This image is never complete, not even in the form of the most glamorous billboard poster or the most refined live recording which always refer the viewer or listener to the fact that the star him/herself is not there. Thus, the star image perpetuates a promise whose fulfilment is always deferred, with film stars as well as rock stars or sports stars: the promise of the fan's communion with the star in the moment of performance, imagined as an impossibly intimate, unmediated face-to-face encounter.

> The star is an impossible image (. . .) The star is tantalizingly close and similar, yet at the same time remote and dissimilar. Further, the star is a legitimate object for the desire of the viewer in so far as the star is extraordinary, unlike the viewer. There is a complicated game of desires that plays around the figure of the star: every feature in it is counteracted by another feature. The male and female star can be desired by either sex, yet that desire has access to its object only on condition that its object is *presented as absent.*[10]

As Ellis argues, the star functions similar to what he calls the "photo effect": Like the photographic image, that "always carries its referent with itself"[11] without ever coinciding with that referent, the star image points towards an allegedly real person that remains inaccessible for the admirer. The promise of presence, of a consummate communion, can never be fulfilled, not even in the moment of live performance. For what Edgar Morin has stated long ago with respect to film actors holds true for rock stars just as well. The moment of performance is that point in time at which the private individual and his/her professional role coincide, but always only temporarily: "Once the film is over, the actor becomes an actor again, the character remains a character, but from their union is born a composite creature who participates in both, envelops them both: the star." The star is hence neither the empirical person who performs nor the role that is performed by that empirical person; the star, instead, is a fusion of both. This 'composite creature' is held together by the fans – both as individuals or as lateral taste communities[12] – or more precisely by the fans' desire to bring the star's duality into alignment, to make the publicly visible persona of the performer coincide with the invisible private person that does the performance.

The construction of such an identity is, evidently, a fan's preoccupation: one that is all the more difficult to achieve when the star in question is a chameleon like Bob Dylan, who has consistently staged himself as arbitrary, inscrutable and unpredictable, i.e., beyond categorisation. Even in the first years of his career Dylan systematically subverted precisely that image that he had just established for himself; hence his transmutations from the passionate protest folk singer to the mid-sixties electric rock Dadaist; from the psychedelic freak to the conservative country musician; from the early-seventies existential songwriter to the evangelical fundamentalist proselytiser. This stance of unpredictable mutability, along with the fact that Dylan has always kept his private life secret, makes it naturally more difficult for the Dylan fan to project a coherent image of that "master of disguise"[13]; Dylan's notoriously arrogant habit of not communicating with his live audiences does not help either. Even at his most relaxed, Dylan never associated with his audiences. He never gave himself away to his fans. He mocked the naive expectations of communion and by this mockery seems to have intensified, on the side of many of his fans, the desire for such communion. From the late sixties on, Dylanologists have not only been following Dylan for long stretches on his tours, or trying to arrest the inconclusive exegesis of the master's scriptures and gestures in some transcendental ultimate meaning, but in some cases browsing through Dylan's garbage cans in order to catch a glimpse of genius there.[14] Dylan became the first artist around whom an entire parallel industry and economy of bootleg publications gravitated. Thus, the album that in the mid-70s was officially released as *The Basement Tapes* had been circulated for years as an unauthorised – or as the substantial community preferred to put it: liberated – Dylan album. The Dylan bootleg catalogue these days amounts to some 500 entries. What do these mostly unbearably lo-fi amateur recordings stand for if not the fans' desire to somehow come closer to their star by possessing one more collector's item?

Yet to be sure, stars are by definition difficult to decipher. In Richard Dyer's analysis, the star image forms a *structured polysemy* comprising "the multiple but finite meanings and effects that a star image signifies".[15] On that reading, the image of the 'composite creature' articulates heterogeneous, often contradictory meanings and functions as a site at which these multiple meanings can conjoin and fuse. Thus, the star image for Dyer serves to ideologically reconcile the contradictions of the society it stems from. Generally, Dyer suggests, the star as a cultural institution serves to both reassert and simultaneously question the notion of individuality: On the one hand conspicuously exceptional and hence 'individualistic' to the point of idiosyncrasy, but on the other hand commonly available as cultural signs, stars appears to straddle the gap between the individual and the generic. In that sense, the star image is structurally fissured by the performative contradiction of enacting a mass-produced aura. All this, again, leads back to the *fort-da* logic that governs the relation between star, both similar and dissimilar, and fan.

Dylan may not have introduced this logic into the field of pop music, but he is certainly one of its pioneers and most ingenious practitioners. The Dylan effect of a permanent tension between disclosure and concealment has by now been normalised in the world of pop but when Dylan introduced it, it still caused a wide range of irritations and complex fascinations. What I mean by "the Dylan effect" is the precise employment of the photo effect: the interplay of presence and absence, of availability and withdrawal. With the publication of the first part of his autobiography, Dylan seems to have conceded to his fans' desire, offering his constituency precisely the 'biography' that he had hitherto deliberately withheld.

III

Dylan's *Chronicles: Volume One* ends on a note that at first sight appears to preclude the form of the chronicle that the book purports to be. At the end of the first volume, the very young Bob Dylan – recently invented as it were – sets out to become that prolific and innovative songwriter that all his readers are supposed to know him for. Having recorded only one long-player so far, young Bob is already feeling confined within the conventions of his self-chosen genre of artistic expression: folk music.

> The folk music scene had been like a paradise that I had to leave, like Adam had to leave the garden. It was just too perfect. In a few years' time a shit storm would be unleashed. Things would begin to burn. Bras, draft cards, American flags, bridges, too – everybody would be dreaming of getting it on. (. . .) The road out would be treacherous, and I didn't know where it would lead but I followed it anyway. It was a strange world ahead that would unfold, a thunderhead of a world with jagged lightning edges. Many got it wrong and never did get it right. I went straight into it. It was wide open. One thing for sure, not only was it not run by God, but it wasn't run by the devil either.[16]

Dylan fans will immediately recognise this 'thunderhead of a world' as the monumental landscape of such classical vast-canvas Dylan songs as "A Hard Rain's A-Gonna Fall", "Chimes of Freedom", or "Gates of Eden". All its vaguely apocalyptic overtones notwithstanding, it is definitely not a theocratically ordered universe that, as Benjamin insists, forms the ground from which the chronicle as a narrative form emerges. Run neither by god nor devil, this world apparently does not endow happenings with an always already given significance. Or does it? Is *Chronicles* actually a chronicle, or does it only *pretend to be* one? How does this genre-related issue tie in with the status of its author as star?

Right from the start it is understood that the book is not conclusive but forms only the first part of a series. Rumour has it that at least two sequels are in the pipeline. *Volume One* consists of five chapters that show Dylan in the late 50s/early 60s while taking his first steps into the folk scene of Greenwich Village / New York; then in the late 60s on the run from his superstardom; and in late 80s New Orleans during the recording sessions for his album, *Oh, Mercy*. These episodes appear to be largely disconnected especially as they are presented as self-enclosed and self-sufficient narratives in their own right; at the same time they permanently refer to a larger narrative that the book itself, however, does not at all relate: the story of Dylan's exceptional career as a pop superstar. This is particularly striking in the chapter entitled "Father of Night" (set in the late 60s) that is about Dylan's short collaboration with the poet, Archibald McLeish, but more than anything about his attempts to escape from the pitfalls of high visibility stardom. It is crucial that Dylan's cult status is heavily associated with the role of a public leader of the countercultural movements of the day. It is *against* these largely political implications that the Dylan of the late 60s asserts that he be nothing but a musician:

> What I had to do was *recondition my mind* and stop putting the blame on external forces. Whatever the counterculture was, I'd seen enough of it. I was sick of the way my lyrics had been extrapolated, their meanings subverted into polemics and that I had been anointed as the Big Bubba of Rebellion, High Priest of Protest, the Czar of Dissent, the Duke of Disobedience, Leader of the Freeloaders, Kaiser of Apostasy, Archbishop of Anarchy, the Big Cheese. (. . .) I couldn't just lie there, had to take the bull by the horns myself and *remodel the image of me*, change the perception of it anyway. There aren't any rules to cover an emergency of this kind. This was a new thing for me and I wasn't used to thinking this way. I'd have to send out deviating signals, crank up the wrecking train – create some different impressions. (C 120)

What is interesting here is not so much Dylan's pose of disclaiming the politics of his own classical 1960s body of work; in all Dylan biographies from Scaduto to Webb, this disclaimer at the turn of the decade has already been canonised as one of the crucial turning points in the vita of the star. What is strikingly new in the passage quoted above is rather the transparency with which Dylan posits himself as a self-engineer: It is not only the strategic displacement of the established star image ("remodel the image of me"), which in itself must have been complicated enough; it is also the "reconditioning of my mind". If mind and image are the objects of this necessary revamping, who would be its agent? This intriguing question points straight at the crucial dilemma behind everything in *Chronicles*: Who, beyond the indubitable congruence of author, narrator and protagonist, *is* the subject of this piece of writing?

The first two sections, "Markin' Up the Score" and "The Lost Land", are set in the period right before Dylan's first record contract with Columbia in 1962; they show the emergence of 'Bob Dylan' from Robert Zimmerman:

> What I was going to do as soon as I left home was just call myself Robert Allen. As far as I was concerned that was who I was. (. . .) Then sometime later, unexpectedly, I'd seen some poems by Dylan Thomas. Bob Dylan looked and sounded better than Bob Allyn. The first time I was asked my name in the Twin Cities, I instinctively and automatically without thinking said, "Bob Dylan". (C 78-79)

"Instinctively and automatically without thinking": certainly an excessive assertion of pre-rational and pre-discursive 'decision' with which the name that will finally stick – Bob Dylan – gets consolidated. This is not the technology of the self-engaged in deliberate automorphosis; it is rather the self that is driven by some deeper or ulterior force. *Chronicles*, despite the laconic and understated oral-style tone of its narrative, is in its deep structure formatted by this reliance on such deeper forces. At the end of the opening of the book, the young and down-and-out Robert Zimmerman (not yet Bob Dylan) is working cheap in second-rate Greenwich Village folk clubs; but by the end of the first section, he has already managed to get friends with the influential Dave Van Ronk and has finally got a foot in the door at the "Gaslight", one of the hottest joints of the folk scene. The chapter ends like this:

> I'd soon be hired to play at the Gaslight and never see the basket houses again. (. . .) I was heading for the fantastic lights. No doubt about it. Could it be that I was being deceived? Not likely. I don't think I had enough imagination to be deceived; had no false hope, either. I had come from a long ways off and had started from a long ways down. But now destiny was about to manifest itself. I felt like it was looking right at me and nobody else. (C 22)

True, this sequence is not entirely devoid of self-irony and partly, no doubt, an attempt to recreate the blue-eyed-boy excitement of a 19-year-old provincial just finding a foothold in New York bohemia. Destiny about to manifest itself, therefore, might well be Robert Zimmerman's and not Bob Dylan's phrase, free indirect speech of the protagonist/focaliser rather than narrator's or authorial discourse. The autobiographical pact clearly allows for such discrepancies. Whose, however, is the first sentence of the sequence: "I'd soon be hired to play at the Gaslight"? Is this again the free indirect speech rendition of Robert Zimmerman's wishful thinking while walking home from his first encounter with Dave Van Ronk? Or is this not just as much Dylan the author-narrator giving us a prolepsis, a foreshadowing of things to come – things that we as good Dylan historians are anyway supposed to have known all along? The destiny talk partakes of this same ambiguity: one cannot clearly decide as to who produces this discourse – protagonist or author/narrator.

The structure of the book is such that the final chapter, "River of Ice", returns to these opening sections and even repeats the very same events. The text does not come full circle, though, but rather rehearses a repetition with a difference. We are taken back to the Greenwich Village beginnings, to Van Ronk, to the Gaslight, to the first record contract. But while these events were presented at the first time in the mode of the chronicle with only very rare occasions of destiny talk, the second time does not come as farce but as *bildungsroman*. "River of Ice" is in fact the portrait of the artist as a young man. It is in this final section that Dylan delineates the genealogy of the artist Bob Dylan, with the understanding that this artist figure never coincides with that much more evasive fiction, the 'person': Earlier in the book, but chronologically much later, Dylan relates his difficulties with the producer of his *Oh Mercy* album (1989); the producer "was looking for songs that defined me as a person, but what I do in the studio doesn't define me as a person" (*Chronicles* 199). In the "River of Ice" chapter, Dylan recounts his initiation into serious folk music when listening, for the first time, to a Woody Guthrie record:

> For me it was an epiphany, like some heavy anchor had just plunged into the waters of the harbor. That day I listened all afternoon to Guthrie as if in a trance and I felt like I had discovered some essence of self-command, that I was in the internal pocket of the system feeling more like myself than ever before. (C 244)

"Feeling more *like myself*" – as a consequence, the narrative goes on with young Bobby's attempts not simply to emulate but virtually to *become* Woodie Guthrie until a ruthless "folk snob" critic brutally punctures his dream by asserting that "you're trying hard but you'll never turn into Woody Guthrie" (C 250).

Greenwich Village in the early 60s, however, appears to offer some remedy for such fixation on unattainable role models. The folk scene is anyway a culture of collective authorship, the recycling of traditional or other peoples' material, and all variants of imitation. Young Dylan is fascinated with a local celebrity precisely because he could "imitate just about anything. He could imitate singers imitating other singers. One of his more outrageous imitations was Dean Martin imitating Little Richard" (C 259). It is a culture of collage, a culture of hybrid identities that are not centred on some deep, essential self. The discovery of Brecht and Picasso feeds into the sharpening of the profile of Dylan, which finds its provisional conclusion with the appropriation of Rimbaud in yet another epiphany:

> I came across one of his letters called 'je est un autre', which translates into 'I is someone else'. When I read those words, the bells went off. It

made perfect sense. I wished someone would have mentioned that to me earlier. (C 288)

Destiny has clearly gone up the chimney by now. The world is run by neither god nor devil. But it is full of revelations, epiphanies, and shock-like truth-events. But only that which is otherwise concealed can be revealed in the first place. Dylan's book can for most of its parts remain a chronicle because it is written on this assumption of a meaning in hiding that at times reveals itself – in Woody Guthrie records, in Brecht/Weil's "Pirate Jenny" song, in some Picasso paintings, in Rimbaud's visionary letters, in the foghorns of the big ships in the harbour. Dylan's chronicles do not rely on the theocracy of the medieval chronicler but on the Romantic and High Modernist expectation and experience of flashes of significance, moments of being in the dense time of the now. Meaning, though never questioned as latency, is never fully revealed. It is disclosed in a flash and concealed again. The world of these chronicles is wide open. Its narrator refuses to shoulder the burden of explanation. All he can and has to do is to account – in the mode of the chronicler – for those moments of revelation. This mystical relation between the Dylan of *Chronicles* and his world seems to be the relation that Dylan offers his readers, those who want to see through him. In the late 80s chapter, Dylan sums up his difficult relation with his producer in terms that might well serve as a formula for his relation to his fans in general: "I know that he wanted to understand me more as we went along, but you can't do that, not unless you like to do puzzles." (C 218)

NOTES AND REFERENCES

1. See http://www.bobsboots.com/CDs/cd-a25.html. Downloaded on 5th November 2007.
2. Walter Benjamin, "The Storyteller: Reflections on the Works of Nikolai Leskov", in *Illuminations: Essays and Reflections*, ed. & intr. Hannah Arendt, trans. Harry Zohn, (New York: Schocken, 1968), pp. 83-109, here pp. 100-01.
3. Philippe Lejeune, *On Autobiography*, ed. John Paul Eakin, trans. Katherine Leary, (Minneapolis: University of Minnesota Press, 1989), p. 4.
4. Frank Kermode (1966), *The Sense of an Ending: Studies in the Theory of Fiction*, (Oxford: Oxford UP, 2000), p. 46.
5. Peter Brooks, *Reading for the Plot: Design and Intention in Narrative*, (New York: Knopf, 1984), p. 19.
6. Cf. Hayden White, *The Content of the Form. Narrative Discourse and Historical Representation*, (Baltimore & London: Johns Hopkins University Press, 1987), p. 5.

7. Benjamin, "The Storyteller", pp. 95-96.
8. E.M. Forster (1927), *Aspects of the Novel*, (London: Penguin, 2005), p. 44.
9. Fredric Jameson, *Postmodernism, or, The Cultural Logic of Late Capitalism*, (London & New York: Verso, 1991), p. 1.
10. John Ellis, *Visible Fictions: Cinema, Television, Video*, (London: Routledge & Kegan Paul, 1982), p. 97.
11. Roland Barthes (1980), *Camera Lucida: Reflections on Photography*, trans. Richard Howard, (London: Virago, 2000), p. 7.
12. See Rick Altman, *Film/Genre*, (London: BFI, 1999), p. 165.
13. Stephen H. Webb, *Dylan Redeemed: From Highway 61 to Saved*, (London & New York: Continuum, 2006), p. 32.
14. See Anthony Scaduto, *Bob Dylan*, (New York: Grosset & Dunlap, 1972), p. 272.
15. Richard Dyer, "Stars as Images" in *The Film Studies Reader*, ed. Joan Hollows et al., (London: Arnold, 2000), pp. 121-24, here p. 124.
16. Bob Dylan, *Chronicles: Volume One*, (New York: Simon & Schuster, 2004), pp. 292-93. All quotations from this edition are cited in the text as C + page number.

ROMIT ROY

Theory as Autobiography: Music and Childhood Reminiscences as Autobiographical Elements in the Works of Theodor W. Adorno

I. AUTOBIOGRAPHY IN THE ABSENCE OF AN AUTOBIOGRAPHY

Theodor W. Adorno did not write an autobiography, but there are a few works that are based on autobiographical motifs.[1] Apart from his correspondence with friends and colleagues (for example, letters to Walter Benjamin, Alban Berg, Ernst Køenek, etc.), there are a handful of published texts that he wrote with autobiographical candour in mind, like "Der böse Kamerad", "Amorbach" and "Vierhändig, noch einmal". Here and there, in an interview or in an aphoristic passage, he would refer to personal experiences during various stages of his life. Occasionally, autobiographical elements – personal anecdotes, impressions of childhood and reflections on music – found their way into his *œuvre.* Personal experiences became illustrations for his theory, and theory made experience intelligible, throwing light upon the relation between the particular, personal, private and the general or public. They provide glimpses into his life, even as they weave his *œuvre* into a comprehensive narrative, giving an insight into why he wrote about particular things in a particular way. His work as a whole and writing itself emerge as a sort of autobiographical inscription.

Although a sociologist and a philosopher by profession, about half his work – or probably even more than half, if one includes unpublished manuscripts and speeches – is on music. Among the better-known works on music by Adorno are *Philosophie der neuen Musik*[2] and the controversial essay "Zeitlose Mode. Zum Jazz" in the collection of sociological and cultural essays *Prismen.*[3] Apart from these, volumes 13 to 19 of his *Gesammelte Schriften* in 20 volumes are on music and musicians. Also, there is a sizeable body of unpublished manuscripts and speeches on music – such as the speeches "Von musikalischer Bildung", "Zum Problem der musikalischen Analyse", and the manuscript titled "Theorie der musikalischen Reproduktion".[4] Another incomplete manuscript, *Beethoven - Philosophie der Musik*, was published in 1993 as a part of Adorno's *Nachgelassene Schriften*, edited and published by Rolf Tiedemann for the Theodor W. Adorno Archiv, Frankfurt a.M. Music also constitutes an essential aspect of works like *Ästhetische Theorie* (GS 7), of various essays in collections like *Kulturkritik und Gesellschaft* (GS 10.1 and 10.2), and even of works like *Negative Dialektik* (GS 6), "which is far removed from all aesthetic themes".[5]

Music dominates not only quantitatively. In fact, musical thought, reflections on and insight into music inform even his non-musical work. Writing on music had two implications in Adorno's œuvre, both somewhat autobiographical. First, Adorno may have tried to compensate for his decision not to become a professional musician. In theory, through the theoretical passage from and back to music, he may have tried to restore his childhood attachment to music, as if trying to atone for not taking up music as a career. Secondly, writing from the standpoint of music-philosophy, the recurrent motif of music in his writing became an act of revisiting and rehabilitating a utopia he believed he had known through music – and this personal utopia was transformed into the antithesis of a self-destructive modern culture.

Adorno had learnt music, i.e., piano and composition, under Bernhard Sekles, Eduard Steuermann and Alban Berg. It was Alban Berg who had warned him that one day he – Adorno – would have to choose between Beethoven and Kant, between music and philosophy.[6] He became a philosopher and sociologist, but he continued to write obsessively on music. He decided not to exercise the choice put before him by his "revered and beloved master" and friend Alban Berg. Writing on music, he brought the two realms of music and philosophy together, reconciling their differences that kept them apart in a culture of specialization and segregation of the arts and the sciences. The reconciliation of music and philosophy in writing, or writing as the simultaneity of musical and philosophical thought – not exactly Adorno's invention – was on the one hand an answer to the political, economic, social and cultural problems of his times, and, on the other hand, on a personal, autobiographical plane, an answer to the challenge his teacher Berg had put before him.

II. MUSIC, PHILOSOPHY AND RECONCILIATION: AUTOBIOGRAPHICAL MOTIFS

In his music-philosophy, Adorno dwelt on the same theme of violent confrontation between tradition and modernity, which was the central issue addressed in the collaborative work of Horkheimer and Adorno, particularly in *Dialektik der Aufklärung*.[7] In fact, Adorno wanted his *Philosophie der neuen Musik* to be read as an elaboration upon *Dialektik der Aufklärung*. The analysis of the dialectics that governed the relation between tradition and modernity was an essential dimension of Adorno's music-philosophy.

Adorno, while rejecting orthodoxy and uncritical devotion to traditions, insisted that substantial progress in music was possible only if one had a true understanding of one's traditional source. One must be aware of what one's tradition meant, of what its limits were in present times, of where it would lead to, its possibilities and impossibilities, and its consequences.[8] One must look at tradition not as a museum relic, but as a dynamic process, as something perpetually growing and developing through its immanent dialectics and by absorbing influences from outside. Schönberg was his ideal in this sense. He was a composer who brought about far-reaching technical innovations in European music without overstepping its boundaries; he merely had a keen sense for the music that demanded to be composed within that very tradition after traditional tonality had exhausted its possibilities. Schönberg had consistently realized those possibilities and necessities with scant regard for popular acceptance. The age of Schönberg and his foremost pupils Alban Berg and Anton Webern would remain for Adorno the golden age of musical progress the way he understood it. Writing obsessively on Schönberg, Berg and Webern, he saw in their compositions the best possible cultural alternative in an age where making music and listening to it was rapidly degenerating into consumerism, even as his own childhood experience of music remained for him the utopia of culture, utopia as music in the moment of its realization within an intimate circle – a sharp contrast to the culture-industry, a profit-making venture of immeasurable proportions, which had nothing to do with music as such, which mass-produced music as entertainment merely for amassing profit through its mass-consumption.

III. NAMING THE 'I'

Born on 11 September 1903 in Frankfurt am Main, Adorno's childhood was spent in idyllic domesticity, in an atmosphere of intimacy and innocence, of genteel and cultured upbringing. In music, the communion between parent and child took place in its most intimate form within the Wiesengrund household. Mother Maria, née Calvelli-Adorno delle Piane, and her sister Agatha, both accomplished professional musicians, made music together at the piano while Teddie looked on, listened, and was allowed to leaf through the pages of the manuscripts.[9] This little family scene, warmly sheltered in music, innocent, idyllic and far removed from the professional and commercial world of music, would remain for Adorno a utopian dream. Strangely, the figure of the father, the Jewish wine merchant Oscar Alexander Wiesengrund, is absent from this picture of domestic idyll. His shadowy presence shrank into the cryptic 'W.' – Adorno's middle name, the lyrical, pastoral, musically resonant 'Wiesengrund', a name rehabilitated and conserved for posterity through a literary reference in Thomas Mann's novel *Doktor Faustus*[10]; a name which the son used to sign his letters with until the late 1930s, but which he, during his exile in America in 1937, was about to stop using, but retained it in the hyphenated form 'Wiesengrund-Adorno' only because his mother insisted.[11] To posterity, however, he would be known as the philosopher Theodor W. Adorno, or simply Adorno. The sheer variety of names adopted by the private person and public author to sign personal testimonies and public texts – the intimate Teddie W(iesengrund) in the letters to Alban Berg and Benjamin, the more formal Teddie Wiesengrund-Adorno, the provocative pseudonym Hektor Rottweiler, under which he wrote a notorious early essay on jazz,[12] the posthumous-sounding Theodor W. Adorno – do they not also seem like minute autobiographical inscriptions, leaving the reader to wonder if it was the same person hiding behind the patchwork of names?

IV. AMORBACH

As a child, Adorno would occasionally travel to Amorbach with his parents to spend the weekend. It is a smallish town about eighty kilometers from Frankfurt am Main. To the child Teddie, this quaint little town set in the idyllic landscape of the Odenwald seemed to have sprung out of mythical times, from the times of the Nibelungen.[13] Years later, it seemed to him like the place most likely to resemble that which he, as a child, barely sensed as reconciliation. The theme of reconciliation motivated Adorno's writing in later years, particularly after Auschwitz. If in Amorbach, away from the busy Frankfurt am Main, he experienced peace and quiet amidst natural beauty, at school in his native city he was daily subjected to the brutalities of class-bullies who probably could not stand that precocious little boy for being so bright, for standing first in his class, for securing double promotions.[14] As an adult, Adorno came face to face with persecution once again, this time at the hands of the Nazis, who seemed to be grown up versions of the bullies at school. He took care to make a theoretical connection between his classmates who bullied him and the Nazi monsters of the 1930s and 1940s.[15] The theme of reconciliation, which he had perceived in the structure of music, became for him a recurrent motif in formulating a philosophy for the conclusion of the project of Enlightenment: reconciliation between the subject and the object, the individual and totality, reconciliation as the necessity of the subject perceiving the objective world in the way it would reveal itself from the location of redemption.[16] In the last passage of *Minima Moralia*, Adorno was in fact theoretically revisiting Amorbach while extending an invitation to the alienated subject of modernity to follow him there, leaving behind a life that was irrevocably damaged. Amorbach, a place seen through the eyes of a child and conserved in memory as one of perfect tranquility and devoid of hatred, was the exact opposite of Auschwitz. The romantic strain in Adorno's writing is unmistakable. The fictitious Amorbach[17] – a place seen in childhood, revisited in remembrance and theoretically reconstructed as utopia – has a special significance *vis-à-vis* Adorno's theory, which in fact increasingly puts on an elegiac tone: critique as lamentation for a lost place, the imagined Germany that he believed in, the *Kulturland* destroyed by fascism and the culture industry. Amorbach is for Adorno that lost Germany both as cultural as well as personal idyll, a place that never really was but existed as imagination, sometimes vaguely experienced in the fleeting moments of childhood. It represented in his fantasy the lost space of well-being and happiness in the company of loved ones. The piece called "Amorbach" is a reconstruction of a fantasy of a place Adorno believed he had seen and been in as a child. The written Amorbach – as even much of his theory – reclaims that ideality constructed in memory. Adorno's theory reclaims in its negative image that ideal Germany as the ideal cultural landscape, presupposes its presence as dream and its absence or loss as reality. The memory or dream of Amorbach energizes his culture-critique, becoming an accusation levelled at modernity for its unwillingness and inability to sustain such a dream.

However, the complex motif of reconciliation (*Versöhnung*) that pervaded "Amorbach" should not be misunderstood as abject reconciliation of the victims with their tormentors. Reconciliation, a legacy of idealist philosophy, was for him a theoretical device – a moment of rupture in conventional thinking that had calcified into the dichotomous, hegemonic relation between subject and object. It was for him a factor that was meant to liberate thought from the endless cycle of dominance, violence and retribution.[18] This almost Gandhian mode of thinking was reiterated towards the end of his life in the *Spiegel*-interview of 1969 where he stated that he had severe reservations against any form of violence; that he would be found guilty of betraying his own life and of denying all the injustices he had experienced and observed under Hitler and Stalin if he did not renounce the eternal cycle of using violence against violence.[19] It was almost as if Adorno, defying reality and history and the comically tragic alienation that he had to suffer in the last year of his life, was thinking of the utopia he had known during childhood: within his family, at the piano, in musical manuscripts, in a place like Amorbach, in the sounds of freedom that he heard in Schönberg's free atonality. The personal, private and subjective visions of utopia are objectified in theory and encrypted in works like *Negative Dialektik*, *Ästhetische Theorie*, *Philosophie der neuen Musik*, even as they resurface in the subjective and aphoristic language of *Minima Moralia*:

> Der spezifische Ansatz der Minima Moralia, eben der Versuch, Momente der gemeinsamen Philosophie von subjektiver Erfahrung her darzustellen, bedingt es, daß die Stücke nicht durchaus vor der Philosophie bestehen, von der sie doch selber ein Stück sind. Das will das Lose und Unverbindliche der Form, der Verzicht auf expliziten theoretischen Zusammenhang mit ausdrücken.[20]

V. THE PHILOSOPHER AS BILDUNGSBÜRGER

In the mid-1920s, Adorno was for a short while undecided about choosing between music and philosophy as career. It seems though that he had resolved this dilemma early enough, deciding not to become a professional composer, but with no intention of giving up composing and writing about music.[21] He did continue to write about music professionally – as a critic and philosopher of music. But during the rise of the Nazis and after Auschwitz, defending and rehabilitating the purely personal in the light of a philosophy of reconciliation – in the light of philosophy *as* reconciliation – became an ethical, not to say political necessity. This shift of accent can be traced back to his experience as a victim and witness of fascism. He was a half-Jew, a liberal leftist thinker at that. Yet, even after escaping with his life from the Nazis, he remained an exile and an outsider in America who would not renounce his German and European past – a recalcitrant and unrepentant Bildungsbürger with very strong and particular musical tastes and a decidedly German attitude towards academics, based upon the idea of speculative, interpretative and critical thought rather than upon learning as compilation of facts and figures. Adorno saw education and culture as *Bildung*, as *Geisteskultur*. Even after returning to Germany in 1949, he would be destined to continue in the role of the outsider, as a relentless critic of the system.

Adorno's writings are of a hybrid nature, combining reflections on aesthetics, music, philosophy, society, culture, politics and psychology. They are speculative as well documentary, secular bordering on the religious. This nature of writing bears the imprint of his personality – of the multifaceted Bildungsbürger, aesthete and humanist, the last of them in fact, one may argue. But the cultural milieu that would sustain such a personality was gone. The standpoint of the *Bildungsbürger* was at best an anachronism in the 20th century: the supremacy of the culture-industry had reduced all other forms of cultural existence to meaningless pedantic exercises, whereas fascism had appropriated and ideologically falsified that very cultural heritage of Germany that Adorno would never renounce, even after Auschwitz. His work was an attempt at conserving this endangered culture under the shadow of the question of how it could have spawned the monstrosity called fascism. Hovering between obsolescence and utopia, Adorno's location on this narrow ledge where diverse disciplines converged was the space where the theoretical and the personal coincided.

VI. THE DIALECTICIAN

There is a kind of fragility in Adorno's personality and his work. And he was aware of it, facing it with disarming honesty coupled with a clever dialectic turning of tables when he once said that he was not at all afraid of contradictions, that the ego stood the test of strength if it showed the ability to admit objective contradictions into its thinking instead of trying to do away with them forcibly.[22] Adorno to some extent treated his writing as a laboratory, where he let such contradictions develop to their logical end. His technique of writing entailed looking at phenomena in such a way that the "confessions of their untruth" would become legible upon their features. This meant looking minutely at the many contradictions that constituted social and cultural phenomena as well as intellectual and artistic products. Once these had "confessed to their untruths", one would imagine that the negative image of the truth would gradually emerge in the developing process of Adorno's writings. But the readers' hopes are belied when they find that Adorno himself was not primarily trying to provide us with an apocalyptic vision of the final truth. He who had categorically said that knowledge had no other light except that which shone upon the world from redemption, refrained from trying to make even a cursory suggestion towards what that redemption should be. Of course, after Auschwitz, redemption could have only one meaning: to undo what had been done and to ensure that such things did not ever happen again. Towards this end, one could only try to understand culture itself as one had known and practiced it in order to discover what it was that allowed such a thing to happen. The purpose of knowledge as the light of redemption was thus to show how culture, as the transition from barbarity to civilization, could at the height of its technological development regress into the most heinous form of barbarity. Such knowledge would be meaningless and merely perpetuate barbarity if its principal tool, critical inquiry, was allowed to degenerate into an inquisition, looking for enemies and always hoping to identify them somewhere else, among some other people, in some other culture. Knowledge must therefore be self-reflective; the subject of knowledge must look at himself. He must ruthlessly look at the contradictions and dialectics within to understand the whys and wherefores of his possible complicity with barbarities like Auschwitz, or, at the very least, he must account for why he looked away, or why he remained silent, or pretended ignorance. Writing in the light of this philosophy, in the light of the 'dialectics of enlightenment', Adorno put himself under its glare allowing his opinionated personality to play out its prejudices and contradictions, to confess to its untruths.

VII. MUSICAL PREJUDICES OF A BILDUNGSBÜRGER

Adorno's writings on music are a study in personal prejudices. This is often misunderstood and dismissed as elitism. In the company of his mother and aunt, Adorno had first heard the 'classics'. As a pupil of Sekles, Steuermann and Berg, he encountered and learnt to appreciate modern music. He would have experienced in his adolescence the shockwaves created by 'atonal' music and would have witnessed the development and systematization of free atonality into twelve-tone music. These were historic developments, and as a witness and a close associate of the New Viennese school of composition, he would forever be preoccupied with this kind of music. He would also have witnessed with bitterness that such music never gained as much appreciation among the musical public as he had expected it to achieve. Instead, the public was swaying to jazz. His bitterness about jazz – which he said was easily integrated into the culture-industry – was however not a result of petty jealousy. Again and again, he tried to explain how jazz was not only musically regressive – many of its perceived progressive elements like syncopation, polyphony and free improvisation, as such rudimentary according to Adorno's estimation, had been preempted and superseded in the previous centuries – but that it was not even the voice of the oppressed Black American slaves, having been appropriated by and seamlessly integrated into the culture industry. Jazz had become for Adorno the archetypical antithesis of 'true' music, that is, of music that consequently unfolded its immanent logic within each strand of its fabric instead of falling back upon entertainment as its sole purpose.

VIII. THE PARTICULAR AND THE GENERAL: CONTRADICTION AS CRITIQUE, ERGO SUM

One must now consider to what extent the subjective and the personal can come together in theoretical formulation without undermining the minimum degree of objectivity that is required, without rendering theory into personal mythology, into a narrative of the private and contingent. The presence of autobiographical elements should on the contrary be such as to give validity to theory, not as a mere source of empirical data, but more as a consciousness, subjectivity, which, as a product of its times and by being what it is, can both testify to history as well as function as a critical instance – in the way Adorno formulated the critical relationship between the individual and the general, a relation he discovered in Beethoven's music and Hegel's philosophy.[23] He had seen that in Beethoven's music the particular (individual themes, the minutest melodic motifs, inspired compositional ideas, the composer himself as inventor, etc.), were by themselves insignificant (*nichtig*); but even as they appeared to be 'something', they achieved their significance only as parts of the whole (the totality of musical form, the traditional repertoire of formal and aesthetic principles that determine musical production and reception, the musical public, etc.).[24] In Beethoven, this relationship was one of mutual respect and distance, and even tension: the particular was never totally and hence never forcibly subsumed under the whole; by virtue of their character and uniqueness, individual motifs resisted total integration, and Beethoven's music abstained from forcing their integration into its formal and harmonic system.[25] In later music, e.g. of Schubert, Wagner and Strauss, the opposite was practiced: the individual elements, melodically richer than those of their predecessor Beethoven, stood out and had to be forced into conforming to the harmonic scheme of the composition. Yet, even in Beethoven, Adorno discovered potentially totalitarian moments in the integration of particulars under the whole – in the symbolic verses of Schiller's *An die Freude*, the text of Beethoven's 9th symphony:

> Ja, wer auch nur eine Seele sein nennt auf dem Erdenrund,
> Und wer's nie gekonnt, der stehle weinend sich aus diesem Bund.

Bourgeois utopia is incomplete without the suffering of the outcast – the one who has no one to love. In fact, like the suitably punished stepmother in the happy endings of fairytales, such figures of loneliness, outcasts, are created by the totality in order to affirm and assert itself as a perfectly happy one, in order to dictate what it meant by happiness and to impose it on everyone while expelling those who failed or refused to conform to its norms.[26]

Adorno had observed the manifestation of antagonism between the individual and the collective in Beethoven's personality: in his monadic personality, in the loud laughter of the demonic, aggressive and sadistic eccentric, in the grim visage and the posturing of the misunderstood and unloved outsider, in his deafness – it even seemed as though Beethoven *wanted* to become deaf.[27] As in music, such extreme contradiction between the two, between Beethoven and his society, marked the contradictoriness of the individual (the artistic genius), itself a product of the times. The individual as artistic genius craves love and understanding, but resists such attention in fear of forfeiting its autonomy by being accepted as 'one of them'. It was almost masochistic and self-chastising, the way Beethoven moulded himself as the one who could never love and call a soul as his own, sneaking out of the congregation of happily love-struck souls. In the context of artistic production and consumption, the socio-economic shift from feudal patronage to open market had resulted in the re-creation of the artistic genius as a pathological case. The genius lamented the lack of cultural knowledge and the lack of understanding for his creations among the new public. This perceived lack drove the genius to desperation, duplicating and amplifying the anxiety every individual must suffer in the face of a totality that overpowered and overrode individuality and imposed uniformity, but to which the individual must belong in order to be one in the first place.

Adorno's work drew attention to the dialectics of individual autonomy and conformism in culture, to the debilitating effect of the culture-industry upon the individual and to the unimaginably brutal suppression of individuality in fascism. Adorno's writing focused on the ideological aspect of social integration, the compulsions of conforming to customs and principles of a society, the mechanisms of reward for those who did and punishment for those who wouldn't. Analyzing the troubled dialectic relation between the individual and the whole unfolded the notion of the individual as the eternal outsider who could not be seamlessly integrated into the totality of social existence.

IX. THE ECCENTRIC

The idiosyncrasies and eccentricities of Adorno's personality have found their way into his theories and philosophies of music, culture, society, politics, pedagogy and academics. They manifest themselves not only in his choice of subject-matter and what he wrote about them but also in his language and style. Yet, without these qualities, theory would perhaps not be possible at all, or perhaps it would be possible merely as formal description, incommensurate with the purpose of theory as critique, as *bestimmte Negation*. Indeed, after Auschwitz, theory could be possible and justifiable only as critique, or *bestimmte Negation* – that is, not as mere evaluation of the aesthetic or pragmatic worth of an object, but critique as deciphering the "confessions of untruth in every feature" of every object,[28] critique as vigilance, watching over the tense relation between the individual and totality. Such critique could perhaps be sustained only if the theoretician lived through the pain, memory and consciousness of being an individual, the potential other, different to the point of being idiosyncratic, eccentric, personal, and endangered.

Adorno's own position as an intellectual, as a survivor of fascism, and as a crusader against the culture-industry made him appear like an eccentric. Sometimes, one has the impression that, like Beethoven, he cultivated the image of a recalcitrant and unrepentant intellectual. In his self-assessment as a theoretician, he expressed his reservations about practicing sociology as amassing and classification of data and information. He saw his role in academics, particularly as a sociologist, as one of interpreting phenomena, rather than merely describing and classifying them.[29] He also arrogantly insisted on his role as a theoretician who, even under collective pressure, would not succumb to current political tendencies and become a social activist: "I am a man of theory who perceives theoretical reflexion as exceptionally close to his artistic intentions."[30] He defended his position as an inhabitant of the ivory tower of theory, and protested against those who imposed uniformity of thought and action upon others who thought differently. He asserted that he on his part would continue to analyze phenomena ruthlessly, even at the risk of being alienated for writing on aesthetic theory in times of violent political upheavals.[31] Indeed, in the foreword to *Philosophie der neuen Musik*, Adorno asked whether after what had happened in Europe and which still threatened the world, squandering time and intellectual energy on esoteric questions of modern compositional techniques might not appear cynical. And yet he believed that only modern music could reflect the truth about life precisely because it was not a familiar manifestation of life, because it kept its promise to humanity by paradoxically going back on its promise of delivering what people most expected from it: by refusing to provide an asylum from the pressures of unbearable norms.[32]

Adorno's political standpoint was defined by the uncompromising critique of totalitarian and authoritarian tendencies. And yet, the intensity of his relentless critique must have been at least partly influenced by the fact that he had once naively tried to survive within fascist Germany by burying his head in the sand like an ostrich.[33] He had even tried to merge with the fascist crowd by writing disparagingly about jazz in a language spiced with phrases reminiscent of totalitarian and racist jargon – like *Kulturbolschewismus* and *Einfluß der Negerrasse auf die nördliche ausmerzen* – the intention being, however, to defend new music and to help it to *hibernate* during the Third Reich![34] His hope that fascism would blow over in a few years without much ado was soon belied when the Nazi authorities refused to renew his *venia legendi*. Then, after witnessing the growing violence of the criminal regime, he decided to immigrate to America, responding to an invitation from Max Horkheimer who had already relocated the Institut für Sozialforschung there.

Probably as a gesture of defiance to prove that his critique of jazz was not a lame attempt at ingratiating himself with the fascists, Adorno never revised his position on jazz. He maintained throughout that its claim to being the music of the oppressed (the Blacks) was only partially true, since it had been taken over by the culture-industry. In fact, he claimed that its musical structure was symptomatic of the isolated and mutilated modern subject masochistically trying to ingratiate itself with authority. In terms of its musical structure, it was a rehash of obsolete techniques of European music. Jazz was neither politically nor aesthetically progressive; it should not be confused with the values forced upon it. Rather, it should be regarded as what it was: as politically tame, even conformist entertainment, as commodity.

X. THE ASCETIC AND THE AESTHETICS OF THE SPIRIT

The frequent suggestion that Adorno disliked jazz for its overt sensuality[35] must be understood in relation to his aesthetic philosophy instead of leading to a hastily drawn conclusion about his prudish middle-class character. In fact, Adorno emphatically rejected any suggestion that would identify him with petit bourgeois types "who giggled at the sight of bare breasts" – he was after all against any kind of erotic repression and sexual taboos.[36] Whatever he may have had to say against music of the "culinary" variety, he was certainly not averse to taking pleasure in the good things that life had to offer. He appreciated roast venison by candlelight in rustic surroundings, and good French wine that tasted of the earth, water, air and sunshine of the province where it was made, and even wistfully admired American society for its abundance that gave its children the freedom to have as much ice cream as they craved.[37]

Adorno the aesthetician accorded to sensual elements the place they deserved in the work of art. Only, he subordinated them to the overall aesthetic scheme – the totality of any given *œuvre* that is to regulate everything else within its parameters. They were not to have any independent function, i.e., sensuality and pleasurable effects were not to serve any autonomous function, especially since he suspected that such elements could be manipulated by the culture industry to increase sales of cultural commodities and to make profit:

> (. . .) ein wesentlich Geistiges durch seinen sinnlichen Repräsentanten vermittelt zu sehen, und nicht diesen Repräsentanten selber in den Geist aufzunehmen, ist infantil. (. . .) Es liegt keinerlei Gründe dafür vor, den sinnlichen Klang von Musik für diese für wesentlicher zu halten als den sinnlichen Klang der Worte für die Sprache. (. . .) Während jede Aufführung von Musik fehlbar ist, kann die wirklich präzise Vorstellung beim Lesen das Ideal der Aufführung geben, das als solches nicht erreichbar ist. Das musikalische Werk wird gleichsam von der Zufälligkeit seiner Realisierung gereinigt. (. . .) Das Aufführen von Musik hat an sich etwas Aufschwätzendes, Überredendes, Propagandistisches und zeigt sich damit der heute herrschenden Kulturindustrie verschwistert. Übertrieben könnte man sagen, jede Aufführung eines musikalischen Werkes hat etwas von Reklame für dieses. Dem gegenüber würde die Realisierung der Musik in

> der Imagination das Werk selbst rein darstellen, ohne dem Wirkungszusammenhang [das] leiseste [Zugeständnis] zu machen.[38]

> [Es gibt] ja in der modernen Musik unendlich viel, was gar nicht klingen soll, weil der Klang selber ja eine Dimension der Darstellung der kompositorischen Idee, des kompositorischen Gedankens ist, und ob das nun reizvoll und angenehm klingt oder nicht, das hängt völlig ab von der geistigen und musikalischen Funktion, die die Dinge haben und darf nicht isoliert genommen werden.[39]

> So wenig ein Geistiges an [den Kunstwerken] zählt, das nicht aus der Konfiguration ihrer sinnlichen Momente entspränge – aller andere Geist an den Kunstwerken, zumal der philosophisch hineingestopfte und angeblich ausgedrückte, alle gedanklichen Ingredienzien sind darin Stoffe gleich den Farben und Tönen –, so wenig ist ein Sinnliches an den Werken künstlerisch, das nicht in sich durch Geist vermittelt wäre. Noch die sinnlich betörendsten französischen Gebilde erreichen ihren Rang dadurch, daß sie ihre sensuellen Momente ungewollt verwandeln in Träger eines Geistes, der in der trauervollen Resignation zum sterblich sinnlichen Dasein seinen Erfahrungsgehalt hat; (. . .) Rücksichtsloser stets determiniert [der Geist] die Kunstwerke und reißt alles bloß Sinnliche, Tatsächliche daran in seinen Bereich. Dadurch werden sie säkularer, feindlicher der Mythologie, der Illusion einer Wirklichkeit von Geist, auch der ihres eigenen.[40]

Adorno criticized sensuality not for what it was or represented, but because he believed that such elements were manipulated by the culture industry to promote a culture of consumerism to the detriment of all other values and practices. Sensuality sells more and more easily than intellectuality: this is the thumb rule by which the culture industry functions. Adorno saw in the reduction of culture to sensual pleasure a fascist tendency, which encouraged and even forced people to reject all other forms of artistic / aesthetic realization.

It can also not be ignored that Adorno regarded with apprehension a particularly virulent cult of physicality that the Nazis patronized, which was expressed not only in their absurd theories of race and evolution but also in their attitude to sporting activities[41] – something which continues to brew even today in the unholy alliance between sports, commercial establishments, popular culture and nationalism.

And yet, Adorno's critique of fascism takes the considered view that the bourgeois suppression of physicality / sensuality may have resulted in a backlash against the culture of *Vergeistigung*, against a culture that is predominantly intellectual in its orientation. Fascist cultural values tried to destroy intellectualism, substituting it with a corrupted notion of the German spirit, but also overturned sensual pleasure into the glorification of extreme physical pain realized through sport, warfare and the physical torture of dissidents and of those racially profiled as different. On the other hand, overt sexuality and titillation characterizes the advertisement of products of modern popular culture in its bid to monopolize the market. Adorno's conciliatory philosophy as negative dialectics therefore considers the possibility of liberating what cannot be reconciled or subordinated to culture – by simply letting go of them. This is consistent with Adorno's view of culture, which as *geistige Kultur* does not imply total eradication of unformed nature and its substitution with the human and the civilized. On the contrary, *geistige Kultur* meant for Adorno *Aufhebung* of the natural in and as culture, and its conservation (*Pflege*) in various cultural forms. Sensuality, to which Adorno deliberately provided a problematic role in his theory, would be redeemed and would as such redeem a philosophy antithetical to it if philosophy learnt to let sensuality be, and not try to suppress it or wish it away.

XI. EPILOGUE: THEORY AS AUTOBIOGRAPHY

Adorno's work is infused with what I would like to call involuntary autobiographism. As such, it surfaces sporadically, never as a consistent linear narrative, more as sketchy references and impressionistic memories. Adorno the private person and the public figure of the star theoretician and author merge into a single personality in the light of the autobiographical elements that characterize his work. His music-philosophy had a Janus-like perspective: one face turned toward music, the other facing humanity, scrutinizing its relation to nature and to itself. Music-philosophy, which was both a philosophy of music as well as philosophy per se, which survived because the moment of its realization had passed by,[42] a philosophy formulated from the point of view of music, became a critique of an "enlightening" culture that sustained itself by destroying the individual, the heterogeneous, the non-identical.

The outbreak of fascism brought into sharp focus the endangered survival of the individual and heterogeneous within totality. In order to survive within the totality of all forms of human existence, the individual was forced to compromise on its autonomy, whereas totality was poised to bring heterogeneous individual existences into its fold, to make them identical with totality – forcibly and through coercive methods. While studying different cultural manifestations, such as the dialectics of Beethoven's musical form, Schönberg's twelve-tone music, the Enlightenment, the culture-industry and even fascism, Adorno focused on different aspects of the fragile relation between the individual and totality. This determined his idea of the purpose of theory itself. To him, theory was no longer possible in its naively optimistic form, which believed that truth would reveal itself on the basis of the mere positivistic accumulation and description of facts. It had to step out of its self-imposed epistemological asceticism into the realm of critique in the form of *bestimmte Negation*: the recognition of the dialectics of every image, text and object, unraveling their cryptogram, deciphering the confessions of their inherent untruth written on their features. Critique as *bestimmte Negation* – the sensitivity towards such confessions – created the foundation for a philosophy that, through contemplation of suffering, developed into the idea of *Negative Dialektik*: philosophy as anti-system, philosophy from the point of view of the heterogeneous and non-identical, of those who lay outside the realm of conceptual uniformity.[43] It diagnosed the malaise of human subjectivity as the absolute dissociation of subject and object – a consciousness, from which the subject could no longer escape, which determined all its thoughts and established and perpetuated the hegemonic relation between subject and object. And yet, such cold dissociation could end with reconciliation – it could liberate the heterogeneous (*das Nichtidentische*) from the uniformity into which conventional subjective thought had forced the object, it could simply let the diversity and difference of the other be.

> [Versöhnung] gäbe das Nichtidentische frei (. . .) eröffnete erst die Vielheit des Verschiedenen, über die Dialektik keine Macht mehr hätte. Versöhnung wäre das Eingedenken des nicht länger feindseligen Vielen (. . .) Versöhnung dient Dialektik.[44]

Through such a reversal of the function of philosophy, Adorno hoped to bring about a reversal of consciousness itself, so that it would no longer look upon the world as an object to be conquered and controlled. The subject, once reconciled with the world, would see things in the way they would show themselves from the standpoint of redemption.[45] Redemption and reconciliation, autobiographical motifs that became cornerstones of Adorno's later philosophy, spanned over the space for rehabilitation and restoration of what was cherished in his childhood and lost in the march of history, but was never to be forgotten and betrayed. Formulated in this manner, philosophy inevitably provided a space wherein the personal, subjective and idiosyncratic aspects of the theoretician confronted the objective world.

Is theory then involuntary autobiographism? When does it become voluntary? Perhaps in times of extreme danger like fascism, when writing theory with clinical detachment from the object, as if nothing had happened, would seem dishonest. Fascism created the awareness of how lives of real individuals became endangered, not only as victims but also as perpetrators of barbarity, of how real people got entangled in the mess, knowingly or unknowingly. Fascism created the resolve to restore that life wherein individual existences would not be threatened with extinction and would not be pressurized into giving up their autonomy and conforming to injustice. Theory, "*die Lehre vom richtigen Leben*" shaken out of its complacent esoteric slumber, became an assertion – the hopeless defence of the individual and of the individual's right to say "I am".

NOTES AND REFERENCES

1. See Hartmut Scheible, *Theodor W. Adorno*, (Reinbeck bei Hamburg: Rowohlt, 1989, 4th Edition, 1996), p. 7.
2. Theodor W. Adorno, *Gesammelte Schriften 12*, ed. Rolf Tiedemann, Gretel Adorno, Susan Buck-Morss and Klaus Schultz, (Frankfurt a.M.: Suhrkamp, 1997). The *Gesammelte Schriften* are referred to as GS with the volume number in the following.
3. GS 10.1.
4. "Von musikalischer Bildung", lecture at the Hochschule für Musik, Frankfurt a.M. 23 February, 1962. Tape-recording in the possession of the library of the Hochschule. Tape-recording catalogue numbers 14, 15, 16 and 17. Unpublished.

   "Zum Problem der musikalischen Analyse", lecture at the Hochschule für Musik, Frankfurt a.M., 24 February, 1969. Tape-recording in the possession of the library of the Hochschule. Tape-recording catalogue number 102. Unpublished in the original version, tape-recording destroyed, no known copies available. An English translation by Max Paddison, "On the Problem of Musical Analysis", was published in the journal *music analysis*, Oxford, July 1982.

   "Theorie der musikalischen Reproduktion", typescript in the possession of the Theodor W. Adorno Archiv, Frankfurt a.M. Catalogue numbers of the Archive: Ts 49470-49564. The typescripts were written over a period of about 25 years. The earliest were written in 1927, the rest from 1946 to the mid-1950s.
5. See *Negative Dialektik*, GS 6, p. 10.
6. Alban Berg to Theodor W. Adorno, Vienna, 28 January 1926. See Henri Lonitz (ed.), *Theodor W. Adorno – Alban Berg. Briefwechsel 1925-1935*, (Frankfurt a.M.: Suhrkamp, 1997), pp. 66-67.
7. Max Horkheimer and Theodor W. Adorno, *Dialektik der Aufklärung* in Adorno, GS 3. Adorno mentions that this "philosophical fragment" was the result of twenty years of collaborative philosophical work with Horkheimer. *Philosophie der neuen Musik* was to be taken as an elaboration (*augeführter Exkurs*) upon *Dialektik der Aufklärung*. See *Philosophie der neuen Musik*, GS 12, p. 11.
8. Cf. e.g. "Von musikalischer Bildung".
9. See "Vierhändig, noch einmal", GS 17, p. 303.
10. See Thomas Mann, *Doktor Faustus*, (Frankfurt a.M.: S. Fischer Verlag, 1956) pp. 75-76. See also, Mann, *Die Entstehung des Doktor Faustus. Roman eines Romans*, (Frankfurt a.M.: Fischer Taschenbuch Verlag, 1984), p. 36.

11. Scheible, p. 13.
12. The article "Abschied vom Jazz" of 1933 (GS 18) was followed by the longer essay "Über Jazz" (GS 17) in 1936, published in 1937 in *Zeitschrift für Sozialforschung V* under the pseudonym Hektor Rottweiler.
13. "Amorbach", GS 10.1, p. 303.
14. Cf. "Der böse Kamerad", in *Minima Moralia*, GS 4, p. 219.
15. Ibid.
16. Ibid., p. 283.
17. This was a suggestion by Prof Anil Bhatti who was chairing this session. I include this retrospectively and elaborate upon it as a reply that could not be given at the venue of the discussion due to a shortage of time.
18. See *Negative Dialektik*, GS 6, p. 18: "Dialektik entfaltet die vom Allgemeinen diktierte Differenz des Besonderen vom Allgemeinen. Während sie, der ins Bewußtsein gedrungene Bruch von Subjekt und Objekt, dem Subjekt unentrinnbar ist, alles durchfurcht, was es, auch an Objektivem, denkt, hätte sie ein Ende in der Versöhnung. Diese gäbe das Nichtidentische frei, (. . .) eröffnete erst die Vielheit des Verschiedenen, über die Dialektik keine Macht mehr hätte. Versöhnung wäre das Eingedenken des nicht länger feindseligen Vielen (. . .). Der Versöhung dient Dialektik."
19. See "Keine Angst vor dem Elfenbeinturm. Ein »Spiegel«-Gespräch", GS 20.1, p. 406.
20. See *Minima Moralia*, GS 4, p. 17.
21. See Adorno to Berg, in *Adorno – Berg Briefwechsel*, letters dated 6 January 1926, p. 60, and 30 January 1926, p. 69.
22. See "Kritische Theorie und Protestbewegung. Ein Interview mit der »Süddeutschen Zeitung«", GS 20.1, p. 399.
23. See Adorno, *Nachgelassene Schriften, Abteilung I: Fragment gebliebene Schriften, Bd. 1: Beethoven. Philosophie der Musik. Fragmente und Texte.* ed. Rolf Tiedemann, Theodor W. Adorno Archiv, (Frankfurt a.M.: Suhrkamp, 1993).
24. Ibid., p. 46.
25. Ibid., p. 50.
26. Ibid.
27. Ibid., pp. 56-57.
28. See *Dialektik der Aufklärung*, GS 3, p. 41.
29. "Wissenschaftliche Erfahrung in Amerika", GS 10.2. p. 703.
30. "Keine Angst vor dem Elfenbeinturm", GS 20.1, p. 403. (My translation)
31. Ibid., pp. 402-9.
32. Cf. *Philosophie der neuen Musik*, GS 12, p. 11.
33. See Heinz Steinert, *Die Entdeckung der Kulturindustrie oder: Warum Professor Adorno Jazz-Musik nicht ausstehen konnte* (Vienna: Verlag für Gesellschaftskritik, 1992), p. 36.
34. Ibid.
35. This refers to a question that was raised during the discussion after the presentation of this paper. Prof. Bhatti and Prof. Manfred Stassen provided

much of the inputs by way of replies; I include mine in this written version of my paper, again retrospectively.

36. Cf. "Keine Angst vor dem Elfenbeinturm", GS 20.1, pp. 406-07.
37. Cf. "Kultur und culture", unpublished lecture, Hessischer Rundfunk, Frankfurt a.M. 1957, and "Europa nach der Emigration", radio-interview with Erika Mann and T.W. Adorno, Hessischer Rundfunk, Frankfurt a.M. 1958.
38. Theodor W. Adorno: ["Theorie der musikalischen Rerpoduktion"], typescript in the possession of Theodor W. Adorno Archiv, Frankfurt a.M. Quoted from typescript no. Ts 49562, early 1950s.
39. Cf. "Von musikalischer Bildung".
40. *Ästhetische Theorie*, GS 7, pp. 135-36.
41. See "Erziehung nach Auschwitz", GS 10.2, pp. 674-90.
42. See *Negative Dialektik*, GS 6, p. 15.
43. Ibid., p. 10.
44. Ibid., p. 18.
45. *Minima Moralia*, GS 4, p. 283.

ROSY SINGH

Kafka's Letters to Felice Bauer: A Lover's Discourse

The genre of autobiography is a constructed narrative where there is invariably some *a priori* manipulation of events depending on how an author wants to presents his self to others. This raises the question of sincerity and legitimacy of any autobiography which, by definition, claims to be a collection of facts. Would it then not be reasonable to say that the real and authentic autobiographical accounts are those which are not written specifically with an eye at publication but are later put together from various sources, like pieces of a jigsaw puzzle? The letters of Kafka (1883-1924) belong to this category. This study concentrates on Kafka's letters to Felice Bauer. It throws light on one of Kafka's most intense relationships and thus provides an insight into the inner universe of one of the most important writers of the 20th century. Apart from the motif of classical love, some other autobiographical motifs explored in this paper are Kafka's writing mania, the very act of writing, his Jewishness, his preferences in daily life and hence, his general state of mind.

Kafka "discovered"[1] Felice Bauer at a get-together in Prague in August 1912 after which she returned to Berlin. It appears that Kafka was simply mesmerised by this solitary meeting with her. Unable to forget the *Berlinerin*, as he calls her, he writes to her a month later on 20 Sept. 1912, addressing her formally as Fräulein Bauer and introducing himself as follows:

> In the likelihood that you no longer have even the remotest recollection of me, I am introducing myself once more: my name is Franz Kafka, and I am the person who greeted you for the first time that evening at Director Brod's in Prague, the one who subsequently handed you across the table, one by one, photographs of a Thalia trip, and who finally, with the very hand now striking [typewriter] keys, held your hand, the one which confirmed a promise to accompany him next year to Palestine.[2]

The reference to the Palestine trip is clearly a pretext to write. This chance encounter with its subtle intimacies was the beginning of an extraordinary relationship in the form of a regular exchange of letters which sustained more than five years (Sept. 1912 to end of 1917), involved two engagements and two dissolutions of the same, indeed a story of "epical dimensions."[3] Later on Felice Bauer married another man but she remained faithful to his memory, the proof of which is that she kept Kafka's letters safely with her for more than four decades till they were acquired from her for publication in 1955. It goes to her credit that she preserved the letters, more than a thousand in number, in those extremely turbulent times of the Holocaust, the exile and the two World Wars, also despite family pressures and dislocation when she moved to Switzerland and later on to America. She died in 1960, seven years before the letters were eventually published. Her letters to Kafka have evidently not survived.

I. FETISH OF LETTERS

"I am an erratic letter writer" wrote Kafka in his first letter to Felice. This is indeed a rather strange remark from a writer like Kafka who is known as much for his fictional writing as for his letters. In fact one gets the impression that he was more comfortable writing letters than meeting the very people with whom he was corresponding. He even avoided talking over the telephone. With Felice, too, it was more of a pen-friendship. The actual time they spent together was meagre. In fact, merely an hour spent in each other's company led to the correspondence. The second meeting was eight months later on Easter, March 1913 in Berlin and that too only for an hour. The meeting was a disappointment, at least for Kafka. The third meeting was in May 1913 and soon after, they announced to their respective parents their engagement.

The long-distance (Prague-Berlin) relationship appears to have suited Kafka. He begins the letter-writing hesitatingly. On receiving the first letter from Felice, he writes to her that he arrived at his office humming. In response to her second letter, he writes that her letter had descended upon him as if from the clouds, to which he had been gazing up in vain for three weeks. Once Felice begins reciprocating, there was no stopping him. He inundates her with letters. Letters are sent by ordinary mail but out of sheer nervousness and alarm that the letters could be lost, he would often send her registered letters. In the letter dated 24 October 1912 he requests her not to be annoyed by the daily signing of receipts. As there was no delivery of ordinary mail on Sundays, which he describes therefore as "unfortunate", he would send her express letters, sometimes even telegrams. In the initial few months she is bombarded with letters twice a day, written either from the office, mostly typed on the Institute letterhead, or from his home in the evenings. It takes him three months to realise that it is not possible to sustain this dizzy pace of letter-writing and then dashing to the nearest letter-box. Then the correspondence is reduced to "only" one letter a day. He would complain bitterly about lost letters or late delivery of letters, cursing the mail for its incompetence but also praising the same when two letters would arrive on the same day. A few remarks cited below reveal the *amours difficiles*. There are many such remarks all of which cannot be cited for lack of space:

> (. . .) no letter arrived today. But what do I do? I hover around the corridors, stare at every clerk's hands, issue unnecessary orders simply to send someone down especially for the mail (for I am on the fourth floor, the incoming mail is sorted downstairs, our postmen are unpunctual, in addition we are in the midst of our board elections, the incoming mail is immense, and before your letter is extracted from the silly pile I might have died of impatience upstairs); finally, prompted by my distrust of all and sundry, I myself rush down and, needless to say, find nothing; had something arrived I should have got it in no time, for I have enlisted three people to bring your letter up to me before any other mail. (15 Nov. 1912)

> But this morning I had to use very different means to attract the postman. Our postmen are so unpunctual. Your letter didn't arrive until 11.15; ten times I sent various people from my bed out on to the landing, as though this could entice him to appear: I didn't dare get up, but finally at 11.15 your letter really was here, ripped open, and read in one breath. (17 Nov. 1912)

> [our] postman happened to be standing next to me, with your letter on top of the bundle; I grabbed it with such force that I nearly upset the whole lot. (30 Nov. 1912)

Sometimes Kafka would also reproach Felice for delay in replying, accusing her of neglecting him and indifference. In one letter he implores her to drop her letter in the mailbox even if she does not happen to have a stamp. In utter despair and misery at not receiving a letter he would turn aggressive with words, baring his teeth. In the next letter he would be overcome with remorse and make amends. Here is a little illustration of his confusion in the state of languor, not uncommon for people in love:

> No letter again today, neither by the first mail nor the second. You do make me suffer; While one written word from you could make me happy! You've had enough of me; there is no other explanation (. . .) I shall expect no further letters. (20 Nov. 1912)

At night, the same day, his self-reproaches and apologies:

> Please, dearest, forgive me! (. . .) All I can say is: Stay with me, don't leave me. And should one of my enemies from within write to you as he did this morning, don't believe him, just ignore him and look straight into my heart.

The next day:

> Dearest, according to today's two letters it seems you are prepared to tolerate me a little longer. Please, please, don't let yesterday's letter change your mind. (21 Nov. 1912)

The Berlin-Prague correspondence develops through a tumult of anxieties, understandings and misunderstandings and even catastrophes. But the two also come closer as is evident from the progress from 'Dear Fräulein Bauer' to 'Dear Fräulein Felice' to 'Dearest' and even 'My dearest child'. Once he even tries to shorten her name to 'Fe' (in German 'Fee' is a fairy) but changes his mind in the later letters because Fe "is too short. It doesn't give one's breath time to linger" (16 March 1913) and "Felice means more, it is like a proper embrace" (17 to 18 March 1913). He remarks that their names sit well and snugly together. When she writes, she is a "model sweetheart"; otherwise she is trying to humiliate him with her silence. The arrival of a letter from Felice clearly sends him soaring from the "depth of misery" to the "heights of bliss" (18 Nov. 1912). The bells toll only when there is a letter from her (1 May 1913). There is no doubt that the letters become his life-line, bring him cheer and keep him going. He clings to them. He pleads with her not to abandon him in his "terrible loneliness". He often calls her letters "kind" as if he did not really deserve them. He wonders whether she writes out of compassion or love. They also exchange photographs. His first story, *The Judgement*, is dedicated to Felice (he always refers to it as "your short story"). This story was written during the period when he met her for the first time. Felice was not a writer or intellectually his match but it would not be incorrect to say that the relationship inspired the most creatively fruitful phase of his life.

Kafka's child-like delight at receiving a letter from his beloved, his jubilation at receiving two letters together, his anxiety, panic and suffering at the non-arrival of a letter for a day or two and his frustration over a lost letter are amazing, especially as they come from a modern 20th century writer famous for absurd and grotesque writing! The passion and the excess in the love letters present a sharp contrast to the anti-romanticism in his novels and other narratives. One need only think of the erotic scenes in his novels like K with Frieda (*the Castle*), Joseph K. with Leni (*the Trial*) or Brunelda in a bath-tub (*America*). If one did not know the thirty-year-old author of these letters, it would be easy to mistake them for a teenager's first flush of love!

II. THE WRITING MANIAC

The initial letters are sweet, cheerful and flirtatious. He would ask her questions like "who tries to undermine your health by giving you sweets?" (28 Sept. 1912). "How long can chocolate be kept before it goes bad?" (27 Oct. 1912). "How do you manage to write in bed? Where is the inkpot? Do you hold the paper on your knees? I couldn't do that, yet your writing is firmer than mine when I am sitting on my desk. And don't your blankets get spattered with ink? And your poor, poor back! And your precious eyes are bound to be ruined." (4 Dec. 1912) His concern for her is evident when he tells her not to over-exert, not to write by candlelight or at night when she should be resting.

This happy phase, however, does not last long. The letters often become sad and reflect his extremely unhappy disposition. He refers to his untidy attire, lack of any desire to talk at meals or even otherwise. There are complains of frequent headaches, the "buzzing" and the "twitching" in the head, the "throbbing" and "aching" in his temples, insomnia and ill-health although he neither smokes nor drinks alcohol, coffee or tea. He does not even eat chocolates. There is no dearth of negative adjectives he attributes to himself – inadequate, hopeless, peevish, miserable, sickly, taciturn, unsociable, morose, gloomy, selfish, a hypochondriac. Sometimes he describes himself "sad like a lost dog" gazing around with imploring eyes. He always repeats that he is in poor health, that he knows he would never have children. He talks of his "weariness", "wretchedness" and "eternal exhaustion". (7 to 8 March 1913) Many letters are full of melancholic remarks like, "It is I who am being flogged, and again it is I who do the flogging" (23-24 Jan. 1913). Or: "For it is I alone who carry all anxieties and fears within me, as alive as snakes." (22 August 1913).

It is evident from the letters that his writing meant the world to him. Without writing he was "fit for a dustbin" (1 Nov. 1912), or like an "old horse shut up in its stable" (12-13 Feb. 1913). His happiness and unhappiness were both related to his writing.

> (. . .) nur der Wellengang des Schreibens bestimmt mich (1 Nov. 1912)
> (. . .) my life is determined by nothing but the ups and downs of writing
>
> Meine Lebensweise ist nur auf das Schreiben hin eingerichtet und wenn sie Veränderungen erfährt, so nur deshalb, um möglicher Weise dem Schreiben zu entsprechen, denn die Zeit ist kurz, die Kräfte sind klein, das Bureau ist ein Schrecken, die Wohnung ist laut und man muss sich mit Kunststücken durchzuwinden suchen, wenn es mit einem schönen geraden Leben nicht geht. (ibid)
> My mode of life is devised solely for writing, and if there are any changes, then only for the sake of perhaps fitting in better with my writing; for

> time is short, my strength is limited, the office is a horror, the apartment is noisy, and if a pleasant, straightforward life is not possible then one must try to wriggle through by subtle manoeuvres.
>
> (. . .) der Teufel, der immer in der Schreiblust steckt, rührt sich eben zur unpassendsten Zeit. (Night of 15-16 Dec. 1912)
> (. . .) the demon inhabiting the writing-urge begins to stir at the most inopportune moments.
>
> Liebste, ich bitte Dich jedenfalls mit aufgehobenen Händen, sei nicht auf meinen Roman eifersüchtig. Wenn die Leute im Roman Deine Eifersucht merken, laufen sie mir weg, ich halte sie ja sowieso nur an den Zipfeln ihrer Kleidung fest. Und bedenke, wenn sie mir weglaufen, ich müßte ihnen nachlaufen und wenn es bis in die Unterwelt wäre, wo sie ja eigentlich zuhause sind. Der Roman bin ich, meine Geschichten sind ich, wo wäre da, ich bitte Dich, der geringste Platz für Eifersucht. Alle meine Menschen laufen ja, wenn alles sonst in Ordnung ist, Arm in Arm auf Dich zu, um letzten Endes Dir zu dienen. (From 2 to 3 Jan. 1913)
> Dearest, whatever happens I implore you, with hands raised in supplication, not to be jealous of my novel. If the people in my novel get wind of your jealousy, they will run away from me; as it is I am holding on to them only by the ends of their sleeves. And imagine, if they run away from me I shall have to run after them, even as far as the underworld, where of course they really are at home. The novel is me, my stories are me – where, I ask you, would there be the tiniest corner for jealousy? In any case, when everything else goes well, all my characters come running arm in arm towards you, ultimately to serve you.

The letters provide fascinating insights into the all-encompassing role of writing in Kafka's life and also into the very act of writing. He equates his whole being, his existence to "nothing but literature" and describes how writing creates havoc in his head like "monkeys leaping about in the treetops". It would not be an exaggeration to say that Kafka was possessed by the demon of writing. Then there are references to the kind of problems he faces in writing, like the effort in keeping the umpteen characters of his novel together and the lack of sufficient time for uninterrupted writing. At times the "inkpots fly", at others he can only "scan the ceiling" or "look out of the window". His stories are treated organically, like at one point he writes: "Many stories, dearest, are drumming their marching tunes in my head". (10-11 Jan. 1913) At the same time he acknowledges that it is the relationship with Felice that gives him the inspiration and the stability to continue writing.

Most of Kafka's stories are inspired by the circumstances in his office and family although he paradoxically considers both a nuisance because they come in the way of his writing. Office is often described as wretched, hellish and a horror. According to Kafka, writing and office contradict each other because the former is all about "depth" whereas the office is simply the "surface" of life. He talks of his status as the first-born vis-à-vis the late-borns, the three younger sisters, father and mother. There are also references to his extended family (including the canary), the engagements and marriages of his sisters and of his friend Max Brod and his anxiety and alienation from such bourgeois activities although he paradoxically aspires for the same.

Scanty nevertheless significant references to Kafka's ambivalent relationship with Judaism can be found in a couple of letters. His childhood memories include visits to the Prague synagogues where he would "almost suffocate from the terrible boredom and pointlessness" of the exercise. (16 September, 1916) The hours spent in the synagogue were "rehearsals staged by hell" for his later office life. He goes on to explain to Felice that owing to his origin, education, disposition and environment he was not able to develop any tangible connections to the Jewish faith. At the same time he was curious about the "dark complexities" and the mystical traditions in Judaism, but more as an intellectual than as a believer. He confesses that he has his reservations about Zionism but then "Zionism is not something that separates well-meaning people". (12 Sept. 1916) Kafka's diaries have more references to Judaism than his letters to Felice. So far as his fictional writing is concerned, Jewish characters or direct references to his Jewish roots are conspicuous by their absence. Prominent exceptions are two stories *Schakale und Araber* (*Jackals and the Arabs*) and *In unserer Synagoge* (*In our Synagogue*), where the titles themselves are an indication of Jewish motifs.

One gets to know some queer personal habits of Kafka through the letters. There are many likes and dislikes that he refers to like his inability to appreciate music and flowers. Then he mentions his aversion to meat. He comes across as a fanatic vegetarian who recommends vegetarian diet to all and sundry and is ruthless on meat eaters. He goes to the extent of declaring that deterioration of teeth is due to meat-eating as tiny shreds of meat between the teeth produce germs of decay and fermentation no less than "a dead rat squashed between two stones". He also has tremendous faith in natural therapy which he practices zealously. His dislike of modern medicine is clearly expressed and once he even vehemently refuses to bandage his severely bleeding thumb preferring to let it heal naturally even if it takes ten times longer. Then he also proudly declares that he sleeps with the window open, even in winters, in a room without heating. It is indeed an irony of sorts that this person who recommends exercises, vegetables and lots of sleep to others, himself led an unhealthy way of life and frequently suffered from insomnia, indigestion and headaches!

In the letter written in breaks, between 10 and 16 June, 1913 Kafka proposes to Felice. In the same letter he reminds her of the sacrifices she would have to make like losing her job, exchanging Berlin for a provincial place like Prague with a language unfamiliar to her, giving up her friends and in return all she would get is a moody and sick husband who does not earn enough. She apparently accepts the challenge and then Kafka goes house hunting. He becomes a member of co-operative building society. The two discuss the location, the size and the cost of the various apartments available in Prague. In April 1914 Kafka visits Felice in Berlin and they become formally engaged. They even try to decide on furniture for their new home. To Kafka's great annoyance, Felice shows a preference for heavy furniture, in tune with the traditional bourgeois taste of that time, whereas Kafka likes the more modern stuff. When Kafka visits Felice in July the same year, everything goes wrong as Felice attacks him verbally with some accusations (Grete Bloch, a girlfriend of Felice, with whom Kafka was exchanging letters, was also present and was somehow involved. Apparently she showed Felice Kafka's letters in which he had expressed doubts about the marriage) and the engagement is abruptly broken. Gradually they pick up the threads again and thus begins the second, more mature phase of their relationship in which the frequency of letters is reduced to once every two weeks. In July 1917 their second engagement takes place in Prague. In September, however, Kafka's tuberculosis in both the lungs is diagnosed. Thereafter, the engagement is annulled and the five year old relationship, which began as love at first sight, comes to an abrupt end. Kafka describes laconically the annulment as an *Erleichterung* / a relief.

III. VARIOUS INTERPRETATIONS OF THE LETTERS

Some Kafka critics have tried to present a sexist Kafka who was unfair to the women in his life. A close reading of the letters to Felice shows, however, that this is far from truth. What emerges clearly is that he is very honest with Felice and treats her as an equal partner in the relationship. In fact in several letters he does not hesitate in expressing his complete surrender to her. Erich Heller's interpretation of these letters as *Minnelieder*[4] (Minnesongs) is, in fact, a more appropriate reading.

Zilcosky[5] situates Kafka's love letters to Felice and later on to Melina, in the context of historical developments, technological and bureaucratic, in Germany and Austria towards the end of the 19th century. The *fin de siècle* technologies of pneumatic mail, the telegraph, the telephone and the wireless and, of course, the railways, planes and automobiles influenced, transformed and even determined, at times, the course of relations or as the author says, the "construction of modern love". Kafka notes in his letters to Melina that the world was divided technologically into two groups, the technologies of human presence (train, automobile, etc) and the technologies of absence (letters, telegram, etc). The 'technologies of presence' promote *natürlichen*, i.e., physical *Verkehr* (contact) between humans, while the 'technologies of absence' promote a *Verkehr mit Gespenstern*, i.e., a ghostly interaction.[6] Kafka chooses the latter to sustain his relationship with Felice and later on in life with Melina. Zilcosky calls Kafka a "letter-addict". Today the world has new *fin de siècle* technologies of e-mails and mobile phones which are again transforming the nature of relations.

Deleuze and Guattari[7] have called Kafka a dracula, a vampire who remains awake at night and writes letters which they equate with bats. This outrageous interpretation in the well-known book, *Kafka. Pour une littérature mineure*, translated into German as *Kafka. Für eine kleine Literatur*, is substantiated strangely enough with scenes from Kafka's fictional works: Gregor Samsa kissing the bare neck of his sister (*Metamorphosis*) and K.'s kiss on the neck and face of Frl. Bürstner (*The Trial*). Further proof is cited: Kafka describes himself as *blutarm* (anaemic), hence his attraction towards the *blutreich* (healthy) Felice in order to suck her blood through the letters which then gives him the strength to create stories. The exchange of letters is described by these learned critics as "truly Kafkaesque love" where the protagonist meets the girl only once and then forces out of her two letters a day and this is the "devil's pact". This is the psychoanalytical interpretation from the famous French team of a philosopher and a psychiatric. Lacan, whose seminars Guattari attended, must be turning in his grave. Lacan's own literary criticisms are few but excellent (refer to his analysis of Poe's *Purloined Letter* and Sophocles' *Antigone*). Lacan reads literary texts in order to understand something of human nature. However traditional psychoanalytical literary analysis, despite Lacan's efforts to give it a philosophical and even poetic twist, is still off the mark as is obvious from Deleuze and Guattari's far-fetched interpretation. My aim is not to belittle psychoanalysis. In fact, I conclude my essay with some noteworthy remarks of C. G. Jung.

Similarly, Reich-Ranicki finds Kafka's relationship to Felice "masochistisch".[8] In fact, most Kafka critics refuse to read Kafka's letters to Felice Bauer as a classical discourse of love. Why is it so? This is apparently related with modernity which considers the sentimental discourse and with it the sentimental lover outdated. In seminars, the sufferings of Werther often invoke amusement among the students. Roland Barthes calls it a historical reversal: it is no longer the sexual which is indecent, it is the sentimental, censured in the name of what is in fact only another morality. Love, according to Barthes, falls outside of interesting time. Everyone will understand that X has problems with his sexuality but no one is interested in those Y may have with his sentimentality. Love is obscene today precisely in that it puts the sentimental in place of the sexual.[9]

IV. PSYCHOLOGY OF AN ARTIST

C.G. Jung has written an excellent essay on the psychology of an artist, "Psychology and Literature". I quote here a section of it because it is so appropriate in the context of Kafka.

> His [the artist's] life cannot be otherwise than full of conflicts, for two forces are at war within him: on the one hand the justified longing of the ordinary man for happiness, satisfaction, and security, and on the other a ruthless passion for creation which may go so far as to override every personal desire. If the lives of artists are as a rule so exceedingly unsatisfactory, not to say tragic, it is not because of some sinister dispensation of fate, but because of some inferiority in their personality or an inability to adapt. A person must pay dearly for the divine gift of creative fire. It is as though each of us was born with a limited store of energy. In the artist, the strangest force of his make-up, that is, his creativity, will seize and all but monopolise this energy, leaving so little ever that nothing of value can come of it. (. . .) A special ability demands a greater expenditure of energy, which must necessarily leave a deficit on some other side of life.[10]

Kafka's letters to Felice Bauer, one could call them mobile signifiers, reveal exactly this state of mind where social acts like job, home, marriage, children on the one hand and the creative urge on the other hand are locked in a combat. He is to a great extent indifferent to the World War I but he is very much aware of the war within himself. In fact he keeps Felice informed of the progress of this psychological warfare through the letters. Both the selves wrestle with each other but they are also interdependent and they cannot be changed unless both were to be destroyed. He is apprehensive that a conventional bond between the two of them may become an obstacle to his writing and his routine and his unhappy disposition may in turn make the woman he loves unhappy. He feels safe with a long-distance relationship but faced with the prospect of marrying the woman in his life, faced with the realities of life, he dithers. Will the actual person be different than the letter writer? At the same time he needs her, at least needs her letters badly, but fears that the relationship might ruin her life as well as his creativity. He is a tyrant and a considerate lover at the same time. So sometimes he tells her enthusiastically to get her trousseau ready, at others he warns her of the hardships awaiting her in Prague; sometimes he pleads with her to go on loving him, sometimes he asks her to hate him. The two requests are sometimes made together like the following declaration at the end of a letter: "And now, dearest, take me as I am but don't forget, don't forget to throw me out at the right moment!" (7-8 March 1913)

He writes that he needs her but does not deserve her. He can neither live with her, nor without her. He suffers in this existential predicament of dual feeling where the development of a harmonious relationship is existentially blocked and it is clear why he recommends to Felice, in all seriousness, Goethe's *The Sufferings of the Young Werther*! Kafka projects himself in Werther, the unhappy lover, who loves with an obsession and a madness characteristic of the classical lovers. But Kafka tries to slip between the two alternatives of hope and non-hope through his writing. He behaves exactly like the Man from the Countryside, the immortal character he created in *Before the Law*, who stands at the threshold all his life. In Kafka's case the threshold is – marriage.

The horror of office is also to be understood in the same context. It is true that the office exhausted him and left him with little time for his creative writing. Writing articles on cylindrical safety cutter spindles, safety cutter heads, annual reports for the Institute, doing accident related insurance was indeed painful for Kafka when unborn stories in his infernal head were pressing for delivery on the paper regardless of all the compulsions. But Kafka did not realise that the office also provided him with raw material for his creativity. The Bureau can hence be counted as his weakness as well as his strength.

The letters are intense, personal and sincere, with very few references to the historical events of his time. In contrast to his letters to Max Brod and his other acquaintances or friends, the letters to Felice Bauer present a different facet of Kafka. They document more so his love life apart from his inner conflicts and existential dilemmas. One could call it a reflection-related autobiographical narrative in contrast to the action-related autobiographies. These tender letters may disappoint those readers who look for more substance, for they reveal mostly Kafka's moods and feelings, are full of abstractions, are self-contradictory and often repetitive. After all this discourse is uttered by a subject who does not know that 50 years henceforth a book will be made out of it. But no one can deny their importance as truly autobiographical accounts because, firstly, it is in the letters to Felice that he lays his inner self or selves bare; and, secondly they were written even more regularly than his diaries. In terms of its sheer volume as well as aesthetic quality, this correspondence is simply magnificent. One cannot but agree to Anthony Powell's assessment (at the back cover of the book in English) that "Kafka's letters to Felice, written without the faintest idea that they would be published, read like a well-constructed novel – a somewhat harrowing one". The latter half of Powell's assessment is not quite correct, for at least some letters, especially the ones in the initial phase of the courtship, express sweet nothings and can in no way be classified as harrowing. The frequency of the letters and their fire and passion are enough to make any sensitive reader giddy. In fact, no book of love letters is complete without including Kafka's letters to Felice where they are placed alongside the famous letters of Abélard and Héloïse who set the twelfth century conservative France on fire with their intellectual and passionate relationship.[11] It is as if there were two Kafkas: the non-romantic, non-lyrical fictional writer of *Trial, Metamorphosis* and other stories; and the lyrical Kafka, who creates in his letters to Felice a discourse of love and longings, of separation and anguish. Barthes rightly considers the lover's discourse as one of "extreme solitude".[12]

V. CONCLUSION

In the end the reader cannot help but feel ashamed of behaving like a peeping Tom. We keep our own private correspondence in lockers and give a confidential password to our e-mail, protecting it from prying eyes but we do not hesitate reading the letters of another person, particularly when he is dead and is in no position to protect his privacy. The only justification could be that Felice herself submitted the letters for publication. But the author's permission is still missing. Would he have permitted his letters to be published? It is well known that he instructed Brod, in a testament, to burn his letters, diaries and unpublished manuscripts. This brings us back to the debate surrounding Kafka's testament, the disregard shown to it by its legal executor, Max Brod, and the consequent publication of his posthumous works, letters and diaries. Some critics like Walter Benjamin have defended Max Brod for disregarding the wishes of his late friend and have praised his painstaking efforts in saving the manuscripts of a great writer. He is highly critical of Ehm Welk who first raised the issue of conscience and ethics with respect to the publications. Benjamin dismisses it as *Kavaliersmoral* (cavalier's morality), and further: such a person needs to "climb down from his high horse". According to Benjamin, Kafka was "shy" of publications because many of his writings were incomplete.[13] On the other end of the spectrum is Milan Kundera[14] who calls it an act of bad faith, an "indiscretion" that is "inexcusable". According to Kundera, it was the "shame" of leaving private things, particularly letters and diaries, lying about for the eyes of others, family and strangers, that was the reason for his testament. Kundera is so infuriated by this betrayal that he goes to the extent of giving a biting title to his own book, *Testaments Betrayed.* Michel Foucault, too, had "little sympathy" for Brod's decision and was determined "to prevent anyone following that famous example". His letter in regard to his own works is very clear: "No posthumous publications".[15]

What is the correct position? Is the publication of letters by Brod a gesture of affection and loyalty towards his friend or is it an act of betrayal of his last wishes? Can any author actually desire that his (unpublished) works be destroyed? Can one or should one differentiate between the posthumous publication of fictional writing and letters? Perhaps the truth lies somewhere in-between. It is indeed an irony of sorts that Kafka's letters and diaries are so popular with his readers today, because this is the same Kafka, who fought bitterly with his mother for having read one of Felice's letters to him without his permission!

NOTES AND REFERENCES

1. "discovered" is used here in the same sense as Goethe's Werther discovering Charlotte in the famous scene where she is cutting and distributing bread to her brothers and sisters. The comparison is valid also because Kafka recommends to Felice *Die Leiden des jungen Werthers.*
2. Franz Kafka, *Letters to Felice*, ed. Heller & Born, trans. Stern & Duckworth, (London: Vintage, 1999), p. 13. All subsequent citations from the book are given as dates on which the letters were written.
3. Marcel Reich-Ranicki, "Franz Kafka. Seine geschriebenen Küsse", in *Sieben Wegbereiter. Schriftsteller des Jahrhunderts*, (Stuttgart, München: Deutsche Verlags-Anstalt, 2002), p. 208.
4. Erich Heller, "Einleitung zu Kafkas 'Briefe an Felice und andere Korrespondenz aus der Verlobungszeit'", in Heinz Politzer, (Hrsg.) *Franz Kafka. Wege der Forschung*, (Darmstadt: Wissenschaftliche Buchgesellschaft, 1973), pp. 431-58, here p. 432.
5. John Zilcosky, "The Traffic of Writing: Technologies of 'Verkehr' in Franz Kafka's Briefe an Milena", in *German Life & Letters*, July 99, Vol. 52, Issue 3, p. 366.
6. Kafka, *Briefe an Melina*, (Hrsg.) Heller & Born, (Frankfurt a.M.: Fischer, 1983), p. 302.
7. Deleuze, Guattari, *Kafka. Für eine kleine Literatur*, Überz. Kroeber, (Frankfurt a.M.: Suhrkamp, 1976), pp. 42-44.
8. Reich-Ranicki, *Sieben Wegbereiter. Schriftsteller des Jahrhunderts*, p. 208.
9. Roland Barthes, *A Lover's Discourse. Fragements*, (London: Vintage Classics, 2002), pp. 177-78.
10. C.G. Jung, "Psychology and Literature", in *The Spirit in Man, Art and Literature*, (CWJ, 15), (London: Rou1edge & Kegan, 1966), pp. 102-03.
11. See Antonia Fraser, ed. *Love Letters*, (London: Weidenfeld & Nicolson, 1969). See *The Letters of Abelard and Heloise*, trans. Betty Radice from Latin, (London: Penguin, 1974).

12. Barthes, *A Lover's Discourse. Fragments*, p. 1.
13. Walter Benjamin, "Kavaliersmoral", in *Gesammelte Schriften*, IV.I., (Frankfurt a.M.: Suhrkamp, 1972), pp. 466-68.
14. Milan Kundera, *Testaments Betrayed*, trans. Linda Asher, (London & Boston: Faber & Faber, 1995), p. 264.
15. David Macey, *The Lives of Michel Foucault. A Biography*, (New York: Vintage, 1995), p. xix.

PATRIZIA RAVEGGI

The Text as a Renewed Self-Portrait: Giorgio De Chirico's *Memories of My Life, Hebdomeros, Mr. Dudron*

(. . .) De Chirico has one or two or three faces? No, one must know that he is something equivalent to the mythical Hidra.[1]

In the immediate post-WW II years, the dirty and pathetic landscape of the Eternal City – remote outskirts, the ruins caused by bombings, the sciuscias, the tragedy of hopelessness – revealed an Italy smelling of death, privation and hardship. The horrors of the Nazi occupation were still fresh in everyone's memory: *Rome, Open City* was fiction as well as real life. Nevertheless, in the ruins were a cheerful people and a great deal of activity in all fields.

The field of painting was no exception. At first glance, this seemed almost unbelievable, for one could neither guess where a painter could get colours, brushes and the various other materials of his craft, nor who, in the evident misery of the country, could afford to buy works of art. The conclusion: painting has much less to do with economics than with faith. The tragedy of war had, in fact, strengthened the Italian faith in arts and aesthetics – painting, literature and cinema.

It is in these very years and all through the '50s and the '60s that the real dramatic change in artistic criteria and parameters takes place. The advent of new expressive forms fiercely opposes the traditional harmony of shapes and colours arranged in aesthetic compositions on the long-established, time-honoured, conventional canvas, frame not excluded, even when the explosion of abstract art swept away centuries-old artistic criteria.

The new expressive forms are based on conceptual, theoretical and noetic elements: not any longer the "good painting" still practised even by some pop artists (Rauschenberg, Jasper John, whose sensibility to pictorial and plastic values and to compositional rules is still meant to reach a traditional artistic result). The new ways of approach to reality and to the world find their way through different media: rags, wood (which can be burnt, to allow fire, the natural transforming element par excellence, to occupy the place of wear and tear of time, destroying and re-creating inert matter), soil, blood and plastic materials. The new artists use these materials to provoke or to unmask. The predominance of the aesthetic is over.

In the immediate post-WW II period, on the field and confronting each other there are three generations of intellectuals: those born at the beginning of the twentieth century (or even earlier) who have a quite long *cursus honorum* behind them; those born around the first decade and who are now beginning to strive for a destiny of (so far barely perceived) glory; and the twenty-year-olds, about to come out and make their debut. Traditional and avant-garde painters, actors coming to the fore of cinema or theatre stage, writers making their debut with a young success not yet confirmed, men of many talents and often of no quality, art critics who would not actually know what to choose between poetry and painting, intellectuals who are now looking at the world through a one-sided political watershed and who consider as cast-aways all those who think in a different way. It is a riotous and war-like crossroad, where intellectual rivalries and envies are now seasoned with the strong scent of political ideologies. It is the war of all against all.

Whatever had been achieved in the cultural and creative field in the '20s and '30s has been nullified by the tragedy of war: metaphysical painting, eremitic poetry, rationalism in architecture, magic realism. All the "isms" and cultural trends are currencies with no value. Nothing can be bought with them. To look for the sin of collaboration has (understandably) become a sort of national sport – searching, if not for the beam then at least for the mote in one's brother's eye for having paid homage to Fascism.

I. DE CHIRICO AND MODERN ART

In these same immediate post-World War II years, in Rome, on a balcony facing the Spanish steps, there is a big gun aimed at the Rome artistic world. Behind that balcony is Giorgio De Chirico's studio.[2]

Born in Tessaglia in 1888 (his brother Alberto named Betti, was born three years later in Athens), De Chirico gained fame and recognition in a measure equal to the great masters like Picasso and Matisse with his metaphysical works of the '10s. In the '20s, he broke with his former friends, the surrealists, who had exalted him as a god and now called him a traitor and a debauched. De Chirico fought back, insulting them, denouncing their lack of skill in painting and drawing, and their (im)morality, calling them all sort of names.

[a] bunch of depraved rascals, daddy's dears, onanists, spineless idlers, self-named surrealists blathering about a surrealist revolution and a surrealist movement. This group was headed by the would-be poet André Breton assisted on the field by another would-be poet, Paul Eluard, a big, dull, common boy with a crooked nose and a face between the onanist and the mystic idiot. André Breton himself was the typical kind of preposterous ass and impotent social-climber.[3]

From 1925 onwards, De Chirico overtly declares that the Paris of fifteen years before was an absolute negative. He feigns surprise and a certain disdain when the so-called "Paris School", confined by Stalin regime in the basements of the Museums, is exhibited with all its "masterpieces" (Matisse, Cezanne, etc.) in Hermitage's many halls after Stalin's death.

Many are the rooms of the Hermitage Museum now devoted to the pseudo-painters from Paris. This happens, because in the sickle-and-hammer-country there are many who even today are nostalgic of 'la Ville Lumiere'; the same happened in Italy during Fascism.[4]

De Chirico, as an artist, belongs to the years '10s of the 1900; he continued to produce in the '20s, was a well known and sought after author all through the '30s and '40s in Europe and in the USA.[5] After WW II, De Chirico, like many others, had to withstand the changes in the artistic taste and inspiration.

He had always liked heavy artillery in his polemics; those shots aimed at destroying all his enemies in one go. In his *Memories* he writes that "my paintings and Isabella Far's writings were like gun-machine bullets in a zoological garden's aviary."[6] He was still living in Mario de' Fiori St House when *1918-1925, Ricordi di Roma*, published by a tiny Roman publisher (Ed. Roma: Cultura Moderna, 1945) had been a real volley of firearm.[7]

In the successively modified and widened version of the same book,[8] De Chirico extols his own life and intelligence, his technique, his own way of painting and his own personality. At the same time he pathetically insults whatever smells of modernity: Picasso, to start with, and then Le Corbusier, Max Ernst, and all the Italian critics who wrote positively about modern art (Lionello Venturi, Palma Bucarelli, not to mention his archenemy, Roberto Longhi, the critic who, on the occasion of the exhibition "Noi metafisici" in Anton Giulio Bragaglia's Gallery in 1919, wrote the famous article *To the orthopedic god* running De Chirico down and at the same time sharply catching the peculiarities of his fantastic world).[9]

An anecdote: one day, in one of Margutta street cafés, De Chirico was shouting against all his cronies and against all modern art; he even insulted Modigliani.[10] The painter Sante Monachesi (in his earlier days a very hot futurist painter) scorned him blowing a scurrilous sound. De Chirico got hold of a chair to beat Monachesi up.

Invited to give lectures, De Chirico uttered the most unheard of inanities against modernism and the French school in various occasions and in various parts of Italy. The texts of those lectures of the '50s and '60s can still be found in some antiquarian bookshop. They are painfully unreadable. Vanni Scheiwiller, a famous Italian publisher, said that De Chirico was something between the Genius and the Idiot. As a matter of fact, De Chirico was a genius who did his best to appear like an idiot, well succeeding sometimes in the process.

He was a genius in almost all what he painted for half a century.[11]

He was a genius when in 1929 in Paris he wrote *Hebdomeros, le peintre et son genie chez l'ecrivain*[12] (Hebdomeros, the painter and his genius in the writer), an autobiographical text and a self-portrait. All De Chirico's iconographic production finds its place in *Hebdomeros*, painting after painting, vision after vision. The described images are in the same order given by the author to the paintings: a space with 'n' dimensions in a time expanding and contracting itself; the images form fragments revolving one over the other. In *Hebdomeros*, the painter and the writer, the face of the author and the features of the things recall each other, like in a mirror which folds into itself and becomes a mirror over and over again. The artist is on the border, dividing the real from the mirrored, on the threshold of infinity: Infinity (and the nostalgia of it) is the subject of the first metaphysical paintings. A metaphysical gesture translates now the image into words.

He was a genius in the way he replied to the young leftist painters reproaching him for not being socially engaged. In the Rome of post-WW II years, when fights between realism and abstract art were raging and social engagement was being progressively identified with realism, De Chirico's reply was that it does not make any difference whether you portray a lady in an evening dress having a good time or a poor worker suffering and sweating. What really matters, what is important, is to produce a good painting.

To issue such statements in that period meant a lot: it meant war.

De Chirico considered himself a great painter (the greatest of all times), and a great writer. Literature for him was neither a divertissement nor a *violon d'Ingres*. He has not left many books, his first known pages go back to 1911. In the first manuscripts of the 1911-1915 period (Manuscripts of the Eluard-Picasso and of the Paulhan collections), the written word is the equivalent of the image and both echo his interior world. In his lyrical and theoretical writings of this first Paris period, De Chirico meditates at length on the act of painting; many are the thematic and visual references to his own and to others works, to Van Gogh, to the impressionists, to the nature of painting, which has nothing to do with nature but only with intuition and revelation. It is in these manuscripts that the whole pictorial world of De Chirico can be found in its state of lyrical intuition – all his fundamental concepts, the demonic essence of the common things, the revelation, the importance of the geometric aspect of things, signs interrelating with other signs, the concept of architecture, history and time; and most of all, the perception of the primeval value of the artistic creation, at the basis of his idea of classicism: a primeval emotion searching for origins, not originality.[13]

II. INSPIRATIONS AND REVELATIONS

Under the vigilant eyes of Nietzsche, Schopenhauer, Rimbaud and Savinio, De Chirico is alternating painting and allusive visions, never explaining how the ones and the others are in a continuous process of overlapping. He considers his source of inspiration the painters A. Bocklin (surprising, disquieting solutions in a classicism filtered through Romanticism) and Max Klinger, the creator who gives a new meaning to things just changing their place, in visions of an unfathomable and paradoxical nature; Bocklin and Poussin (De Chirico's source of inspiration as well) have been able to bring the work of art "beyond all paintings"; the work of art which is necessarily deprived of common and logical sense. Substituting "beyond" with "meta", its Greek equivalent, the metaphysical research gets its definition.

The same operation of pictorial invention becomes an explanation of reality of universal order, deeply rooted in critical and philosophical thematic, and in close analogy with the images created in literature. According to Schopenhauer, the intuition of truth is an intuition of a world unknown to all. Listening to it means listening to "the language spoken by the things of this world". This language is made of phonemes: "the strange, unknown revelations which can be translated into images". De Chirico reflects on the revelations at the origin of every immortal work of art. Quoting Schopenhauer's *Parerga und Paralipomena* (Revelations and Intuitions):

> To have original, extraordinary, maybe immortal ideas, it is sufficient to isolate oneself from the world in a way so complete that for some instants the most common things and facts appear completely new to us, unknown, revealing their truthful essence.[14]

Then he goes on to explain how he had the revelation of a painting which he exhibited that year at the Salon d'Automne, titled 'Enigma of a fall afternoon'. During his Florence period while reading Nietzsche and Schopenhauer, De Chirico discovers the strong and mysterious feeling of beautiful fall days in Italian cities in the afternoon. Through Nietzsche he has deepened the idea of many unknown, solitary and strange things which can be translated into painting: the language of the things of this world, the hours of the day, the meaningless things. In Florence this special mood becomes stronger.

> In a clear fall afternoon I was sitting on a bench at the centre of Santa Croce square in Florence. It was not the first time I was sitting there, but, recovering from a long and painful disease, I was in a state of morbid sensitivity. The entire world around me, the marble of the buildings, and of the fountains, looked as convalescent to me. At the centre of the square there is a statue of Dante, in a long robe, tightly holding his works to his chest and meditatively reclining his laurel crowned head. The statue is in white marble, but time has given it a very agreeable grey shade of colour. The autumnal sun, warm without love, lightened the statue and the façade of the temple.
>
> In that very moment I had the feeling that I was looking at those images for the first time, and I had the revelation of the painting in the eye of my mind. Now, every time I look at that painting I see that moment again. A moment which is still an enigma for me, that's why I named enigma the work which resulted from it.
>
> Dante Alighieri in the middle of the square, with a long robe and his works held tightly to his chest, and laurel on his thoughtfully bent head. The sun is still strong and lights up the facade of the church. In this very moment, De Chirico feels like he is seeing everything for the first time, and the composition of the painting reveals itself to his spirit. The church becomes a Greek temple, small, but with the closed curtains of the oracle; the statue becomes a standing figure without arms; on the background, a ship far away on the horizon.[15]

In one of the texts in French of the 1911-1915 period:

> [t]owards evening when the light-house shadow will be long on the jetty, when the oriflammes will rustle and the white sails will be round and hard like breasts swollen by love and desire, in the evening, when the light-house shadow will be long on the jetty (. . .)

This was a revelation, the sort of Nietzsche revelation which can arrive when you do not expect it, provoked by a building, a road, a garden, a public place, just by itself. Nietzsche wrote, 'I was surprised by Zarathustra'; in this 'surprised' there is all the enigma of a sudden revelation. The painting is made. Giorgio cannot explain what has happened. It is inexplicable.

> Every time I look at that painting I live those moments again. The moment is an enigma for me, because it is inexplicable. I like to call 'enigma' also the work resulting from that moment.[16]

Fig. 1. Santa Croce Square, Florence.

A work of art is an immortal masterpiece only if it overcomes human limits, and if it is illogical and deprived of common sense. Reading *The Adventure of Pinocchio* De Chirico experienced the same sensations he had when reading *Also sprach Zarathustra* – a strange similarity which reveals the depth of the work, nothing to do with primitive artist's artlessness or spontaneity. There is something like the strange feeling of a child, but created on purpose. A painting, to be really deep, should achieve this effect. Bucklin and Poussin have reached the limits; one more effort is needed to attain the painting which will lead us beyond all the paintings. (meta = beyond)

The painting was bought by Paul Eluard, but it is now lost and references are made to copies taken by Max Ernst. The reproductions of the painting show a complete transfiguration of the reality elements: the church becomes a gothic temple, the square is compressed, Dante becomes a classical statue, and a sail appears on the horizon. There is a memory of the things, not their real portrait; things are studied and analysed in their ancestral roots, in their hidden meaning.

The story behind the 'revelation' shows the family again on the move, this time from Milan to Florence. The thematic of travel and of being let down is very close to De Chirico. He travelled first with his parents. Father Evaristo was a rail road engineer. The children followed the family in countless

Fig. 2. Enigma of a fall afternoon, 1910.

houses and countries, and then to pursue his own studies and interests from Athens to Munich and then back to Italy and to Paris, etc. This continuous moving made of De Chirico a displaced person, but at the same time it exposed him to a multi-faceted culture and gave him a first-hand knowledge of different traditions.

De Chirico has been for some time in physically bad shape; he is very weak and accuses cramps and pain in the abdomen. When he walks on the street, he is afraid of fainting and so he walks along the walls. In his room, on his table, there are many drugs with evocative names, very Greek: epatina, coreina, zimatrax (. . .). Melancholy, Nietzsche's melancholy, is his regular mood. From Vallombrosa – where a physician had sent him to cure his abdominal pains – he comes back to Florence with no results:

> In Florence we remained not more than one year (. . .) my brother had the idea to travel to Monaco to perform his music. My health did not allow me to afford a trip so long, so I remained in Florence (. . .) then my brother went to Paris which was then considered the city for excellence giving encouragement to young artists and young promises, full of life, movement and intelligent people (later on, I realized that this exists only in the fantasy of people and that in Paris people do not understand anything more than in Rome, London, Madrid, Berlin or Pernambuco). I was still very depressed; my health was not getting any better; I was very

weak and I was fighting against all sorts of physical troubles. I went to see a notorious physician of those times, prof. Grocco. He prescribed to me no drugs, but a resort in Tuscany, Vallombrosa, where good air should cure me. In Vallombrosa it rained non stop, a terrible humidity penetrated in the room (. . .) the bed sheets were wet, and mushrooms grew in the cupboards and chests of drawers. My intestine troubles increased, and so did my nervous depression; I was caught by a strong melancholy and when I could not take it any longer I ran away from Vallombrosa and went back to Florence; after Vallombrosa, I realized that sometimes, on some occasions, mountain fresh and healthy air can be damaging. Bruno Barilli told me that when he was in Paris, around 1930, (I was there as well in the same period), he got invited by his publisher and friend Pierre Levy (who later on published my Hebdomeros in French). Levy invited Bruno in a small property he owned near Paris; for those few days Bruno ate only the freshest food; fresh-laid eggs, fresh-milked milk, fresh-picked salad from the orchard; after sometime all these utmost fresh products poisoned him severely; so that when he came back to Paris he ran to those filthy price-unique eateries where they serve food in advanced state of decomposition. Thus, Bruno Barilli put back in place his organism purging it of all the toxins accumulated by the excessively fresh products.[17]

During the war, in the years between 1916 and 1918 (the so-called Ferrara period), De Chirico's works are inspired, lyrical and prophetical of the new art which De Chirico was hoping to organize in the Italy of the post-war period with the help of the few intelligent ones like Soffici, Papini,

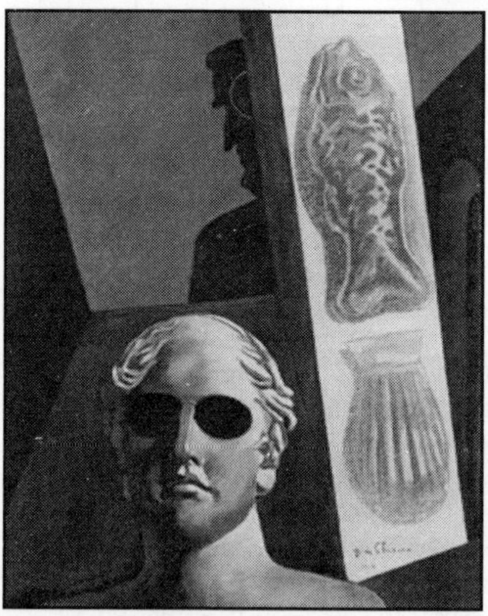

Fig. 3. Apollinaire's Portrait, 1914.

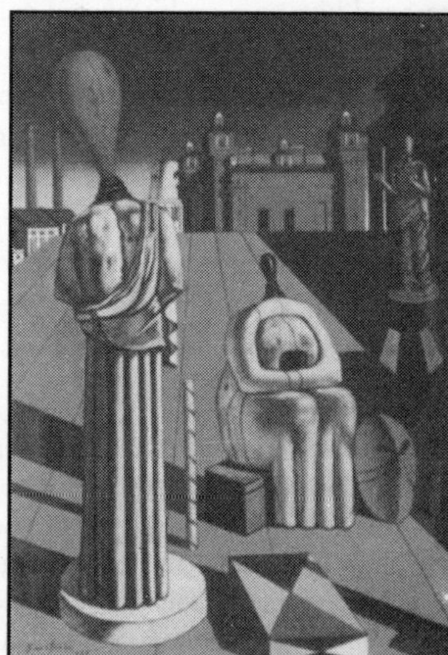

Fig. 4. The disquieting Musae, 1918.

Fig. 5. Le reve de Tobie (Tobie's Dream)
(Ferrara period, 1916- 1917).

and together with Savinio, Carrà and Broglio. De Chirico seems to enter in competition with his friend Apollinaire who, according to De Chirico, had been able to understand the complicated demonology of the new painting.

Max Ray's photo-portrait (Fig. 6) had been carefully planned, the presence of the painting *Le reve de Tobie* behind the head of André Breton is not casual. From the left, standing: Baron, Queneau, Naville, Boiffard, De Chirico, Vitrac, Eluard, Soupault, Desnos, Aragon; sitting: Simone Breton, Morise and Soupault's wife.

In all De Chirico's texts, even if not explicitly, one realizes that he is always writing about himself, that every text is a sort of self-portrait and a meditation over his work. From the texts, by way of lapsus, some revelations

Fig. 6. Max Ray, photo-portrait of the Surrealist group, 1924; published on the cover page of the magazine "La revolution surrealiste", 1st number.

on his themes and inspiration can be easily detected: the subject of his painting otherwise would never be openly revealed, according to De Chirico, it should remain a mystery (*mysterium mirabile*).

De Chirico's point of view on the themes of the *toys and of the mannequins* emerges in texts absolutely above suspicion. There are many such revelations: on the iconography of the *archaeologists*, the value of the *furniture in the valley* and *the temples in the room.*[18]

One of De Chirico's most surprising texts regards Turin, inhabited by statues, as the ideal city for metaphysical aesthetics.[19] In the first page of a late 1939 critical essay occasioned by a Paola Levi Montalcini's exhibition, De Chirico enlightens his experience of this city, the emotions which lead to many of his best works of the metaphysical period.

> Turin is not in the road map of tourism like Venice, Florence or other small cities of Umbria and Tuscany. Turin is the deepest, the most enigmatic, and the most disquieting city not only in Italy, in the whole world. Friedrich Nietzsche was the first one to discover its hermetic beauty; he was the first one to feel the infinite poetry of this city built on the two sides of a river slowly flowing like the life of men slowly flows, now grey

now sky blue. Friedrich Nietzsche guessed the enigma of those straight roads, the arcades, under which one can discuss poetry and philosophy even if it rains. (. . .) nobody else has perceived the beauty of Turin apart from Friedrich Nietzsche and me (. . .) and it is a beauty which can be fatal. Friedrich Nietzsche already weakened by a life of intense interiors emotions and discoveries, could not afford for long the beauty of Turin and sank in madness during one of those afternoons in the Fall when the long shadows, the stillness of the sky, the atmosphere of quietness and convalescence expressed by nature after the criminal violence of spring and the exhausting fevers of summer bring the hidden beauty of Turin to its highest degree of expression. It is then that the whole people of marble or bronze, the great men who stand still for the whole year on their low pedestals in the middle of the come-and-go of vehicles and passers-by, slowly and painfully descend from their pedestals and after stretching their limbs start off to the famous Piazza Castello where their mysterious gatherings take place. Turin lives under the sign of the Taurus. Its first inhabitants had a Taurus as an emblem; they were the Taurinorum Gens, hence Turin. Now everybody knows that the most anthropomorphic animals are the ass, the hen, the cock, the bull. And it is not for nothing that in Greek mythology a man with Taurus head has been a guard to the most mysterious construction that ever existed in the world of legend.[20]

All De Chirico's visions thirty years ago (1912-1914) flow before our eyes with some new element of the great Nietzschean afternoon in the

Fig. 7. La tour rouge (The red tower), 1913.

Fig. 8. Carlo Magliocchetti monument to Emanuele Filiberto in Torino (last photo right); Mole Antonelliana (photo above it).

melancholic city; themes come to the surface "on dove's wings" as Nietzsche would say. Arianna gets a new light, the wise and melancholic heroin of the *gaya scienza* reveals her connection with the surrounding space, those squares as far as time, the hour which stands, the wrong hour, and a dreamed-of Italy, and its Lybic dream, as far as space.

From the very beginning, De Chirico has correlated Arianna with the labyrinth; and the labyrinth with Theseus; after Theseus' flight, De Chirico has overlapped the Dionysian aspect to Arianna's melancholy and to the Minotaur. Thus, Arianna finds her proper surroundings in Turin (*Augusta Taurinorum*), a sort of metaphor of Knossos with its sacred bull. One small tessera more, filling up De Chirico's enigmatic cosmos.

The dreamlike atmosphere of *La tour rouge* results from an irrational perspective – the lack of a unified light source, the elongation of shadows and a hallucinatory focus on objects. The Italian Piazza bound by arcades or classical facades is transformed into an ominously silent and vacant setting for invisible dramas. The absence of events provokes a nostalgic or a melancholic mood. The half shadow of a knight and the arcades recall the Carlo Magliocchetti monument to Emanuele Filiberto in Turin; the tower itself recalls the Mole Antonelliana.

In the years around 1920, De Chirico's articles appeared in several magazines (*Valori Plastici*, *Il Primato artistico italiano*, *Il convegno*, *La Ronda)*, the magazines of the "coming back to order" type. In this period of the "terrible artistic European renaissance",[21] De Chirico's critical texts and essays are so many and of such a good quality that they overtake even his pictorial research. De Chirico addresses those who are repentant for having been avant-garde with a paternalistic tone, e.g. in the text *Noi metafisici*[22] (*Veniet felicior aetas*, my friends; with this hope (. . .) I end my rebuke and quietly go back to my own work); usually, he preaches with much heavier tones, labelling their work as "massonic painting", "coloured masturbations" and "pederast gymnastic trainer's way of painting"; he puts the accent on his superiority interspersing his writing with excessively polite and considerate French expressions like *par delicatesse*, or *savez vous*; on the contrary, when he gives advice to the young painters, his tone becomes imperative, and his advices are very similar to orders ("Copy the ancients! Make moulds of ancient models! Go back to academic models!" etc.)

Coming back to Paris in 1924, while the mannequins change style and give birth to cities or to toys, becoming more human than the Ferrara ones, De Chirico introduces Attic horses and gladiators in his new fantastic world; his pages become visionary, the style is lighter, more subtle. Now he speaks in parables, or through feigned characters dream-nets. The top prose of this period is the 1929 masterpiece *Hebdomeros, le peintre et son genie chez l'ecrivain* Editions du Carrefour.

Born as a seven months' child, just like Apollo with whom he identifies himself, De Chirico is the leading character of the book, amongst Gladiators, the Triumphs and characters transformed into mannequins. Hebdomeros is a long visionary labyrinth, a maze on which De Chirico has been working for the last couple of years, 'unmasking the great game of the eternal': some excerpts had appeared in the magazine "Bifur" in the same year, a few months earlier. The surrealists, his former friends and present enemies, love the book as well; they have split up this same year; Breton has published the second *manifesto* of the movement but is not able to hold his ex-followers in check; they attack him with a motto, thrown at him like a stone: "You are a corpse." Aragon will write in *La peinture au defi*, 1931 that *Hebdomeros est un ouvrage interminablement beau* (the genius of the painter is expressing itself in writing, nowadays, when he abandons the tricks of his trade to trust his intelligence); Breton and Henry Miller think that it is a work of an absolute beauty and Bataille that it is of an absolute greatness.

In 1928 De Chirico publishes a pictorial technique treatise (*Piccolo trattato di tecnica pittorica* Ed. Scheiwiller, Milan 1928, which has a Prague edition in 1931: *Mali Traktat a Malirske Techniche* on the occasion of a personal exhibition in the capital), going from pedantry to irony, very different from the new polemics of the '30s, played in a heavy anti-modernist key (*The painter's trade*, 1933 published in a local Turin paper (Gazzetta del Popolo); *Quelques perspective sur mon art*, 1934 published in Prague; *Vox clamans in deserto* and *Ambrosiano*, 1938). Some of these texts will be collected by De Chirico himself in a small book *Comedy of modern art* (Rome 1945) rich in omissions and censorship.

III. DEFINITION OF ARTIST

Georgio[23] is famous. His paintings are exhibited and sold all over Europe and in the USA. 1931 onwards, his life will be on the road, travelling without pause. In an article published in Paris on the occasion of one of his exhibitions, the critic of *Petit Parisien, (Argus de Presse)* launches into a daring comparison: De Chirico's works are paralleled to Joyce's interior monologue; the abrupt insertion in the middle of the page / painting of fragments of conversation or descriptions of the character's thoughts, both the intimate and even the casual ones.

In the midst of this notoriety and glory, there are many who doubt De Chirico's present creativity. His old friend Waldemar George writes an article *Vie et mort de Chirico* describing De Chirico as a living corpse, a brain without soul: "At the beginning, his work opened a new way of knowledge to his contemporaries, he led the way, he was a real pioneer. Why then did he write those cruel and pedantic pages? Why does he talk so much about morals, having confirmed to be beyond morals?"

There are other moments when De Chirico writes to clarify to himself his own aesthetic ideas (and this is the case of the many excerpts of the French period, not meant for publication, at least not all of them). In the various periods anyhow, there is a constant in his writings: a balance between lyrical inspiration and polemic argumentativeness. His writings sound different, even formally, in the different literary periods: the French period, the Ferrara period (during the war), and the after-war period.

Memories of My Life (modified and published several times since 1945) is certainly the most important piece of literature. For historical reasons, but not only: re-running the phases of his life, perfectly overlapping the phases of his artistic work, De Chirico feels himself at the centre of the world and of the history of art, and reveals the reasons of his life-long polemics with his cronies, the other artists, and in particular with those of them who had been well received, and had a good success. After many years of good relationship with the avant-garde, De Chirico decided to cut whatever connection declaring himself the only heir of the European and the Italian tradition, portraying himself as the superior being who had been allotted the task of protecting art and literature against those ex-friends of his, who had chosen career, success and money. It was a kind of war, long and with intervals, filled up with progressively radicalising declarations and anathemas based on morals and reasons. De Chirico's aim and purpose was the reform of Art[24] but at the time of his historical declarations he cancelled his own work from the history of Art, going back to tradition and to the great models of the past, which he was not afraid to be compared with.

His autobiography is a *Bildungsroman* at all effects, starting with his childhood and adolescence to the years spent in Munich (1906-1909) looking for new ways of doing Art until the avant-garde movements recognized him as the MASTER and the dominating figure in world art.

Fig. 9. Self portrait with a XVII century costume, exhibited in London in 1949 (half-length).

Fig. 10. Self portrait with a XVII century costume, exhibited at the Biennale di Venezia 1956.

Fig. 11. Self-portrait with a XVII century costume, 1959, of redundant taste, very close to bad taste, theatrical and self celebratory, a painting which is "rich" in decorative details like the embroidered collar and the small figure of the knight in the background.

De Chirico begins writing his own biography in 1919: *Auto presentation* in *Valori plastici*, 1919; the booklet *Souvenirs of Rome 1918-1925* (re-published by Edizioni della Cometa in 1988 and revolving around the Roman cultural system of the *Valori plastici* years, the "Ronda" magazine until Fascists came to power) is an exhilarating satire, later integrated in the *Memories*, mocking those men of letters who were regular visitors of Caffé Aragno and denouncing those who joined forces to suggest that De Chirico should leave Italy for Paris in 1925. The conclusion of the booklet was

> (. . .) I have decided to stay and work in Italy and (. . .) maybe in Rome itself. Yes, yes, it is here that I want to stay and work, work ever more and ever better, work for my glory and your damnation.[25]

De Chirico devotes the year 1945 to the definition of the Artist; he represents himself as a superior being whose task is to defend art and literature from mistreatment and abuse by those who are only seeking success and money. Self-portraits, autobiographies, and theoretical treaties are all published in 1945. It is the artist defining himself as an individual who becomes Master of the Art, intellectually and practically. He appears to our eyes as a Rubens or a Van Dyck; in his writing he mixes autobiography (*Memories*), autobiographical novel (*Mr Dudron*) and theoretical treaty (*Commedia dell'arte moderna*) with personal narrations, historical judgements and pictorial technique.

Memories of My Life follows the publication of the booklet *1918-1925, Souvenirs of Rome. An Adventure of Mr Dudron* is published in 1945 as well as *Comedy of Modern Art* on art theory. The exhibition in Rome of the "Naked Self-portrait" and "Self-portrait in a costume of the XVII c." also takes place in 1945. The sequel of self-portraits increases: they were born with De Chirico's first metaphysical production and go along with the artist's poetics, like "comments", frequently from 1945 onwards.

In 1962, year of the second edition of *Memories*, a new chapter 'Technique of painting' is added to the book and chapters from the *Comedy of Modern Art* are inserted even in a new edition of *Dudron*. All this is done with the purpose of filling De Chirico's utopia with solid practical and theoretical elements: knowledge is dominating and works are perfectible.

Technical perfection and moral vocation are the basis of the written works. De Chirico condemns modern art after having been such a great part of it and his life and work belong to modern art on the whole. His denouncement comes in the 40s, between the end of Fascism and the conclusion of WW II. De Chirico completes the first draft of his *Memories* while the nuclear explosion is rumbling in Hiroshima; in 1962, when he starts writing the *Memories* again, he very keenly notes this detail. His judgement of Fascism and America, Nazism and Communism, faces of the same disfigured prism, is equally severe.

The purpose of the *Memories* is to found a future for Art on a historical judgement regarding society. De Chirico gives a new turning to the kind of Vasari's artist-biographies. His point of view is "I am the metaphysic painter, my moral and technical qualities are superior to everybody else's. I am attacking this system to create a better one." His *Memories* are a political biography, the system reacts, his admirers are disappointed and desert him, and it is war.

A literary equivalent of De Chirico painting after 1940, *Memories of My Life* is a linear autobiography, whose purpose is to create De Chirico's own myth. When De Chirico resorts to Isabelle Far, "a unique woman with a philosophical intellect", and the only person who understands his painting, it is in order to undergo the heavy task of self-description and self- representation.

Complementary themes to the biographical ones are the pamphlet against modernity, the apology of pictorial techniques and the elegy of childhood. One can hardly miss the pretentiousness, the pompousness of the self-centred narrator of his own *Memories*, but at the same time there are many pages of good narrative – ironical, light and pleasant. The narration of De Chirico's meetings with Longhi on a Firenze's street and in Rome are examples of good writing with an ironical vein in it and an assertion of De Chirico's awareness of his own undisputable sacred greatness.[26]

Hebdomeros and *Mr Dudron* are the other two works where De Chirico shows his qualities as a writer, the wealth of De Chirico's fantasy following the lines of his creations. It has been observed that from a certain point of view, De Chirico does in literature the same he was doing in painting: he deceives the reader, as he deceived the art critic, mixing his passions, the real ones and the faked ones, often made up only for polemical reasons. In his many self-portraits as well, De Chirico gives space to the most obvious part of the representation, but at the same time he makes us understand that his real soul is NOT in the colours and lines of that painting.

De Chirico was not very far from his hated surrealists who used reality but only on the condition that it had undergone a strong correction according to the violent contradictions between a work of art and life. Re-reading one of the many strong De Chirico's outbursts against modern artists, and the Italy of his day we realize that these tirades are most probably an excuse for not giving a good reason to his change of direction, from avant-garde to classical art

> [w]here the highest spiritual things, the arts, literature, poetry, music, are dragged into the mud by a bunch of abject flatterers of the foreigners, emasculated and illiterate, who have turned every form of art and thought to an obscene aping of what most decayed, empty, frivolous was being done outside Italy, especially in Paris.[27]

IV. CONCLUSION

What De Chirico has not explained: why and how he had passed from modern avant-garde art to yesterday Italy, why he had decided to change his path. Why does he never explain this critical earthquake? It is a mystery not sufficiently explored and De Chirico was too intelligent not to know that such a behaviour and change of direction – which he insisted was due to Isabelle Far's extraordinary intuition – was going to rouse reactions more than explanations and interpretations. From this point of view his challenge was against fashion and the winning party. The more he inflated the magnitude of this universal decadence the more he was provoked to aggression, not to discussion. One could add that these memories are a *mea culpa* where he condemned first of all his first experiences, his first enthusiasms and fights, knowing very well that nothing was going to change and he was going to be the never-ending "monomaco" and loser, even if from outside he could appear as a Roman Emperor coming back home decorated with medals and acknowledgements.

In his lonely moments, in his last fights De Chirico must have felt that he had been part of history for a long time already and that everything was allowed to him: mixing moral ideas and mockery and plans of renewal.

It has been noted that one more key to his *Memories* might consist in interpreting them as a great laugh and a *cupio dissolvi* where he made the balance of *La sconfitta che l'arte anche nei suoi momenti più alti sopporta sotto la ruota implacabile del tempo* (the defeat suffered by art, even in its highest moments, under time implacable – wheel).

NOTES AND REFERENCES

1. Maurizio Fagiolo Dell'Arco, *Vita ed opere di De Chirico attraverso incisioni e litografie,* (Milan: Interarte, 1980), p. 2.
   "Through the cycles of lithography one can reconstruct a career of surprising inventions and programmatic replicas, a life under the sign of contradiction."
2. The Spanish Steps apartment hosts today the De Chirico Foundation displaying De Chirico's paintings. De Chirico moved here in 1947 from Mario de' Fiori Street. He had always loved the Spain Steps and the surroundings, especially Caffé Greco.
   Giorgio De Chirico, *Memorie della mia vita*, (Milano: Tascabili Bompiani, 2002), pp. 210-11.
   "(. . .) Spain Steps are close to all those places which we visit, more or less frequently. There are first rate drugstores, banks, international book-shops, travel agencies, movers, luxury hairdressers, art galleries, shops for ladies and gentlemen, (. . .)" (English trans. mine)
   "from the balcony of my studio at the fifth floor of Piazza di Spagna, I see splendid sky shows, clear skies and clouded skies, fire sunsets, moon nights and night effects of yellow circled clouds, as one can see in some marines of Flemish and Dutch painters. I am always ready to take note of these natural views (. . .) Corot said *La nature c'est le meilleur maitre* (Nature is the best teacher), even if nature cannot teach anybody to produce a masterpiece. The only way to progress is to learn from the master painters. Only after having studied and copied many times the works of the masters one is allowed to copy from nature." (English trans. mine)
3. Ibid., p. 142. (English trans. mine)
4. Ibid., p. 223.
5. Amongst the many works commissioned to De Chirico due to his notoriety: Frescos on the theme "The culture of the time" for The Triennale di Milano (1933); Scenery-paintings for "IPuritani" by Bellini, at the Maggio Musicale Fiorentino (the film-director Max Reinhardt single-handedly appreciated these scenery-paintings; so far as the performance is concerned, it was booed by the public for three nights); 66 lithographs for his friend and appraiser Apollinaire's Calligrammes (1930); Ballet costumes and scenery-paintings (Boris Kochno's scenes of Le Bal for Djagilev' Russian Ballets performed in Montecarlo and in Paris in 1929); Cover page for *Vogue.*
   De Chirico participated with the "Italians of Paris" in the Venice Biennale 1932 and held personal exhibitions in Genoa, Turin, Milan, Florence, Zurig, etc.
6. De Chirico, *Memorie della mia vita*, pp. 190-91.
7. All books were tiny in those years for lack of money: *Bicycles thieves*, *Furor mathematicus*, etc.
8. De Chirico, *Memorie della mia vita,* (Roma: Astrolabio, 1945).
9. Roberto Longhi, *To the orthopaedic god*, (Rome: Il Tempo, 22 February 1919).
   "Pushed by his hand of cruel engine-men, the horribly disfigured and unavoidably mannequined mankind (. . .) in the midst of squeaks and whines

appears on the wide deserted stages constantly watched by the heavy big boxes of the hot and dark house-buildings. Here, the "homo orthopaedicus" / *sgrana con voce di carrucola una sua parte impossibile* / shells out in a pulley voice his own impossible role / to the disowned statues of ancient Greece. Under the clammy emerald colour of a sky pretending to be Mediterranean, the guillotined Hellenic myths hand over their credentials to Cavour's statues; civilizations echo one another; factory's smokestacks line up with medieval fortresses, while Pirelli and Borso from Este agree at the first sight of their one only artificial eye (. . .)" (my translation)

10. In 1924, just before his second Paris period (1925-1929), De Chirico affirmed in one interview that
"in Italy there is no modern art movement. No merchant, no galleries. There is no modern Italian painting. There are only Amedeo Modigliani and myself, but we are both almost French." (English trans. mine)
In the *Memories* (1945), nevertheless, De Chirico accused those who liked 'Modi' and his 'daubs' of being snobbish.

11. De Chirico's first known painting dates back to 1908. He never stopped working all his life - a life almost Picassean in length - and even in his old age, end of the '60s, he found new sources of inspiration by way of rethinking all his own previous works; he again expressed himself in a fresh genuine sprouting of creativity revisiting his own works without the tired repetitions and quotations of clichés of the '50s. Eighty years old, he finds a new creative moment assembling excerpts of his previous works, mainly theatre scenery-paintings and graphic works. As a matter of fact, there is a sort of reunification of the different plans of research of the '30s and '40s. The 'squares' and 'interiors' of the Ferrara period, the 'rooms with archaeologists' of the '20s, are combined with the motives of De Chirico's works in scenery-painting of the '30s, or with the sun and the moon of the litho for Apollinaire's Calligrammes of the '30s. Going back to his past in an unburdened peaceful climate he creates a delicious play-mood with stylised, neither heavy nor ponderous figurines. (see Rome: Ebdomeros, Bestetti Publishing House, 1972. De Chirico's illustrations; here below, "Ebdomeros departure")
"One who would seek the dark atmosphere of the metaphysical works, would be disappointed: here the colours are light and airy. Pale yellows, luminous okras, clear neat sky blues, delicate pea-green, somehow close to cartoons' colours or children's room decoration (. . .) a sort of final catwalk where whatever has been done in the course of the show is called back on stage and all the actors and extras parade together (. . .)" (Bruno Barilli, 1974) (English trans. mine)

12. Giorgio De Chirico, *Hebdomeros, le peintre et son genie chez l'ecrivain,* (Paris: Carrefour, 1929). The title itself echoes the sentence prefaced by Apollinaire *Et moi aussi je suis peintre* to his Calligrammes (poems shaped as figures). On the cover page of the first edition the name of the author, De Chirico, is well in evidence; the signature of the painter is close to the double image of Hebdomeros, with classical vestiges in the background.
Hebdomeros is a sort of "rendering of accounts" with the surrealist movement, a book De Chirico will never forget, written directly in French, and very well received even by his former friends, the surrealists, now his enemies. Aragon wrote: *Hebdomeros* was a work of an infinite beauty / *un ouvrage interminablement beau.* Bataille wrote: *il rayonne d'une absolute grandeur* / it oozes an infinite greatness. As a consequence, the book was consecrated as a masterpiece of the surrealist literature, with or rather without De Chirico's consent.
In 1942 De Chirico translated and published the first Italian edition of *Hebdomeros.* Then, in 1957, he printed at his own expenses a second edition dedicated to the sacred memory of his brother Savinio, who had died in 1952. A third edition was brought out by Longanesi in 1971 with a sharp back-of-the-coverpage write-up by Giorgio Manganelli (*Ebdomero*, Ed. Abscondita, 41, (Milan: Carte d'artisti, agosto, 2003). Manganelli:"*Hebdomeros* is not a character and *Hebdomeros* is not a novel: the first one is an intentional name, the second is an itinerary, a deposit of images, a catalogue of symbols, a collage of dreams, landscapes, home-interiors, drawing-drafts, all of them lighted up by a phosphorescence smelling of memory, vision, hoaxing. *Hebdomeros* fairy-tale stretches like a proliferating labyrinth, a building able to reproduce itself, to project new wings, quarters, entrances and exits: it would be useless to look for a beginning and a conclusion, privileged peaks, pivotal discoveries. In one building, a space, a compact dead city, an accurately, lavishly secularized temple, every point is pivotal, it inaugurates and seals. This infinitely corny, unoriginal place (*infinitamente spurio*) mythological and devious, of centaurs and blind alleys, is described in a discourse which can be defined "objective monologue": that meaning the transcription in an uncaring, at the most worried or slightly crossed prose, querulous and peevish at times, a tale which does not proceed from event to event but passes from one image, from one word to another, from an analogy to another: thus, along a route, two points are necessarily contiguous but by no means either of them can be inferred from the other or can they be reciprocally foreseeable (. . .) far from being a dream and far from being interior monologue (. . .)"
13. Paolo Baldacci, De Chirico 1888-1919. *La Metafisica*, (Milan: Leonardo Arte, 1997), p. 58.
14. De Chirico, *Meditation d'un peintre, Que pourrait etre la peinture de l'avenire*, (Paris: Manoscritti Paulhan, 1911-1915), in M.F. Dell'Arco, *Il Meccanismo del pensiero* (Einaudi, 1985), p. 13 ff.
15. Ibid.
16. Ibid., p. 17.
17. De Chirico, *Memories*, p. 80.

18. Giorgio De Chirico, *Discorso sullo spettacolo teatrale* "L' Illustrazione italiana" (Milan, 11 October 1942); Revelations on the iconography of the *archaeologists, furniture in the valley & temples in the room,* are also to be found in *Statues, meubles, et generaux,* 'Bulletin de l'effort modern', ottobre1927, in M.F. Dell'Arco, *Il meccanismo del pensiero*, p. 471.
19. Ibid., p. 321.
"*Quelques perspectives sur mon art*": "Turin inhabited by statues is the ideal city for metaphysical aesthetics. Turin has inspired all my works from 1912 to 1915. Nietzsche, whom I read passionately, is my inspiration as well. He wrote *Ecce Homo* in Turin, before madness clouded definitely his mind. It is in the fall that Turin expresses at its best its metaphysical charm."
20. Ibid., p. 361 ff.
21. Quoted from *Guillaume Apollinaire*, Nov. 1918. Article written on the death of the poet.
22. De Chirico, *Noi Metafisici*, (Cronache d'attualità, Bollettino della Casa d'Arte Bragaglia, 15 febbraio 1919).
23. Giorgio De Chirico signs 'Georgio' (either a Latin or French influence) private and public texts and many of his paintings of the years 1910-1913.
24. De Chirico, *Mr Dudron*, pp. 30-31ff.
The protagonist's meeting with Isabelle Far: "Isabelle Far was a unique case of philosophical intelligence and talent (. . .) a lady writer who considered him, Mr Dudron, the only painter who had understood the mystery of great painting, the only painter capable of bringing back decayed painting to a plan of nobility and beauty."
25. *Memories of My Life*, p. 18.
26. Ibid., pp. 115-16.
De Chirico meets Roberto Longhi, following Giovanni Papini's (author of "*Un uomo finito*", then in Rome to write a "metaphysical novel") advice; he was living in isolation, concentrating on writing but the novel was never born.
"Following Papini's advice, I went to see Longhi. He came to my exhibition, he looked at the paintings, he said nothing, (as Diane Karenne, an actress who had earlier visited the exhibition and whose only comment had been: "What a huge amount of work") and then he went out with me and tried to "make me talk". We reached Bussi, a café'-pastry shop which used to be at the corner between via Veneto and via Buoncompagni; at Bussi's, Roberto Longhi offered a café' to me, pronouncing it "coffee" as an Englishman. I, poor innocent, unaware of everything, candid, trusting, I talked about art, expressing my ideas, my dreams, my hopes, I opened my pure heart, I said it all, confiding myself confessing myself candidly and naively to him, to him who deceitfully, satanically, horribly, was shaping a sinister evil move in the deep of his soul. As a matter of fact, a few days later, on the third page of Tempo newspaper, his article appeared, demolishing me, by the title "To the orthopaedic god". Longhi was trying to write his articles in a style between the perfidious and the brilliant, similar to Barilli's style, but since he did not own the sharpness and the "nerve" of our great national Bruno, there came out certain things, certain

poor withered, stunted, bilious, pretentious, rickety, peevish and hysterical, which as soon as they were born, delivered their soul to Satan.
Since then, Longhi's livid envy has been increasing, for about 27 years. When he meets me on the road his jaws slightly shift and he gets a beginning of facial paralysis. He is capable of magic and supernatural phenomena, he has the gift of ubiquity and the ability to disappear whenever he likes. I remember by the way that about two years ago I was passing under the arcades of the Central Post Office in Florence; I saw Longhi all of a sudden, twenty steps from me, walking towards me. He saw me; in a flash he estimated the distance and reckoned that most probably we were bound to collide like two steamships in the fog. There was no time to loose, he resorted to extreme means, to magic, and he opened his arms and at about twenty steps from me dived into the pavement. I am neither exaggerating nor making anything up: Roberto Longhi disappeared into the pavement.
When I looked around to find out where he ended up, I discerned behind me, far away, at the end of the arcades, Longhi's hinder part: who, rounding off the corners, was disappearing towards via Strozzi (. . .)
Another time, during my staying in Rome, I had gone to Longhi's for a painting (. . .) there arose a discussion between me and him regarding that famous Raffaello's portrait which I found in Florence Pitti Gallery, known as "the pregnant woman". In 1920, I made a copy of that portrait, a copy which I still retain.
Longhi kept on saying that Raffaello had wrongly painted the woman's left hand, I attracted his attention on the fact that the drawing was not wrong, that those disproportions – to be seen in some Durer's works as well, were due to a special character connected to the painting as a whole, and that, far from diminishing the value of the painting, they, on the contrary, increased it. Short of arguments, Longhi fell into hysterics; he started stamping on the floor, *pietiner sur place*, like somebody in urgent need of urinating but who cannot satisfy this need; while he was stamping the floor he kept on repeating with a suffocated voice 'Mr De Chirico, I have the honour to salute you, I have the honour to salute you, Mr De Chirico'. The painter Amerigo Bartoli was present at the scene."

27. Ibid., p. 186.
"leccasedere dello straniero che, vigliaccamente e delinquentemente hanno ridotto ogni forma d'arte e di pensiero ad una oscena scimmiottatura di quello che di più scadente, di più vuoto, di più frivolo si fa fuori d'Italia e specialmente a Parigi."

SANJA ROIĆ

Autobiographical Paradox of Alberto Savinio

My paper attempts to highlight the narrative techniques that Alberto Savinio (1891-1952) used in creating his unique autobiographical discourse in Italian and European literature. Besides the French surrealists, his models were the works of writers and philosophers like Petrarch, Bruno, Vico, Nietzsche, Weininger and Freud. Starting from these intellectual suppositions, Savinio did not content himself with representing the formless and expressing the unconscious, but he wanted to give shape to the formless and to bring awareness to the unconscious. Instead of writing a classical autobiography, he scattered fragments of his auto-ironic autobiography where "I" is at the same time the protagonist and the antagonist: a man sensitive to pain and smell, with a tendency towards depersonalization, visions and explaining typing lapses.

He was born as Andrea De Chirico, the younger brother of Giorgio de Chirico.[1] After finishing his music studies as a twelve-year-old boy he first goes through a phase of strong intimacy with his brother and his work but then he rejects the stiffness of the imposed name and continues to work and live under the name of Alberto Savinio. His journey of life begins in Athens and this first phase includes Venice, Rome, Munich and Paris.

Alberto Savinio is considered "the biggest stranger" among all Italian writers. He wrote: "It's true I'm Italian but I'm also many other things."[2] I will concentrate on the works related with his childhood (*The Tragedy of Childhood* and *The Childhood of Nivasio Dolcemare*), his youth (*Hermaphrodite, Inspired House* and *Achilles in Love*)[3] and articles written for the Italian magazines in the period of his artistic maturity, in order to identify the autobiographical fragments of this multifaceted artist whose field of activities and eventual contemporary reception is entire Europe. It is well known that the turn and the first half of the 20th century in Europe – which are the chronological coordinates of the lifetime of the writer I wish to talk about – were marked by two world wars, while the artistic plane is dominated by the poetics of Modernism, Surrealism, Futurism, Avantgarde and later Neorealism. Alberto Savinio and his brother Giorgio De Chirico were born at the end of the 19th century in Greece, outside the linguistic and cultural milieu of Italy. Their cultural homeland, though, is a large part of Europe: from Athens, "one of the capitals of Balkania", as he liked to call it, through Munich, Paris, Rome, again the Balkans (as Greek translator in Italian troupes), Rome, Paris, Milan, Versilia in Toscana, New York, and finally back to Rome! Savinio understood contemporary poetics in a special way: for him Surrealism (but elaborated from the classical mind!) was giving a form to the unformed, or creating consciousness about something that is still unconscious. Lucid irony and even skepticism in relation to everything that surrounded him are typical of Savinio's views and his interpretation of reality. Mystery present on the canvases of these two artists is manifested in different ways: with De Chirico it is peaceful and fascinating, and with Savinio it is provocative and disturbing. He thought that the supreme victory of style has to be merited in a peculiar struggle and effort.

But Alberto Savinio's literary work did not encounter an equivalent reception as the metaphysical painting of his brother. His books and texts deviated even from new poetical trends. They were prose texts which required great attention from the readers and critics because they "wove" a specific network of meanings. Historical circumstances were such that a large portion of Savinio's texts remained scattered in literary magazines and dailies. That is why Savinio, like other artists such as Kafka, Leopardi, Van Gogh – was discovered posthumously. Italian literature has classified Savinio among its best writers only from the seventies of the 20th century, and a great admirer of his ethics and artistic expression was a Sicilian, Leonardo Sciascia.

I believe that these facts should be kept in mind while approaching the autobiographical component of Savinio's prose. It should be observed as intermedial, together with his painting and musical and theatrical production whenever possible, taking into account the parallel artistic experience of his brother Giorgio, as well as the cultural and linguistic mixture and periods of his life spent in Greece, Germany and France, and, last but not the least, the relation between classical, realistic, surrealistic, abstract and metaphysical in his literary works, although this does not round off the totality of his entire work. In short, Savinio has not written an autobiography which would, according to its characteristics, comply with Lejeune's requirements, although there is a page in the work that can be identified as an invitation to stipulate the so-called "autobiographical pact".[4] The way Savinio wrote his autobiography is closer to the idea of Jean Starobinski according to whom the style of an autobiography is the matter of an individual, or that "every autobiography is an interpretation of oneself".[5]

In the year 1947 Savinio was invited to write a short contribution titled "Writer on the mirror" for "La Fiera Letteraria", an Italian magazine. On this occasion (and it is well known that he condemned the sincerity!) he said that his work is "partly a precise and extensive autobiography", thus opening new possibilities to the literary genre which already had its coordinates. The statement that one's own autobiography can be written as part of one's work, that is, that one's work (at that moment Savinio had five more years to live)[6] should be written as a precise and extensive autobiography meant deconstruction of subsequent narcissism that emerges after a distance in time, as autobiographies were written until then. A specific monument to his "self" constructed by narrative means could now be discerned just as in fragments and segments, similar to "patches of fabric".

Savinio's literary beginnings are linked to the circle around Apollinaire in Paris, and the topic that engrossed him was "half-death" along the tracks of Stoics and Leopardi, but also Petrarch's melancholy (*Les chants de la mi-mort*, published in the magazine "Les soirées de Paris" edited by Apollinaire). "Half-death" is from the very beginning the topic which hints at the search for life as fullness. Savinio was convinced that autobiography should not start from the status of maturity of artist's spirit and intellect; in his writing he was more consistent than some theoreticians (here I have philosopher Giambattista Vico in mind, who considered childhood to be the true poetic period of a life cycle, that is, the history of an individual which progresses in three phases: childhood / adolescence / maturity).[7] Savinio himself denotes the parts of his work which form a "precise and extensive" autobiography, as the following: *Tragedia dell'infanzia, L'infanzia di Nivasio Dolcemare, Souvenirs, La casa ispirata*; then stories *Isabella Hasson* and *La partenza dell'Argonauta* (from his novel *Hermafrodito*), *Achille innamorato* and finally, stories from *Casa "La vita", Ascolto il tuo cuore and città* and *Tutta la vita.*

By compiling these parts, an almost complete history of his life can be obtained. What are the characteristics of these fragments and are they elements which belong to a triple whole? According to me, his last book *Il signor Dido* (*Mister Dido*)[8] should be added to the list, since it will bring the story of "a lifetime" almost to the end. Although he accepted early Freud's theories which explore the tensions in relations with persons near to you, Savinio believed that he personally did not need analysis: "Why should I subject myself to psychoanalysis", he wrote, "when my whole life, my whole work is a discharge of mental material?!"[9]

The question that arises is whether the "I" in *Tragedy of Childhood* can be considered to be Savinio's predecessor, the child who still is not the artist

Fig. 1. "I genitori" (The Parents), 1931.

and who has the name-pseudonym most probably chosen by his brother? Yes, this "I" is the child-artist in the world of childhood, and one of the proofs is that he still is not aware of God Kronos. Childhood knows not dates, it has no chronology, it is uncertain even when it comes to seasons ("was it summer, or perhaps spring?", the narrator wonders), topography is absolute because it does not know any other and parents' personalities assume mythical proportions because they are absolute rulers.

For Savinio, remembrance is the filter of the truth. Whatever is "deposited in us as eternal" remains, because oblivion erases everything that is false. Remembrance is pain, light, darkness, thirst and it is clear as day; and metaphor is cognition, again along the trail of Giambattista Vico's philosophy, the unstoppable torrent of desire for cognition in a child's questions that are uttered only approximately, the babbling of a child, because a child only unsuccessfully imitates the phonology of grown-ups. Childhood is life in the shadow of Mercury, theatre is more authentic than life, the fall into the unconscious state of delirium is possible and diseases that touch upon the limits of beyond, death, and then the return to life follows, like in sinuous courses and recourses (Italian: *corsi – ricorsi*).

The world of adults is afraid of the world of child. Birth is the arrival of little "enemies", and immediately thereafter, the war begins between adults and these tiny people who set out to conquer the world. Childhood is dangerous and creative; it disturbs the order of things. In each child, Savinio believes, there is an Ibsenism which has not yet found its Ibsen. Childhood is the tide of revolution stopped by adults who can be identified as reactionists. There is a loss of illusions and their eventual disappearance. Man is reduced to a pronoun, just as the French, masters of the average, reduced *homo* to pronoun "*on*". Up-bringing is sterilization of the individual. Only an artist can, in a natural way, continue with his childhood and that is why, in order to woo them, they are often said to be "big children". The tragedy of childhood is the victimisation and destruction of that which is primevally childish after which the only thing that remains is the memory of the primeval forest (through which giants roamed, as testified by Vico). Is this primeval forest the same as paradise lost, Savinio wonders? There is no affirmative answer, but he is convinced that only poets are permitted to return to that primeval forest.

Fig. 2. "Autoritratto" (Self-Portrait), 1936.

When Savinio praises abandoning of all poetic conventions including Aristotelian unities, it is clear that by doing so he is pleading the abandoning of conventional literary genres as well. He experiences every fixation of unities as deadly ("unity is Fascism!" is his clear condemnation), and finds corroboration in mobility, movement, fluidity and transforming of the narrative "I" into the anagram of the pseudonym Savinio into Nivasio.

This does not mean, however, that he inclines towards writing an autobiography in third person, which historically is not unusual in the genre. Nivasio will coincide and blend with many new third persons.

Achievement or victory is liberation from the past; that is why Savinio gives priority to childhood which does not know what chronology is. Muse Clio is the "strictest" of all muses, she is the archivist who stores acts of the past and unburdens the subject.[10] The artist (Savinio) is the man, who so long as he creates and works, remains young; he is interested in what he has *not yet* done. Accordingly he considers the straight line superior to the circle because he perceives critically everything that is closed, and the circle is closed or sealed. According to him, the circle is a symbol of sanctity, immortality, and therefore of non-humanity. The straight line is life; segments of it can be observed as segments of autobiographical discourse. Straight lines can form an angle, a rectangle, a square, and that is a positive space, even when the space is a tomb. Self-citations and self-referring with Savinio correspond to constant returns and departures in an open, sinuous form. Who is "I" in fact? – From the unnamed I-narrator in *Tragedy* to fragmented characters called Nivasio Dolcemare, Animo, Malino, Aniceto, Riccardo, Mr. Münster, Omero Barchetta, Mero, Leonato, Proteo, Quintilio Maio, Achille, Mr. Dido and Dodi, the opposite to Dido.

Fig. 3. "Il sogno di Achille" (The Archilles Dream), 1929.

In the land of True Friendship, says Savinio, names are confused, and a former enemy calls his current friend by his own name (. . .).[11] In other words, a man should look upon another man not as an enemy, but as himself, as the other "I", and interpersonal relations are the relations of "I" with the other potential "I". Savinio lays foundations of a new humanism and universal peace, and this is one of the reasons why Italian and European literature rediscovered him in the end of the 20th century in the context of new disturbing and frightening historical events. Lejeune believes that the pseudonym is the author's name, a name that is neither a secret nor a mystification; it is as authentic as the first. The pseudonym is rebirth. But when the young Andrea De Chirico appeared for the first time as Alberto Savinio, he opened the possibilities for other names as well, for different and new aspects of "I". The multiplication of narrators corresponds to the annulment of unity in narration. The polymorphous narrator, the masked narrator marks the escape from fixation to literature. Savinio believes that to fix a portrait of a person in narration would mean to condition that person. A character may be just outlined in order to enable the appearance of another character which corresponds to the transformed narrator. Narration means to focus on one moment, so his self-portraits dating from '27, '34, '36 and '46 are all different.[12]

Savinio's autobiography is writing fragments in which different aspects of narrative "I" are also changing. Autobiography for Savinio means writing it himself all his life. Special attention should be paid to the words, their origin, etymology, because they are at the same time an investigation of origin in general. To write means to investigate even the slips of tongue and of pen, according to Freud.

What is the status of death in the context of permanent writing out a life, "bios"? It is the place where, almost like in a fairy-tale, the narrator believes, the "I" will finally meet its ancestors, where he will meet his father whom he lost when he was a child, the place where he will "for the first time see my sister Adelaide who died six months before I was born, and maybe that is the 'physiological' reason why I constantly carry inside me the thought of death".[13] According to Savinio, death nullifies sin, grants absolution from evil and resolves the dualism of body and soul created by men. It is in fact a "familiar situation" for men, the only certain fact in their lives (both Savinio in *La nostra anima* and Giacomo Leopardi said that people are nothing but walking coffins)[14]. Mr. Münster, mature because of the determinant "Mister", does not conceal his metaphysical need for immortality. On the road from *Tragedy of Childhood* to discourses with Muse Clio, the landscape of the primeval forest is tamed to become a park! Cognition is transferred from without, implanted into Man, and this thesis Savinio has taken from Otto Weininger, who in his controversial psychology in the context of studying "human soul", investigated the following relations: will and value, individual and pure moral principle, man and God, mother and prostitute. Elements of Weininger's learning are evident in some fragments of Savinio's stories written in his youth: valuation of mother and prostitute, rejection of femininity that would lead the woman to a moral principle, her emancipation from the feminine and from what makes her a woman. But since God (along Nietzsche's lines) is dead, man's movement is marked by uncertainty. In his Paris period Savinio has already discovered Metaphysics together with his brother as the other Argonaut (they were also compared to Dioscuri). The artist-traveller had already set out on an anatomical investigation to discover the secret assemblies on the verbal and plastic level. The predecessors of this new sensibility, according to Savinio, were primarily Giordano Bruno, Tommaso Campanella and Giambattista Vico. An artist who has discovered the junction between the physical and the metaphysical is located on the other side of the logical, and objects around him become specific fetishes of new spirituality.

Savinio's wish is to reproduce the eternal idea which stands at the foundation of objects that surround him, and not their individuality. That is why he is riveted by architecture of the end of the 19th century, because of the possibility of citation. He is a poet of will (*der Wille*) who establishes categories of things which can be contemplated (everything that an idea can be derived from).

In Savinio's last book, *Mister Dido*, there is a dream about himself that Mister Dido would like to dream over and over again. The dream is fluid-like in which everything is merged and finally becomes authentic, similar to itself.[15] Mister Dido is convinced that there is continuity between the physical and the metaphysical and that there is no fracture.[16] Savinio gave him a double Mister Dodi on the track of Valery's and Michaux's experiment. Gusdorf's idea, according to which writing of an autobiography is the second, but this time more truthful reading of one's own existence, due to its synthetic nature, can be applied to Savinio's fragments of autobiographical discourse. They manage to shake the reader who nevertheless expects the customary self-cognition. Chronology either does not exist or is shifted, the beginning is not in the beginning: for example, the fragment "At the Bottom of the Sea" from the *Tragedy of Childhood* describes childbirth. And at the end of the opus, the question remains open whether it is truly the end when Mister Dodi, imitating Empedocles, wishes to disappear in the crater of Etna volcano; but there is no confirmation that it actually happened.

If the choice of literary genre is a characteristic of style, to choose autobiography means to select some sort of *super-ego* among literary genres! In Savinio the author, narrator and protagonist are in constant interaction and full of surprises. It is never certain when and how some little detail of the dynamic artist's life can be touched (like in billiards, Savinio's most favourite sport,[17] but is it really a sport, a game or a competition?). The author, narrator and protagonist in *Tragedy of Childhood* is the child, "I", a nameless Being; "I" in retrospection, because at that age the child still does not use this pronoun.

A specific comical relief occurs in the *Childhood of Nivasio Dolcemare* who writes his playful statements in experimental third person, in the period when the narrator could really use "I". Savinio uses the so-called thanatographical view, where the author's body appears to be detached from the *corps* (Derrida). It deconstructs the whole, fragments life (*bios*) and testifies about phases, sequences of life that problematize the whole, do not contribute to its establishment. There are different climates, cultures, languages, arts, characters and voices, views and gestures of women, men, children, close and remote. The author and narrator give up on the first person and choose the third person, like in children's speech. This is the author's and the autobiographical paradox of Alberto Savinio: he truly, as already mentioned by one of his best critics Sciascia, talks with his reader, and in a conversation, it is common knowledge, both parties participate. This paradoxical recourse will enable Savinio to tell even the continuity of the physical and the metaphysical by the assumed leap of Mister Dido into the crater of Etna, because it is fitted into the conversational procedure with the characters in the story, and through them, with the reader.

I would conclude that the status of the writer of this unusual autobiography could be compared to the status of the narrator of the first degree (according to Genette) of the collection of stories in the past, with the important difference that for the reader the challenge is not the action, the shift, reconstruction of events, the witty remark like in collections of stories, but the act of cognition of the fragmentized junction of the author, the narrator and the character, a junction which cannot operate any more like in a "traditional" autobiography. Collections of stories have lost their "framework" a long time ago and have been transformed in many other aspects. Nevertheless, one could say that fragments of Savinio's autobiography are framed by his entire artistic practice which reflects parts of a unique, ingenious "I" who is searching to reconstruct the *corsi e ricorsi* from his personal world: in his case the Greek period of childhood (a forest!), the years spent in Paris and in the Balkans in the First World War (the youth) and the maturity in Italy in the familiar context, writing, painting and collaborating to the theatre. Like many centuries before, the cataclysm of the plague threatened to destroy everything that the world had experienced and created. In Savinio's case, the cataclysm, first a family one and later worldwide, threatened to remove reconstructed fragments from the memory (his father's death, the First and then the Second World War), but they resisted thanks to their stylistic peculiarity, waiting to continue conversation with the person who would read, comprehend and try to reassemble the fragments of Savinio's intentionally scattered pages because they were written by one who explicitly liked dispersal.

NOTES AND REFERENCES

1. Andrea Francesco Alberto De Chirico was born 1891 in Athens as third child in the family of Italian engineers, originally from Sicily and the Genovese *nobildonna.* The father was employed in trail construction in Greece. The older brother Giorgio was born 1888 in Volos, Greece and the sister Adele died before Andrea's birth. The Italian *Dizionario Biografico degli Italiani* classifies both brothers under name 'De Chirico' Andrea De Chirico and Giorgio De Chirico: DBI, Vol. XXXIII (Rome: Istituto dell'Enciclopedia italiana, 1987), pp. 521-29 and 529-38.
   In the surreal paragraph *Una testa vola via* (from *Il signor Dido*, Milan: Adelphi, 1992, p. 50), a baroness Emma Testa di Cuvolo "reunited in her son love for the dead daughter as well. Riccardo became a double character: a man and a woman; a complete creature." The family which is often present in Salvio's writings lacks a brother. Nevertheless, he appears as Giorgio, Andrea's brother in *Trololò* in *Casa «la Vita»*, (Milan: Adelphi, 1988), pp. 183-98 and as "the brother painter" in whose house he encountered Berenice a couple of times, in the paragraph with the same name *Il signor Dido*, p. 85. See also Marié-José Tramuta, *Savinio et l'autre. Étapes d'une identification surmontée* in *Figures del'autre*, ed. Mariella Colin, "Cahiers de Littératures et civilisations romanes", 3, Italien, Presses Universitaires de Caen, 1995, pp. 107-119, that quotes a book of Mihaïl Dimitri Sturdza, *Grandes familles de Grèce, d'Albanie et de Constantinople* (Paris, 1983) who reconstructed the genealogic tree of De Chirico's family. The family came to Constantinople from the Republic and city of Dubrovnik, Ragusa in Dalmatia, in 17th century and its identity was Catholic and Italian.
2. See A. Savinio, *Sorte dell'Europa*, (Milan: Adelphi, 1977), p. 36. (the note was written on 1st August 1944)
   Leonardo Sciasca wrote that Nivasio Dolcemare, one of multiple Savinio's "I" had resolved the problem of internationalism, unity and brotherhood among nations.
3. *Tragedia dell'infanzia*, ed. della Cometa, (Rome, 1937; Torino: Einaudi, 1978); *Infanzia di Nivasio Dolcemare*, (Milan: Mondadori, 1941; Torino: Einaudi; 1973; Milan: Adelphi, 1998); *Hermaphrodito*, (Firenze: Libreria della Voce, 1918; Torino: Einaudi, 1974); *La casa ispirata*, (Lanciano: Carabba, 1925; Milan: Bompiani, 1953); *Achille innamorato*, (Firenze: Vallecchi, 1938; Milan: Adelphi, 1993).

4. See Philippe Lejeune, *Le pacte autobiographique,* (Paris: Seuil, 1975); *Autobiography in the Third Person*, «New Literary History», 9 (1977/78), pp. 27-50.
5. See J. Starobinski, "The Style of Autobiography", in *Autobiography,* ed. James Olney, (Princeton, N.J. 1980), pp. 73-83.
6. He died in Rome in the 1952. The mirror can also be a confirmation of solitude, as he writes in *Idolum patris* (1st ed. In «Illustrazione italiana», 6 July 1924; later a chapter of *Achille innamorato*, pp.48-9). The protagonist is searching for the traces of his father in the Hôtel du Helder in Paris, *ma trova soltanto il proprio spettro con gli occhiali che lo segue* (but finds only the own ghost with glasses who was following him).
7. See Giambattista Vico, *Principii di una scienza nuova intorno alla comune natura delle nazioni*, I ed. 1744 (Milan-Naples: Ricciardi, 1953); see also *The New Science of Giambattista Vico*, (Ithaca, NY: Cornell University Press, 1984). Nivasio (in *Infanzia di Nivasio Dolcemare*, pp. 63-4) tells a story about the way his first pun was created by "spontaneous genesis" similar to the metaphor of the first Vico's man: "(...) the first pun, that nonappreciated form, but form of geniality worthy of appreciation. Bitter-sweet compassion, he thought". A pun is, how he explains it, the most ingenious form of etymology, light projected in the interior of things and at the same time adversary of religions. Also (pp. 77-8) concerning a child's admiration of guns: "Although Nivasio is, as Giambattista Vico says in *Libro degli Elementi*, destined by nature 'to live in Plato's Republic and not to get himself into Romulo's mob', mystery of the firearms irresistibly fascinated him, like all those who possess manly qualities." It is a paraphrase of axiom VI from paragraph *Degli Elementi* (Savinio avoids using the expression «Romulo's scum»). In his later work *Dico a te, Clio* (1st ed. 1939; Milan: Adelphi, 1992) Savinio confirms: "Giambattista Vico was right. Etymological meaning reveals persistence of consciousness about origin in a man", p. 120.
8. 'Dido' in Italian is synonymous of female name Didone, Elissa (who is remembering), protagonist of Virgil's *Aeneis*, but also of melodrama *Didone abbandonata* by Pietro Metastasio. Elissa is one of the seven young girls from Boccaccio's *Decameron* narrating the stories.
9. A. Savinio, *Il fantasma di Freud, Sempre a caccia di verità in Opere. Scritti dispersi tra guerra e dopoguerra (1943-952)* a cura di Leonardo Sciascia e Franco De Maria (Milan: Bompiani, 1989), p. 1503.
10. Savino relates his book *Dico a te, Clio* with his *Tragedia dell'infanzia* (1st ed. 1920). He compares the first one to garden and the second one to forest. (p. 9) He simultaneously relates these two books also with food: the book about childhood can be compared to raw food, and the other one, about maturity, to cooked food.
11. See *Casa «La vita», Occhio n.8*, the eigth 'eye'. (there are in all nine 'eyes' in the book)
12. He was writer, painter, illustrator of books, musician, author in decorative arts and mosaics, designed costumes and theatre scenography. In *Tutta la vita* Savinio said: "Every name has a meaning of its own, a reason of its own, a "spirit" of its own. The name influences our character, determines our destiny, gives form to our life. It is a symbol and a distinguishing mark of a person

who carries it and imposing names on our own children when they do not yet have possibility to express their approval of the names given to them is abuse of power and a hideous act sometimes." He wrote: «I have so little trust in the magical force of the name and the second name that I have changed both my names» in *Opere. Scritti dispersi*, p. 31.

Savinio's wife, Maria Savinio (also their son, Ruggero, well known Italian painter, took the artistic name Savinio) wrote in her book of rememberings, *Con Savinio*, (Palermo: Sellerio, 1987), p. 37: The fame that Giorgio De Chirico won, influenced his brother Andrea to change his name into Alberto Savinio, to prevent any confusion. De Chirico /Giorgio, S.R./ says: "I was the one who found a pseudonym for him in Paris, when we decided to 'differ', by which he later became famous – Alberto Savinio. It would have been better if I had kept 'Savinio' for myself and left 'De Chirico' to him when I think how wrongly my name is pronounced abroad. In France, for example, they say 'Shiricò'.

The critic Marco Sabbatini believes that Savinio needed to liberate himself from his 'double', his brother so he chose the name Alberto, the same as Apollinaire's brother, because of a profound friendship and admiration towards that poet (Savinio and Apollinaire were connected by the same date of birth, 25 August). Cf. M. Sabbatini, *Alberto Savinio: anatomie d'un pseudonyme*, «Cahiers de la Faculté des Lettres», Genève, 1/1991, n. 4, pp. 29-32. Savinio mentions Apollinaire's brother Alberto di Kostrowitzki in the chapter «Apollinaire» (dated Milan, December 1934) in *Souvenirs*, (I ed. 1945; Palermo: Sellerio, 1989), p. 77.

Héctor Bianciotti quotes Savinio's friend Nino Frank, translator of *Tutta la vita* into French who testified that Andrea changed his name, *italianizzando* (making Italian) a name of Albert Savine, French translator of foreign literatures. Cf. Introduction in *Souvenirs*, pp. 12-13.

Adopting a pseudonym can be interpreted in different ways. If something is definite, as it is that Andrea De Chirico became Alberto Savinio, it is also definite that he did that so he could subsequently show faces that were always different and new, thus creating real and actual space of freedom, in clean opposition with Pirandello's unfortunate characters. Savinio spent his life trying to give plausible grounds for the pseudonym, in the sense that he was the author of so many different books, as one of his critics, Walter Pedullà, stated.

13. See *Casa «la Vita»*, p. 15.
14. See *La nostra anima*, p. 34 and Giacomo Leopardi, *Zibaldone de' pensieri*, 4149, (Milan: Newton Compton, 1997).
15. Savino, *Il signor Dido*, p. 66. As early as in his work *Infanzia di Nivasio Dolcemare* in the concluding fragment number 3 Savinio wrote that death is "supreme virginity", p. 163.
16. Ibid., p. 163.
17. See *Il biliardo a carambola*, in AA.VV. *Giuochi e sports*, I quaderni della Radio, V, (Rome: L Ed. Radio italiana, s.a.) pp. 135-38.

SWANTJE LICHTENSTEIN

Lyrical Autobiography: Life, Death and Self in Lyrical Poetry of Heiner Müller and Thomas Kling

Der Tod ist die Maske der Revolution.
Die Revolution ist die Maske des Todes.
(Heiner Müller: *Der Auftrag*)

I. POETRY AND AUTOBIOGRAPHY

The first addressee and destination of an autobiographical text *is* the writer or autobiographer, who *is* the text (in terms of theory of deconstruction). The autobiography lies *within* the readable text, like Nietzsche announces in *Ecce Homo*: "I tell my life to myself," as well as according to Paul de Man's illustrious words, "Autobiography (. . .) is not a genre or a mode, but a figure of reading or of understanding that occurs, to some degree, in all texts."[1] Hence, every text inherits an autobiographical gesture. In the textual system of autobiographical production of texts, the poet is also a placeholder of the *voice* in this text. The voice of the phenomenology, the voice of *hearing oneself speak*, affects the text, the autobiographer and the reader in one. If we listen to this voice, we read the signatures of readable texts close to the author and the reader. It seems there is no difference between author, reader and text. But how does a text or even an autobiography become readable? What do we share if we read a text? Or:

> But what, then, is a readable autobiography? Or rather, *whose* autobiography does one read when reading signatures and the text they sign? It now seems that what is problematic in the sentence 'any book with a readable title page is autobiographical' is less the difficulty of consenting to such an all-inclusive assertion than the difficulty of facing up to the way it

> upsets a basic certainty about the autobiographical work and its signature. By making it a function of readability, de Man does not so much dissociate autobiography from writing and the writer as place it *between* writer and reader, writing and reading. Thus the same gesture *both* allows one to assert that any text is more or less autobiographical *and* prevents a certain attribution of autobiography to reader or writer. Autobiography is an all-inclusive genre precisely to the extent that it remains impossible to conclude whose life is being written – or read.[2]

Thus, even when the text is intended to be autobiographical, it becomes "an all-inclusive genre" and acquires readability.

Lyrical texts are constituted through self-representation, more than other texts and narrations. Self-representation is a figure in itself in a lyrical text. Like the figure of *prosopoeia*, the mask of speech,[3] it is a model of the figurative way we read life or ourselves into a text. To listen to this voice of the text declares the text as intelligible and also as readable. Originally *prosopoeia* means the representation of an absent person as speaking, or of a deceased person as alive and present. The autobiographical text similarly shows the absence of the author, while the fiction of his presence lies in the text.

In lyrical poetry the principle of intelligibility depends therefore on the phenomenologization of the poetic voices. The affected subject of a lyrical text shows the autobiographical aspects of lyric poetry in terms of the implicit tension between the heightened subjectivity and the artificiality of this genre. If we regard a subject or a self as a figurative construction of language, we can say lyrical poetry increases the self- or auto-referentiality of this figuration as much as autobiography does. I start my discussion about autobiographical lyrical poetry from this point. I will observe the correlation of the autobiographical figuration in language in connection with this phenomenon of reference and referentiality of the self.

II. SELF, SUBJECT AND OBJECT

The traditional position of autobiographical writing is explained as:

> From its roots in the Augustinian notion (. . .), autobiography flourished because there seemed to be a 'self' to represent (. . .), a mimetic medium for self representation that guaranteed the epistemological correspondence between 'narrative' and 'lived life', a self-consciousness capable of discovering, uncovering, recapturing that hard core at the centre.[4]

If autobiography is deemed as self-reflection and the understanding of the subject, the self is no longer the term of explanation of the subject in a text. If an autobiographical writer breeds the subject in a text, then it is already given in scripture, and is simply reconstituted and supplemented.

The understanding of the past moments, in the present, is in itself a complex situation.[5] Then the self is a figure of fiction, because the self is, first and foremost, composed linguistically. The fiction is the referent of the self, related to the language. The subject of the speech, the face, the voice is figurated. This is not a natural, but a rhetorical operation.[6] The paper will show the connection between this rhetorical dimension of lyrical autobiographical texts, the self and the metaphor of life and death in poems of Heiner Müller and Thomas Kling. Both survey the presence of their foreseeable death similarly: as the question about subjectivity and self in lyrical texts in general.

III. LIFE AND DEATH (HEINER MÜLLER)

Heiner Müller's autobiography *Krieg ohne Schlacht. Leben in zwei Diktaturen* is a poem on the author himself. It includes the question and the answer of the "I" and the autobiography:

> Soll ich von mir reden Ich wer
> von wem ist die Rede wenn
> von mir die Rede geht Ich wer ist das[7]

Heiner Müller does not even use any punctuation marks. The reader is not able to keep track; therefore, all ways are open for him. This demonstrates the unfixed sense of these lines, and of all texts and the self. If the author is talking of himself, the question is: who is this "self", while he is talking about him? *Ich wer ist das* hints at the same time Arthur Rimbaud's idea of subjectivity *Je est un autre (I is an other)* and of Friedrich Nietzsche, who phrased it in *The Gay Science*: "You are always a different person."

The simplest 'methodological' description of autobiography within the code of current discourse says: the subject of autobiography takes itself as an object. Autobiography contains the identity of the same (thing / object), the iterability of the identification as the *auto* as much as the *bio[s]*, the life not only in biological terms.

The term *bio[s]* brings a scientific relation to the phantasm of objectivity, what is known as the ideal distance of the object. The opposable object of life would be death, or a thanatological, or in this case a thanatographical, text. Life, as an object or thing for the sciences, and the (re-) reading of the term *bio[s]*, incorporates the course of life. It is seen as a process and the unique psychic configuration that *is* the life and no other.[8] If this life / death *happens* as a performance in the text, could this give itself as an example of what it writes? Autobiography here constricts the distance between subject and object and it also opens up a new space, where death inaugurates life as well.[9] It also contains the incorporation of the difference and therefore of a coming together of subject and object. Heiner Müller demonstrates the life of a dissected body:

Im Spiegel mein zerschnittener Körper.
In der Mitte geteilt von der Operation,
die mein Leben gerettet.
Wozu
Frage ich mich beim Blick in den Spiegel.
Für ein Kind, eine Frau, ein Spätwerk.
Leben lernen mit der halben Maschine.
Atmen, essen. Verboten die Frage Wozu
Die zu leicht von den Lippen geht.
Der Tod
Ist das Einfache. Sterben kann ein Idiot.[10]

The fragmentation of the self, the *bio*logical side, separates the body in this lyrical text. Heiner Müller mirrors the new spaces, parts of this subject are already becoming an object. The self learns to live with a machine, learns to die while the text is writing about life: *Für ein Kind, eine Frau, ein Spätwerk* (*for a child, a women, late works*) or what life was thought for.

The following lyrics of Heiner Müller and Thomas Kling reflect on this performance between life and death in an autobiographical way. They *act as if* they were dead while not totally dead. This objectifying of the inner self meanwhile looks at the things and objects in a text also *as such*.

> To relate to an object *as such* means to relate to it as if you were dead. That's the condition of truth, the condition of perception, the condition of objectivity, at least in the most conventional sense.[11]

In the autobiographical pathogenesis of Heiner Müller's poem *HERZKRANZGEFÄSS* (*Coronary Vessel*) the "I" is talking to a "you", who is the "I" itself. Meanwhile it is listening to the voice of the other, the doctor, who is telling the truth about the end of his life. Via pictures on a film he can show *where* the dead is situated at the given present moment, which becomes the only future he has. It is the place of death. The self is called to see by himself the coming death. The lyrical voice declares this as "knowing where God lives". The whole poem of Heiner Müller shows the context:

HERZKRANZGEFÄSS

Der Arzt zeigt mir den Film DAS IST DIE STELLE
SIE SEHEN SELBST jetzt weißt du wo Gott wohnt
Asche der Traum von sieben Meisterwerken
Drei Treppen und die Sphinx zeigt ihre Kralle
Sei froh wenn der Infarkt dich kalt erwischt

Statt daß ein Krüppel mehr die Landschaft quert
Gewitter im Gehirn Blei in den Adern
Was du nicht wissen wolltest ZEIT IST FRIST
Die Bäume auf der Heimfahrt schamlos grün

21.8.1992[12]

For the lyrical "I", time is respite ("ZEIT IST FRIST"). He compares his decaying body to the "shameless green" trees he passes by on the way back home; the world is full of life whereas his own life is coming to an end. The cold, matter-of-fact speech of the doctor, full of medical jargon does not help matters. His words, better dead than a "cripple", are far from comforting.

The approaching death seems to be the evidence of life. The localisation of this is "DIE STELLE" (*point, area*); it is an image of the order of life compared to the death. The incommunicable agony, the mourning and the bereavement are now finding a way out of the body and the self. Through this objectifying of the body, Müller shows the visualisation of communication and their observation as a vivisection.

Another poem of Heiner Müller describes *die Trauer* (the sadness and mourning) of the doctors that they and their machines were not able to conquer the tumour. The tumour is again an objectified part of the subject, and the self is proud of this *Fleisch von meinem Fleisch* (flesh of my flesh):

ICH KAUE DIE KRANKENKOST DER TOD

Schmeckt durch
Nach der letzten
Endoskopie in den Augen der Ärzte
War mein Grab offen Beinahe rührte mich
Die Trauer der Experten und beinahe
War ich stolz auf meinen unbesiegbaren
Tumor
Einen Augenblick lang Fleische
Von meinem Fleisch

12.12.1995[13]

It is also the experience of the other in the self, the tumour *is* the pathos and it gives the self the essential distance to write about it and also makes it readable. The fear of pathos in the lyrical text shows the Being's fear of the end. It is not only an error of style. The fear of ontology makes the text capable of talking about oncology. The "I" becomes on objectified part of the subject.

Rhetorical lectures demonstrate the mechanism of the stratification of a text, where there are always referential constraints. So the connection between body, subject and text is not simply to distinguish one from another, even if we are talking about centrality and selfhood:

> The attributes of centrality and of selfhood are being exchanged in the medium of the language (. . .) [The self] can only persist as a self if it is displaced into the text that denies it. The self which was at first the center of the language as its empirical referent now becomes the language of the center as fiction, as metaphor of the self. What was originally a simple referential text now becomes a text of a text, the figure of a figure. The deconstruction of the self as a metaphor does not end in the rigorous separation of the two categories that allows for their mutual persistence at the expense of literal truth. By calling the subject a text, the text calls itself, to some extend, a subject.[14]

The body is a rhetorical figuration of the text in texts. The model of figuration gives life to them as *prosopoeia*, as giving a face and a voice. So, it is not the subject that bears the autobiography. Then the text is neither inside nor outside the subject, but it is, according to Barbara Johnson, both in one.[15]

IV. AUTOBIOGRAPHICAL EXAMINATIONS (THOMAS KLING)

Auswertung der Flugdaten (*Examination of the Flight Itinerary*) in 2005 by the poet, Thomas Kling, is also an autobiographical legacy of life and death. Kling re-writes the stages of his fatal disease. He describes writing through the noise of his breast as a song. The reiteration of the word "frantic" repeats the incommunicability of death. The stages of search and diagnosis come first. And again the self recognizes the continuation of the world around, while the self is getting used to the thought of not existing forever. Nature is timeless, the subject as an "I" is not. Müller's endoscopy in *Ich kaue die Krankenkost der Tod* and Kling's bronchoscopy in the following poem link the two poems.

> GESANG VON DER BRONCHOSKOPIE
>
> ARNIKABLÄUE
>
> so fran-
> st grafit das hochgebirge aus mir:
> den kopf, die abzählbaren kuppen.
>
> sonne strahlt arnika, trotzdem: frantic,
> reichlich alles. die im blauen kranz,
> herzkranz austobt sich, protuberanzen.

schraffuren erzeugend in blau –
yves-klein-pigment? sei's drum.
wenn diagnose steht ersma' – frantic.

wie man eintäufte in meine brust,
rumfuhrwerkte darin und loren proben
abtransportieren, nix von gemerkt - frantic.
. . .

jetzt ist es. jetzt wird ich:
zum schacht, zum *lungen-*
schacht wird ich.[16]

The writing of this "I" is all in present tense. It is now and not forever, *jetzt ist es. jetzt wird ich: / zum Schacht, zum lungen-/ schacht wird ich.* The present tense is becoming the only future the lyrical "I" is able to think about. The present tense is an autobiographical aspect of the subject.

The *Schacht* (*shaft*) of memory is Hegel's term for describing the commemoration and apperception and the capacity of remembering. For Hegel the memory is first a relationship with the word. Intelligence compiles the images of the view in time and space. Memory is, therefore, for Hegel, the unity of "I" and inwardness. This is called the *Schacht des Selbst* (shaft of self); the memory is lifted from there through the consciousness to the self. This memory is then emblematic.[17] Subjectivity allows productivity to grow. It is the power of "I" to hand it to the being. The part of this subject called "I" in this poem of Thomas Kling is the lung. The lungs are giving breath, conventionally symbol of life. Thomas Kling died of lung cancer. In this poem, his disease is an autobiographical notice of the "I" speaking in this text. Thomas Kling, as the lyrical author as well as the text, is becoming a fragment of his readability. The poem *Inhalator* imparts again the signature of breathing and not breathing to the text:

INHALATOR

anweise atemtelegramm. flatternd.
und wie von polarfuchs heiseres gebell,
das blauflatternde, geflatterte ventil, arnika-

blaue lüfte: das sehr zarte wölkchen
jeweils entlässt; aus emser salz ein wölkchen.
salzbarke, die in see sticht. um sofort

überzugehn in aufste auflösung. über-
gangslos hinflatternd, wie anweise polar-
fuchstelegramm gestossen. bei stiemendem fell

hervorgestossnes: atemmail, wie metal aim
gezähnte lüfte. so lautet inhalt, kurz hall-mail,
so inhaliert der dichter.[18]

The text is exhaling his words, talking of the closure of life and text. The text is still in transition. The presence of writing of the poet shows that he is inhaling yet, he has neither stopped writing nor breathing. It is memory as 'life death'.

> Memory, life death, is at the very least the simultaneous necessity and impossibility of the self-relation. It is necessary that it passes otherwise than phenomenally, eidetically, perceptually, ontologically, for these are the very motions which promise an ideal narcissism of return, closure and 'identification', the objective description of the idea. But it is impossible for it to do so. This is perhaps because – to speak diagnostically – the register of possibility and impossibility already belongs on those motions. To think life as the already dead, as if now surviving, as if a still life of all can be objectified (. . .) Like the proper name it survives already its own inception, leaps over from objectivity, and therefore from subjectivity, into a dimension whose most strictly formal quality is its lack of measure, its verse that goes around the object. No more can one write 'on' life.[19]

The mask of death is unveiled, the subjectivity and the memory of the autobiographical voice in Kling's poems also depends simply on the finitude of memory:

> But this finitude, which is also that of memory, does not at first take the form of a limit, of a limited ability, aptitude, or faculty, of a circumscribed power. Nor does it assume the form of a *limit* which would move us to multiply testamentary signs, traces (. . .), or autobiographical 'memoirs' No, this finitude can only take that form through the trace of other in us, the other irreducible presence; in other words simply the trace of the other in us, the finitude of memory, and thus the approach or memory of the future. If there is a finitude of memory, it is because there is something of the other, and of memory as a memory of the other, which comes from the other and comes back tc the other. It defies any totalisation, and directs us to a scene of allegory, to a fiction of prosopoeia that is, to tropologies of mourning: to the memory of mourning and to the mourning for memory.[20]

Instead of memory, in the present tense, the performance is a productive way to write and read the relationship between self and autobiography. Activated by different theories like speech-act-theory and gender theory, discussion about performance shifted the focus to experiential texts and bodies, and to the actual process of making and unmaking identities and their cultural signature.[21] Thomas Kling writes his autobiographical lyric *in statu nascendi*; selfhood is not solid, not even while facing death. It is the performance as the process of life and death. So, the process of death reflects the process of language as well as the ongoing course of life. Thomas Kling uses the metaphor of the breath, the non-solid gas of carbon dioxide that fills our lungs. The exhalation is not readable but you can listen to it while reading.

III. CONCLUSION

These examples of lyrical autobiography of Heiner Müller and Thomas Kling speak about life and death in terms of the dissected, diseased body. The *auto* and even the *bio[s]* in texts are connected to the writing and reading of the text. Paul de Man further notes:

> We must in short, consider our limbs, hands, toes, breasts (. . .) in themselves, severed from the organic unity of the body (. . .) We must, in other words, disarticulate, mutilate the body (. . .) To this dismemberment of the body correspondents a dismemberment of language, as meaning-producing tropes are replaced by fragmentation of sentences and proposition into discrete words, or the fragmentation of words in syllables or finally letters.[22]

Autobiographical lyrical poetry reflects this dismemberment of language and the rhetorical reading of the body in a text. The figuration of the language and the rhetorical lecture of lyrical poetry show us another way to talk about autobiographical texts, selfhood and subject.

NOTES AND REFERENCES

1. Paul de Man, "Autobiography as De-facement", in *The Rhetoric of Romanticism,* (New York: Columbia UP, 1984), p. 70.
2. Peggy Kamuf, *Signature Pieces: On the Institution of Authorship*, (Ithaca: Cornell UP, 1988), p. 124.
   Cf. Robert Smith, *Derrida and Autobiography*, (Cambridge: Cambridge UP, 1995) (Literature, culture, theory; 16).
3. Paul de Man, *The Rhetoric of Romanticism*, op. cit.
4. Sidonie Smith, "Resisting the Gaze of Embodiment: Women's Autobiography in the Nineteenth Century", in *Fea(s)ts of Memory. The Autobiographical Writings of American Women*, ed. Margo Culley, (Madison: Univ. of Wisconsin Press, 1992), p. 79.

5. Cf. Judith Butler, *Excitable Speech: A Politics of the Performative*, (New York/ London: Routledge, 1997), pp. 1- 41.
6. Bettine Menke, "Rhetorik und Referentialität bei de Man und Benjamin", in *Flaschenpost und Postkarte. Korrespondenzen zwischen kritischer Theorie und Poststrukturalismus*, ed. Sigrid Weigel, (Cologne: Boehlau, 1995), pp. 50-70.
7. Heiner Müller, *Krieg ohne Schlacht. Leben in zwei Diktaturen. Eine Autobiographie*, (Cologne: Kiepenheuer & Witsch, 1992).
8. Cf. Robert Smith, *Derrida and Autobiography*, op. cit., p. 133.
9. Jacques Derrida, *Of Grammatology*, (Baltimore: Johns Hopkins UP, 1976), p. 143.
10. Cf. Heiner Müller, in: Rolf Hochhuth: „Mein letztes Gespräch mit Heiner Müller“, in *Das Sonntagsblatt*, Nr. 3, 1996 (cf.: http://www.sonntagsblatt.de/ 1996/3/4-24.htm).
11. Jacques Derrida, *As if I were Dead / Als ob ich tod wäre*, ed. Ulrike O. Dinkelsbühler et al., (Vienna: Turia & Kant, 2000), p. 18.
12. Heiner Müller, *Ende der Handschrift*, (Frankfurt a. M.: Suhrkamp), p. 57.
13. Ibid., p. 96.
14. Paul de Man, "Rhetoric of Tropes (Nietzsche)", in *Allegories of Reading. Figural Language in Rousseau, Nietzsche, Rilke and Proust*, (New Haven/London: Yale UP, 1979), pp. 103-118, p. 111 ff. Cf. Anna Babka, *Unterbrochen: Gender und die Tropen der Autobiographie*, (Vienna: Passagen, 2002), pp. 77-83.
15. Barbara Johnson, *A World of Difference*, (Baltimore: Johns Hopkins UP, 1987), p. 6.
16. Thomas Kling, *Auswertung der Flugdaten*, (Cologne: Dumont, 2005), pp. 11-14.
17. G.W.F. Hegel, Enzyklopädie der Wissenschaften, in *Theorie-Werkausgabe*, ed. Eva Moldenhauer/Klaus Markus Michel, (Frankfurt a. M.: Suhrkamp, 1969), p. 13, p. 25 (§ 461).
18. Thomas Kling, *Auswertung der Flugdaten*, op. cit., p. 20.
19. Robert Smith, *Derrida and Autobiography*, op. cit., pp. 168-69.
20. Jacques Derrida, *Mémoires: For Paul de Man*, revised ed. and trans. C. Lindsay et al., (New York: Columbia UP, 1989), pp. 28-29.
21. Cf. Susanna Egan/Gabriele Helms, "Autobiography and Changing Identities: Introduction", in *Biography* 24 (1), 2001, p. XX.
22. Paul de Man, "Phenomenality and Materiality in Kant", in *Aesthetic Ideology*, (Minneapolis/London: Univ. of Minnesota Press, 1996), p. 88 ff.

KATHLEEN KERR-KOCH

Autobiography as Critique: De Man and the Realists

Within the human sciences there has emerged a certain degree of self-satisfaction amongst some critical practitioners who after four decades of seeing themselves suffer the performative machinations of scriptors and readers, feel vindicated in their opposition to the modernist and post-modernist critiques of authorship. In this context Sean Burke's book *Death and Return of the Author* was received as a breath of fresh air by a conservative establishment. Not all of the euphoria, however, stems from a wish to reinvoke the boundaries between literature and science, or literature and philosophy or witness the rebirth of a monumentalised European centre. Amongst those grateful for the opportunity to save the author from destruction are historically excluded subjectivities – racial, ethnic, gendered, sexual, class, migrant and diasporic identities largely absent from the memorialised frame of eighteenth and nineteenth century versions of the formation of the mind, especially in the self-writing or auto/biographies ascribed to so-called genius. In the interests of recognition, representation and inclusions, say these critics, it is crucial that autobiography and autobiographical criticism maintain the fact-fiction distinction and a connection with referentiality viewed as the truth of the present, or the truth of consciousness present to itself. According to this argument, autobiography loses its critical force if it forfeits a transparent connection with a real world.

What both conservatives and cultural revisionists are targeting, of course, is the powerful critique of the Hegelian-inspired epic of a temporally developing self-consciousness found, for example, in romantic autobiography. This form of critique involves an emphasis not so much on real time as on textual space, or the constellation of paratactically arranged 'montage of experiences' endowed with significance by 'a writing subject'. As Gerhard Richter puts it in his discussion of the work of Walter Benjamin,

> While the status traditionally accorded to the autobiographical performance names a chronological, hierarchically unfolding of the narrative of a life – on the order of what Adorno would call hypotaxis – (. . .) the space of these [paratactical] constellations can never be outside of temporality, time is here a trope that names not a linear unfolding of a vital trajectory (of the *bios, des Lebens*) but rather a "strange figure", that is a rhetorical form through which time is constructed in the moment of remembrance (*Eingedenken*). This strange figure of time is thus not the product of some natural life, the mimetic product of lived experience, but rather what emerges as the figural image of temporality in the scene of writing autobiography.[1]

From the point of view of realism, inasmuch as autobiography constructs a myth of self-completion wherein an authoritative (and authoritarian) kingdom of thought can reside, it is also a valuable source of human experience and valuable as a genre which can critically intervene and act on the brutality and violence of the modern world. But from a textually based deconstructive critical perspective, autobiography, along with the authoritative subject which it houses, lacks coherence as the borderline between subjective consciousness and textual (and mechanical) technologies is no longer straightforwardly discernable. That these two perspectives are not susceptible to a dialectical synthesis is clear: textually-based deconstructive readings radically eliminate the epistemological ground central to realism, while the force and urgency of real life experiences often demand transparency precluded by a textually-based orientation. This paper will present examples of both of these critical standpoints and suggest that, despite their difference, they are necessarily parallel critical operations.

M.H. Abrams, in his book *Natural Supernaturalism* promoted the view of Romantic life writings as paradigms of the fusion of the sensible and the intelligible through narratives of quest and self-discovery, which ultimately stand as witness to an apocalyptic and cyclical grand narrative of the fall, secularisation and final redemption and restoration. Anne Mellor, author of *Romanticism and Gender*, points out how Abrams uses Wordsworth's *Prelude* as a parable of individualism, conceived in masculine terms, and creates a template for understanding the linguistic conventions which could represent a viable self in literary autobiography.

The extent to which Abrams' reading of the romantic epic of (masculine) self-consciousness contributed to a discourse which functioned to keep the sensible wired to the intelligible in the interests of constructed truths became apparent with the advent of what came to be called deconstruction. Jacques Derrida pointed out, in his ground breaking essay 'Structure, Sign and Play in the Discourse of the Human Sciences', that central to the operations of western metaphysics was the opposition between the sensible and the intelligible. These operations had undergone an event which impinged directly on the dichotomy itself: the event occurred with a displacement of philosophical, scientific, political, economic and technical discourses, in other words, with a cultural decentering brought about by a new political/libidinal economy. Nietzsche's critique of metaphysics, Freud's critique of self presence and Heidegger's critique of onto-theology are all cited as contributors to this epistemologically ground-shattering event. Crucially, the centrality of the 'subject' presumed to be identical with itself and presumed to know was 'deconstructed'. Derrida reads this event into ethnology and the work of Claude Lévi-Strauss and uncovers an impasse in his analysis of the nature/culture dichotomy. Lévi-Strauss, on Derrida's reading, is forced to adjust his methodology, to disentangle the sacred connection between truth and method and become a *bricoleur,* or one who borrows concepts from the text of a ruined heritage. Lévi-Strauss himself describes *bricolage* as a *mythopoetic* approach which contrasts absolutely with a methodology directed towards creating linguistic totalities. Such a methodology is characteristic of 'engineers' who believe they are the originators of their own discourses constructed *ex nihilo.*

For Derrida, Lévi-Strauss's methodological shift is just one example, but an absolutely fundamental example, of a transformative event which displaced European culture and the history of its metaphysics, making it no longer possible to view Europe as the stable fixed centre of reference for all knowledge. Thus, the critique of metaphysics brought in its wake a new discipline of ethnography and the critique of ethnocentrism, that is the belief that a particular European ethnicity is naturally exemplary and therefore legitimately central. Just one consequence of this methodological shift, then, was that literary autobiography – especially its romanticist formulation as a genre attached to genius and endowed with an inner necessity which engenders the writing and ultimately, through the growth of individuality and self-consciousness, historical progress – became subject to a number of critiques. One very powerful critique can be found in the work of Paul de Man, for whom reading itself simultaneously establishes and undoes the autobiographical model.

The question of the autobiographical moment is central to de Man's attempts to read the shapes of self-reflexivity which are characteristic of French abstract knowledge and German romantic mysticism. Thus, it is in the trajectory that begins with Rousseau and ends with Nietzsche that the challenge to the distinction between these two cultural descriptions begins to shatter. For our own purposes, de Man's reading of Rousseau, the writer whose autobiography *Confessions* has been seen along with Goethe, Gibbon,

Cellini, Mill and Spencer's autobiographies as the embodiment and personification of the best of Western culture, will bring us closer to what de Man may have meant when he stated that,

> Autobiography is not a genre or a mode, but a figure of reading or of understanding that occurs to some degree in all texts. The autobiographical moment happens as an alignment between the two subjects involved in the process of reading in which they determine each other by mutual reflective substitution. The structure implies differentiation as well as similarity, since both depend on a substitutive exchange which constitutes the subject. This specular structure is interiorised in a text in which the author declares himself the subject of his own understanding, but this merely makes explicit the wider claim to scholarship that takes place whenever a text is stated to be by someone and assumed to be understandable to the extent that this is the case. Which amounts to saying that any book with a readable title page is, to some extent, autobiographical.[2]

He follows this with the contradictory claim that,

> But just as we seem to assert that all texts are autobigraphical, we should say that, by the same token, none of them is or can be. The difficulties of generic definition that affect the study of autobiography repeat an inherent instability that undoes the model as soon as it is established (. . .) The specular moment that is part of all understanding reveals the tropological structure that underlies all cognitions, including knowledge of the self. The interest of autobiography, then, is not that it reveals reliable self knowledge - it does not - but that it demonstrates in a striking way the impossibility of closure and of totalisation [that is the impossibility of coming into being] of all textual systems made up of tropological substitutions.[3]

For de Man, Rousseau is an important figure because, contrary to mainstream descriptions of his work which present him as a naturalist and primitivist, he represents both the promise of enlightened thought and its failure in the hands of experience, experience which is itself contoured by the empirical self's relation to Being. Rousseau therefore represents 'the crucial moment in the development of Western thought a turning point (. . .) in the history of Western consciousness.'[4] As Rosiek points out, "Rousseau's 'turn' consists in the recognition of the primacy of consciousness or, in other words, the interiorisation of Being as self-consciousness."[5] More than this, the history of philosophy, not to mention literary history, has been misrepresented because of the lack of proper attention to not only Rousseau's writing, but the way that his work is recovered by other writers that follow.

For de Man, contemporary criticism is largely anachronistic in that it has returned to and reified a problem that romantic poetry had from the beginning begun to leave behind. Criticism has to a large extent imposed a very modern scheme on to romantic texts, that of the enmity between an empirical and an ideal subject, which can be understood as a conflict between fiction and reality, or more broadly as an antagonism between an understanding available through literature and a (scientific) truth revealed through analytical philosophy. Critics who use this conflict as the basis of their reading of romantic texts inevitably reveal the very interested nature of their engagement with that text, and it is this problem that he always seeks to address initially. The conflict is a postromantic theme, one taken from twentieth century literature, not romantic poetry. Rousseau's primary importance is in his early portrayal of this modern conflict, but more than this, in his attempt to transcend the problems of the empirical self's relation to the fiction and the personal, ethical and political questions this focus entails.

In Rousseau he finds at times an empirical self in conflict with a fictional self, but at other times an empirical self that is entirely subsumed in the fiction, in other words, an empirical self that becomes one with a fictional or poetic self. It is through the medium of poetic language that the empirical self is thus subsumed. It is only 'when the light of sense goes out', or with the 'death' of the empirical self that the ontological relationship between the poetic particular and the totality of the work is given 'life', albeit temporarily, constantly subject to renewal in the continuance of the poetic. Transcendence occurs only in this flashing or alternating movement between death and life, between the empirical and the aesthetic selves preserved in the medium of poetic language.[6]

De Man's first lengthy reading of Rousseau first occurs in the 1960 essay *Structure Intentionelle de l'image romantique*, translated and slightly revised in *The Rhetoric of Romanticism* as 'The Intentional Structure of the Romantic Image'. Rousseau represents a more expansive understanding of imagery that is available in the eighteenth century and ultimately becomes subject to a reductiveness during the course of the nineteenth century. So in this essay de Man is interested in thinking through the history of Western literature by returning to the changes in the discourse about poetics and the correlative changes in imagery that occur in the eighteenth century. He conducts an initial analysis of what he describes as the 'paradoxical dialectic' of romanticism:

> An abundant imagery coinciding with an equally abundant quantity of natural objects, the theme of imagination linked closely to the theme of nature, such is the fundamental ambiguity that characterises the poetics

of romanticism. The tension between the two polarities never ceases to be problematic.[7]

The example given to illustrate this paradoxical dialectic comes from Hölderlin's *Brot und Wein.* He picks out stanza five to discuss the relationship between the empirical natural object and the poetic word, not based on equivalencies in essences or appearances but in the mode of origination: the 'authentic word fulfils its highest function in naming being as a presence.' On the other hand, it is also true to say that if the poetic word originates like a natural object – that is that its own history is identical with its own being – and that it originates out of itself, then 'existence and essence are identical' and they originate without the assistance of metaphor. De Man concludes that the birth of the poetic word would be the exclusion of all metaphor.[8] He explains just how this works in one of the Gauss seminars of 1967:

> [t]ranscendence means that the self has to get outside its own immanence, that it has to find another entity in which it can structure its own intentionality in such a manner that it can contemplate it as a total figure, instead of being caught up in the inevitable short-sightedness of lived desire. The intention takes on the pseudo-objective aspect of a total entity, centered on a point of origin and circumscribed by an outer limit. But this entity is never allowed to remain static and self-sufficient, like a natural object, or like the perfect artefact that exists for art's sake. For it has to transcend itself anew each time it has achieved a temporary totality in the never-ending process of preserving its autonomy as a self. This is symbolised, in part, by Rousseau's image of Galathea's statue coming to life, not as a part of 'this living universe' but in contradistinction to the static totality of nature.[9]

Contrary to what M.H. Abrams has declared:

> The intent of poetic language is certainly not directed toward empirical insight, nor is it transcendental in the sense that it leads to closer contact with being in general; its intent is ontological, that is, directed toward an awareness of its own particular being.[10]

De Man illustrates the point in a comparative analysis of three writers – one French, one German and one English – who were writing at the end of the eighteenth century. Excerpts from Saint-Preux's twenty-third letter to Julie in Rousseau's *La Nouvelle Heloise,* are read alongside excerpt's from Book VI of Wordsworth's *The Prelude* and Hölderlin's *Heimkunft.* What de Man describes in these texts is the tension between two contradictory types of imagery, between two types of nature, one 'earthly and material' and the other 'mental and celestial', which struggle, but eventually overcome the disturbing conflict and ascend to the mental and the celestial. It is the imagination that facilitates this ascension, but more importantly, it is only in leaving behind the sensuous world, rejecting entirely the exterior world, that 'consciousness can exist entirely by and for itself'. On this reading, the early romantics were in command of an insight that the later romantics and the 'moderns' lost:

> (. . .) literary history has generally labelled 'primitivist,' 'naturalistic,' or even pantheistic the first modern writers to have put into question, in the language of poetry, the ontological priority of the sensory object.[11]

'The Image of Rousseau in the Poetry of Hölderlin' seeks again to contribute to 'a historical definition of the concept of Romanticism'[12] in terms of an analysis of the relationship Hölderlin-Rousseau. Methodologically, this task would involve an identification and exegesis of passages in Hölderlin that unambiguously cite Rousseau, a reading of Rousseau in association with broader, overt and covert networks of themes (festival, wine, fruit, sleep and waking, forgetting and memory, water and voyage) and then a comparison between the interpretation this activity leads to and the historical Rousseau. However, the task of establishing a working methodology is complicated by various factors: contradictory and changing interpretations of the works of both, and a persistent distrust of Rousseau in the German camp which invades the thinking of others and 'disfigures' his work. Thus, the attempt to address a literary historical imperative is blocked by a 'much more profound resistance to a problematic whose importance far exceeds questions of literary history and evaluation', and it is to this 'obstacle to thought' that de Man turns his attention in his reading of Rousseau in Hölderlin.

Insight into this obstacle is found in Hölderlin's relation to Schiller: Schiller's dislike of Rousseau is linked to two orientations in his work, feeling and intellect, orientations that are laudable in themselves, but which, according to Schiller, in Rousseau's hands remain unsynthesised: This failure leads to the two very different orientations of the political writings and the fictional writings. Because of Hölderlin's admiration for Schiller, conventional interpretations of Hölderlin assume that Hölderlin seeks to recover Rousseau's failed energy by making him extinguish inner passion and intellect in order to allow for a transparent perception of creation. As we would expect, at this point, de Man queries whether

> [t]he juxtaposition of inwardness with historical action, of the imagination's reverie with institutionalised thought, a juxtaposition reflected in the confusing structure of Rousseau's oeuvre, constitutes a genuine dialectic or a contradiction, the unfolding of a polarity in the temporality of thought or a break pure and simple.[13]

In 'Madame de Stael and Jean-Jacques Rousseau', de Man indexes Rousseau as an implicit and explicit presence in all of Madame de Stael's work, both fictional and critical/political. De Man's reading is typically idiosyncratic in that he attends to not only the content of the work, but the movement of thought: there is an intuitive affinity between Rousseau and de Stael so profound that at times the two are indistinguishable, 'an alliance so intimate that it becomes impossible to say where the one begins and the other ends'.[14] The ground of this affinity is the seat of passion, but what struggles out of this overwhelming and self-annihilating passion is reflection. For both, the experience of passion entails suffering (for it is also the painful denial of the self), suffering, which if prolonged enough, ultimately enables the constitution of reflection. But the reflection thus constituted out of the duration of pain, cannot overcome the pain, just observe it. Reflection is ambivalently powerless and strong: it cannot act to transcend contingency, but from this inability to act decisively and universally it derives strength in the knowledge of the sheer chaos of the self born out of this space of difference.

On de Man's reading, this emergence of reflection from out of the duration of the contingencies of passion, which involves in the first movement an interchange or merging of subjectivities, is not de Stael's egotistical appropriation of Rousseau, but a motion entirely in keeping with certain other writers of the period in whom the very definition of Being (*Dasein*) is given in the substitution of subjectivities: Rousseau is as much de Stael as de Stael is Rousseau. At the level of the passions, de Stael enters Rousseau's world and in the experience she is subject to him, the inconstancy of his work that moves between enlightened thought and the eroticism of fiction. On the other hand, the establishment of reflection opens up a space of difference between the two, a space of literary creation which distinguishes between the two: for de Man, Madame de Stael's authentic self is constituted in the distance between herself and Rousseau in that space opened by reflection. This space of difference also establishes the difference between two different kinds of aesthetic experience: on de Stael's reading of Rousseau both she and Rousseau suffer with the inconstancy of the self in experience. It is the passionate duration of this suffering, the memory of this suffering that induces reflection, albeit entirely impotent. The memory of her passion yields the conclusion that Rousseau is an example of 'the soul possessed of sensibility'. On de Man's reading, this particular aesthetic experience is to be attributed to de Stael, but not Rousseau. The way the space of difference is articulated by Rousseau differs radically from de Stael.

As de Man explains in 'Hegel on the Sublime' this space of difference can be overcome substantially and positively, as it has been historically, by either law or religion. In this case, memory and judgement – the determination of value (good and evil) through memory, or the determination of limit (lawful and unlawful) through judgement, either through God or a through a subject onto which it has been displaced – enter the discourse.[15] And this is the case with Madame de Stael which for de Man determines her difference from Rousseau. In de Stael's fiction, duration is sustained through a commitment to suffering which cannot be overcome by reflection: it is because of this that she requires a morality of rights and duties in the concrete circumstances of existence to moderate contingency, motivate memory and hence the soul's duration. This, on de Man's reading, is a kind of martyrdom:

> To shift from self justification to self comprehension, reflection must be able to renounce not only the hope of overcoming pain, but even the hope of justifying itself by means of that pain, of making it serve self-glorification.[16]

But this is just one way to negotiate the space of difference, and de Man's reading of Rousseau indicates another orientation. In Rousseau's fiction, in contrast to Madame de Stael's, duration is motivated by an undirected meditation of thoughts or fancies, or reverie, which entails the relinquishment of the private self:

> Far from being an idealisation or a compensation, the fiction, by the intermediary of artistic creation, brings the private self closer to being.[17]

'Rousseau and the Transcendence of the Self' indexes the exemplary importance of Rousseau in de Man's thinking about not only romanticism and literary criticism in general, but in particular the status of the autobiographical self. What constitutes romanticism, for him, is the question of the relationship between an empirical self and a poetic self, a question that he finds explored in some depth in Rousseau, specifically in the early *Narcisse* and the later *Pygmalion*. Again he reiterates the movement of identification and difference with reflection that occurs in the close readers of Rousseau, and advocates this as a model for literary criticism. Like Boris Eichenbaum and the other Russian Formalists, and unlike the structuralists, he views method as an end rather than a tool of criticism 'an endless project that each of us has to begin all over again, each time in his own terms.'[18] This, then, is de Man's anti-theory theory, the model of resistance that he reads into all conceptual categories such as the sublime, transcendence, the self, romanticism and ultimately autobiographical criticism.

Reading such close readers of Rousseau as Madame de Stael, Hazlitt and the more contemporary Jean Starobinski indicates that a very specific relationship develops between Rousseau's readers and his language, which is based on what de Man reads as Rousseau's own experience of duplicity: 'between himself as an empirical subject and another entity who still bears his name but who appears in the works'[19]. For de Man, the distinction between an empirical self and the poetic self is crucial, and the history of misunderstandings of romanticism is based on confusion between the two. He reads in Rousseau the pre-romantic a consciousness of a doubling, which, despite the historical vilification and valorisation of the name Rousseau, cannot be understood in terms of good and evil. For de Man this doubling must be understood in terms of self-knowledge and self-deception.

The affect of this duplicity on the close readers of Rousseau is not confusion, as one might expect (Madame de Stael's work was 'an opaque muddle of erotic and moral confusion', but this was down to 'the relentless power of her own self deception and inconstancy'[20]), but critical insight. Readers as different as de Stael and William Hazlitt – the former being entirely sympathetic to, the latter being hostile to, the kind of interiority that Rousseau represents – at some point through the act of reading, become one with the poetic self and through this merging acquire critical insight into the imaginative source of self-awareness:

> Critical insight seems to occur at the moment when the consciousness of the reader and that of the writer merge to become a single Self that transcends the two empirical selves that confront each other. This encounter forces the reader to leave behind his own everyday self, as it exists at this particular moment of his history, to re-establish contact with the forgotten origin of the self, and to engage the degree of conformity he has maintained with this origin.[21]

De Man's reading of Jean Starobinski's reading of Rousseau is important because it is premised on the Starobinski's own prioritisation of the empirical self. His own epistemological orientation is repeated in his narrative of Rousseau: main themes and tensions in Rousseau's work are seen as signs of an intentionality the source of which is his consciousness, which Starobinski can access with correct interpretation. Thus, it is that he reads in Rousseau a flaw based on a *dedoublement*. Rousseau's move is between the representation of a purely objectified self that he imitates, but does not understand, and a self that is an entirely transparent consciousness capable of observation and interpretation. Starobinski then imposes this analysis of Rousseau's lack of reflective thought on his reading of Rousseau's place in eighteenth century theories of consciousness. Both Rousseau's naturalism and his claim to an unmediated contact with Being through pure feeling are without reflective components: there is a 'passive continuity' between the social and moral aspect of human needs; feeling linked with Being itself is prereflexive.

De Man's reading takes off from Starobinski's reading of the pre-reflexive nature of Rousseau's transparent consciousness. Starobinski's insight here occurs because of a particular blindness in his own critical process, that is in making reflection a necessary component of transparency, without considering that transparency might be linked with another activity of the mind called imagination, or what Rousseau calls fiction. On de Man's reading, the narrative function of fiction can perform both philosophical and literary operations: reconstruct the state of nature or the birth of language, facilitate confessions or the invention of worlds. But the priority of reflection in Starobinski's approach, in particular as regards its absence in Rousseau's 'uncritical' understanding of transparency, is due to a methodology which prioritises the empirical self over the fictional self: the empirical self precedes the poetic self and brings the poetic self into being for its own pragmatic purposes, be they protection or camouflage. From this perspective the empirical self is never really fully detached from the poetic self, never fully disinterested: the poetic self comes into being and exists for the empirical self. According to de Man, Starobinski's own methodology is deeply interested and his reading, therefore, not only confirms his view that Rousseau is a mystified thinker, but that

> [a]rt is a fetishistic, substitutive activity that replaces an unavowable desire by a pseudoinnocent but, in fact, even more self-indulgent gratification.[22]

The philosophical domain is again pre-eminent in a reading that sees the birth of the imagination as merely a pragmatic occurrence which serves the interests of the empirical self. This effectively eliminates the radicality of the double temporal perspective that de Man claims is in place.

De Man searches for another model for the birth of the imagination in the Rousseau *oeuvre* that might counter Starobinski's view of the psychological and pragmatic source of Rousseau's imagination. He looks for places where the interaction between the empirical and poetic self, or the author and the work are explored thematically. He chooses two texts — one a preface to an early play called *Narcisse*, the other a short lyrical scene called *Pygmalion* – which stand on either side of his most productive years, that is the years 1753 to 1762 when he produced *Social Contract, Emile*, and *Nouvelle Heloise*. For de Man, in these texts

> [w]e can capture (. . .) Rousseau's prospective as well as his retrospective meditation on his relationship to the fictional self that gets expressed in his work, and on the nature of the relationship that develops toward this self.[23]

Narcisse or *The Self-Admirer* was put on in Paris by his Majesty's Company of Comedians on December 18th, 1752, but it was not until 1753 that he wrote the *Preface*. The action of the play surrounds the weakness of Valentine, an extremely self-admiring man, and the collusion between two women – his sister Lucinda and her woman Martha – who decide to show up his vanity by draping a portrait of Valentine with female clothing. However, rather than recognising a disguised message, Valentine reads the portrait literally and proceeds to fall blindly in love with his own feminised image, and it takes the entire course of the action to bring Valentine to some realisation and reinvoke his love for his betrothed Angelica. De Man's interest in the play is that it introduces elements that will later figure in 'the complex dialectical relationships' of *Pygmalion*: 'the dialectic of self and other in the act of reflection, the dialectic of self-love and desire, the question of the ontological status of the reflected image',[24] through the relationship between Valentine and the portrait, which he describes as 'one of mutual mystification', is simple, functional and entirely interested, rather than aesthetic and capable of disinterested judgement. In the *Preface* to this play, written one year after the Paris production, Rousseau indicates that in a corrupt civilisation, any insight that philosophers and artists may gain into human nature is immediately forfeited by a self-isolation born out of self-love. In such circumstances art is produced in bad faith and the only reason to produce at all is to test whether or not one is party to 'some sublime geniuses who can penetrate beyond the veils that hide truth'. For de Man, in this,

> Rousseau clearly recognises that the authenticity of an aesthetic consciousness is defined by the ability of the self not to use the product of its aesthetic activity for its own gratification.[25]

De Man reads *Pygmalion* as an exploration of possible relationships between the artist and the work: in the first instance Pygmalion admires, in the second movement he admires, and in the third the relationship between Pygmalion and the work is one of sexual desire, and in the fourth, recovering from the shock of realising that what he believed to be worship was actually desire, Pygmalion lights on the true understanding of the relationship between empirical and poetic self that has some of the structure of sexual desire. Desire and aesthetic consciousness are similar in that both are movements toward something that is lost: '[t]he desire of an aesthetic consciousness is oriented toward authenticity, which is lost in the fallen world of empirical experience. It experiences this desire as a lack, as a shortcoming in itself, which it tries to remedy. What distinguishes sexual desire from the aesthetic consciousness is – as with de Stael who firms up a deficiency in an insecure self by sacrificing fiction for the stability of a private self masterable through memory and judgement – the error in believing that 'the possession of a particular person could be sufficient to fill a void that does not exist on an interpersonal but on an ontological level.[26]

From a theoretical point of view, De Man's work on Rousseau throws up several important issues: first, the duplicitous nature of texts in the world that must account for both an empirical self that experiences, and a private self that can only come into being through forgetting the empirical in the act of memorisation; secondly, that aesthetic consciousness understood as a positive relationship with the other that can then become an object of reflection is really a grounding based on an inability to face the void, the 'nothingness of being'; thirdly, that rhetoric serves not the interests of sublime transcendence, but materially disrupts or undoes the authority of metanarratives, a situation that philosophy has tried to remedy historically by introducing various strategies for domesticating them. The story of this domestication, however, is undone time and again by philosophers themselves who have been implicated in the undoing by their own use of language; fourthly, that the category of the aesthetic, so crucial to the project of passing from formal linguistic presuppositions or poetics to hermeneutic presuppositions, or from form to meaning, depend on the aesthetic to negotiate that passage.

From a practical point of view, De Man's reading of Rousseau highlights a fundamental dilemma in approaching the complexities of autobiography: On the one hand, there is a complicity between autobiography, viewed falsely as the shaping of a past which imposes a pattern on life through a coherent narrative of the an empirical/poetic self, and eighteenth and nineteenth century notions of characterology and racial hierarchy. This complicity demands a radical interrogation of the ground of the assumptions in play in the production and consumption of such a liminal form. On the other hand, such a radical interrogation of autobiography would have to take place by ignoring or bracketing another aspect of eighteenth century thought: that is the extent to which the writing of autobiography as the projection of a life onto the world also came to function as a counter to a racialised aesthetic ideology. When, for example, Thomas Jefferson in his *Notes on the State of Virginia* expressed a concern for what he perceived as the aesthetically inferior properties of black bodies which were linked to an intellectual and spiritual vacancy born out of an inability to sublimate sensuous desire, what was at issue was the potential ability of certain races to advance civilisation, the measure of which would be their track record in the arts and sciences, defined by universal European standards. In eighteenth century discourse, the Negro race in particular is seen as incapable of contributing effectively to the intellectual progress of civilisation, though there are plenty of examples, despite their enslaved condition, of black people writing their race into the developing concept of nation with autobiography. Slave narratives, a crucial resource for white abolitionists, were later claimed to be the most uniquely

American autobiographical writing', created *sui generis* by the conditions of a racially and politically divided country. In this the materially real conditions of enslavement have been central to a history of Black American resistance and its individual and collective expression in life writing.

The critical force of slave narratives finds a modern equivalent in the genre of *testimonio* or oral autobiography which is emerging in areas of the postcolonial world which are riven through with violence, abject poverty and oppression. In India, for example, the work of Mahasweta Devi, far from focussing on the complexities and ultimate impossibility of self-production, which are the concerns of a privileged educated European class, gives voice to the real world experiences of individuals in tribal communities who have old and deeply imbedded traditions, but which have nevertheless paid the price of independence with their bodies and souls under, among other things, a relentless process of dehumanisation disseminated through the bonded labour system. These oral autobiographies speak out to the world with sincerity and urgency though they are necessarily written through the imaginative framework of a narrator.

Oral autobiographies have also become embroiled in the culture wars which have erupted between broadly postmodernist approaches (a category into which de Man's thinking has often wrongly been placed) and the realists who make it an imperative to maintain the connection between life and letters. A case in point is that of Rigoberta Menchu whose *testimonio, I Rigoberta Menchu: An Indian Woman in Guatemala* (1983) not only won her the Nobel Peace Prize in 1992 for its urgent portrayal of the oppressive and violent conditions that individuals like Rigoberta herself were enduring, but sparked off a venomous critical debate when it was revealed that she had not been a witness to some of the events represented in the book as her own experience. Menchu's defenders claimed that she was merely a scriptor, that her words represented the experiences of the community, while others, like the anthropologist David Stoll (who brought the discrepancies in the narrative to light) argued that those subalterns who write testimonies have an ethical duty to make sure that what they say is absolutely verifiable. In his book *Rigoberta Menchu and the Story of All Poor Guatemalans,* Stoll asserts that,

> [w]hen a person becomes a symbol for a cause, the complexity of a particular life is concealed in order to turn it into a representative life. So is the complexity of the situation represented. Sooner or later, in one form or another, what the legend conceals will force its way back into our attention. The contradictions glossed over by a heroic figure will not go away because we wish to ignore them'.[27]

One is reminded here of De Man's critique of Starobinski's reading of Rousseau and his insight that transparency is linked to imagination and fiction and, perhaps most importantly, that 'fiction can perform both philosophical and literary operations: reconstruct the state of nature or the birth of language as well as, facilitate confessions or the invention of worlds.'

NOTES AND REFERENCES

1. Gerhard Richter, *Walter Benjamin and the Corpus of Autobiography*, (Detroit: Wayne State University Press, 2000), p. 49.
2. Paul De Man, "Autobiography as Displacement", in *The Rhetoric of Romanticism*, (New York: Columbia University Press, 1984), p. 70.
3. Ibid., p. 70.
4. De Man, "The Image of Rousseau in the Poetry of Hölderlin", op. cit., pp. 38-40.
5. Jan Rosiek, *Figures of Failure: Paul de Man's Criticism 1953-1970*, (Aarhus: Aarhus University Press, 1992), p. 93.
6. De Man, "Patterns of Temporality in Hölderlin's 'Wie wenn am Feiertage…'", in *Romanticism and Contemporary Criticism: the Gauss Seminar and Other Papers*, ed. E.S. Burt, Kevin Newmark, Andrzej Warminski, (Baltimore and London: John Hopkins University Press, 1993), p. 64.
7. De Man, "Intentional Structure of the Romantic Image", in *The Rhetoric of Romanticism*, op. cit., p. 2.
8. Ibid., pp. 3-4.
9. De Man, "Patterns of Temporality in Hölderlin's 'Wie wenn am Feiertage...'", in *Romanticism and Contemporary Criticism: The Gauss Seminar and Other Papers,* op. cit., p. 52.
10. Ibid., p. 55.
11. De Man, "Intentional Structure of the Romantic Image", in *The Rhetoric of Romanticism*, op. cit., p. 16.
12. De Man, "Image of Rousseau in Hölderlin", op. cit., p. 20.
13. Ibid., p. 23.
14. De Man, "Madame de Staël and Jean Jacques Rousseau", in *Critical Writings 1953-1978*, ed. Lindsay Waters, (Minneapolis: University of Minnesota Press, 1989), p. 172.
15. De Man, "Hegel on the Sublime", in *Aesthetic Ideology*, ed. Andrzej Warminski, (Minneapolis: University of Minnesota Press, 1996), pp. 105-118.
16. De Man, "Madame de Staël and Jean Jacques Rousseau", in *Critical Writings 1953-1978*, op. cit., p. 177.
17. Ibid., p. 178.
18. De Man, "Rousseau and the Transcendence of the Self", in *Romanticism and Contemporary Criticism: The Gauss Seminar and Other Papers,* op. cit., pp. 32-33.
19. Ibid., p. 33.

20. Ibid., p. 28.
21. Ibid., p. 31.
22. Ibid., pp. 37-38.
23. Ibid., p. 40.
24. Ibid., p. 41.
25. Ibid., p. 42.
26. Ibid., p. 45.
27. David Stoll, *Rigoberto Menchú and the Story of All Poor Guatemalans*, (Boulder/Colorado: Westview Press, 1999), p. xi.

AMY WAI-SUM LEE

The "I", "Tibuta" and the "Black Witch" in Maryse Condé's Postcolonial-Feminist-Fictional-Auto/Biographical Song

Perhaps it is a little strange to start a discussion of the development in autobiography after the death of the author by giving information about another author, the author of this paper. But as I believe very much that the death of the single authorial voice also coincides with the birth of a diversity of different voices, my own introduction will sit comfortably within the boundary of relevance in this discussion. To talk about myself is never simply a question of passing on information about my person, but a matter of handing out a network of facts and relationships, origins and progress, sense of belonging and moments of aloneness. I teach at the Arts Faculty of Hong Kong Baptist University. I am not an anthropologist, nor am I an expert on autobiographical research. I am just an average person with an interest in personal stories, and this interest serves me very well in my teaching. Arts and Humanities are not taught through transmission of information from one end to another. For me, it is getting to know my students, talking to them and listening to them. In this process of communication, inevitably, I am also imparting information about myself, my family, my teachers, my friends, even my dogs. As I am telling the stories of literary texts to my students, I am also telling the story of my own discovery of these texts, the story of my own growth, and the story of my dreams. We communicate in stories: voice within voice within voice.

I am certainly not alone in my commitment to stories. The urge to tell one's own story has been as old as time itself. At the time when I saw and responded to this call for papers, Hong Kong director Wong Kar-Wai[1] had just released his belaboured film, *2046*,[2] which took five years, a lot of money, and a lot of reshaping and rescheduling to make. The number 2046 has a special meaning for the people of Hong Kong, as it would mark the 50th anniversary of the 1997 handover from the British government to the Mainland Chinese government,[3] a historic moment for Hong Kong which changed its identity, from being a British colony to a SAR (Special Administrative Region) of China, overnight. Although the Basic Law[4] guarantees that the economic system and all those features leading to Hong Kong's success as a financial centre will not be changed for 50 years,[5] there were still a lot of worries and anxieties about this change of status of the city. This sense of uncertainty manifested itself in the city's cultural scene beginning from the early 1980s, when the British government started to talk about the future of Hong Kong with the Mainland Chinese government. Locally produced drama, publications of local histories, and memoirs of famous citizens who have had an impact in shaping Hong Kong overwhelmed Hong Kong society.[6]

Now, several years after the handover, the fear of a sea change in daily life being over, people have gone back to the "usual" mode of day-to-day existence. The focus of public attention has largely shifted to criticizing and commenting on the performance of the new SAR government, especially on its efforts to maintain Hong Kong's economic competitiveness. The overwhelming urge, before the handover, to generate stories and to recall forgotten histories has subsided. And with this ebbing interest, the personal, the really private areas of individuals seem to have gone out of the picture after the Great Event has passed. Wong's film *2046* seems to be a reminder of this seven-year amnesia, of the existence of the personal, the narrative of the day-to-day existence, the individual human worries and the fears, no matter what is happening outside in industry, in politics, and in the money market.

2046 is an independent story by itself, but the narrative and the stories of some characters are also a continuation of Wong's previous work *In the Mood For Love* (2000).[7] As with Wong's other creations, the characters indulge themselves in repeating the same stories again and again; sometimes one character will be telling the story of another character as if it were his/her own story. In this film, one of the recurring images is a character pushing his/her head into a huge gramophone, whispering a personal story that no one is present to hear. But these secret personal stories have to be told, and be told to *an audience*, making the telling a *performance*. This meticulously made film in postcolonial Hong Kong illustrates for me interesting things about the telling of one's story. (i) Telling one's own story is never just one's *own* story isolated from threads of other people's lives, but always already an intertextual enterprise drawing information, supportive or contradictory, from other equally personal and complicit narratives. (ii) The autobiographical act is always performative, and with the intertextual and interpersonal nature of each of these personal stories, the audience is never simply a passive bystander.

(iii) Finally, the autobiographical act has already spread beyond the medium of the speaking voice, and has manifested itself in more and more complicated mediums: written words, songs, images, and cyberspace.[8]

Having given such a long preamble of how story-telling has a special connection with individuals who have a postcolonial background, I would like to move to the main discussion. The title of my paper is *The "I", the "Tituba" and the "Black Witch" in Maryse Condé's Postcolonial-Feminist-Fictional-Auto/Biographical Song*, a rather clumsy and roundabout way of expressing what Maryse Condé, the author, has done most economically, wittily but powerfully in her 1986 novel, (translated into English in 1992) entitled *I, Tituba, Black Witch in Salem*. In this article, I would like to examine Maryse Condé's novel as an example of a complex performance of autobiographical gestures. Although the book has been sold as fiction, the title, the settings, the protagonist chosen, as well as the author's introduction of the book have all cooperated to give a more complex identity to the narrative. Maryse Condé has made no secret about her personal investment in the figure of Tituba and how her rendering of Tituba's story has a particular relevance not only to herself, but to people of the postcolonial cultural situation. In the course of unfolding the unknown story of Tituba, the author has also drawn from fact and fiction, culture and history, to give footholds to different voices and identities in this multi-facet personal narrative space. In its entirety, the narrative told by the now deceased Tituba, supposedly fresh from the grave, and through the mouth of a twentieth century postcolonial feminist writer, has not only broken a few rules of the genre of autobiography, but has also enriched our understanding of this flexible literary text.

Philippe Lejeune, in his attempts to found principles in the genre of autobiography, proposes to see the unity between the author, the narrator and the protagonist as a basic requirement of an autobiography. Measured by this yardstick, Condé's book definitely does not qualify to be an autobiography: On the cover of the book, we have a late twentieth century female Caribbean writer's name, which does not match with the first person reference of the title. Inside the cover, we are faced with the first person narrator who claims that she was born in the 17th century, and that she will continue to tell us the story of her life. The representation of how this complex narrative comes into existence, however, promises that there is more to it than just a piece of fiction. The voice of the author and the voice of the narrator, seemingly two distinct entities from two different historical and cultural backgrounds, come together in this text to challenge conventional understandings of authority in voices.

Before the preface/story proper starts, we have a signed personal note from the author: "Tituba and I lived for a year on the closest of terms.

During our endless conversation she told me things she had confided to nobody else." Now here we have a unity between the voice of this narrator and the name printed on the cover of the book. The author is making a statement and is adding weight to the statement by signing her name. This statement, again, if believed, should give the story a status of being "real" which means that what has been recorded has really taken place. Not only that, but the name Tituba is a "real" name in the sense that she was a historical figure which had a real existence in New England during the 17th century and was involved in an event which had left a copious historical record. The puzzling aspect is that Tituba was accused of being a witch in the Salem witch trials, and that was more than 300 years ago. How can a living writer tell a story with first-hand information from someone who died 300 years ago?

Putting aside the fantastic detail of the informant's date of birth, then, in one sense, this text can be seen as a biography, for here is a real author writing another person's life with the help of exclusive information from this other person. But when we arrive at the content proper of the text, what we see is a different matter.

> Abena, my mother, was raped by an English sailor on the deck of *Christ the King* one day in the year 16** while the ship was sailing for Barbados. I was born from this act of aggression, from this act of hatred and contempt.[9]

It is a first-person narrative by the protagonist herself, of her life, starting very properly in the tradition of an autobiography, with her ancestors, in this case her mother, even beginning with her mother's name and not her own name. This shift in the narrative voice, and yet displacement of the self by the name of the mother complicates the issue of the identity of the text. While the author's note to assure us of her exclusive information prepares us for a detailed informative piece of another woman's life, the assumption of the first person narrative voice seems to deliberately confuse us concerning the validity and authenticity of the information. Usually with a biography, the biographer, for the sake of authenticity and objectivity, will research the protagonist to fill in the missing gaps or to confirm what is being told by the protagonist herself. But using the first person narrator's voice here, this attempt to be objective seems to play no part.

Yet even when we make allowances and view the text as an autobiography with a shifted voice, or a biography with too little a distance between the author and the protagonist to allow objectivity, the unfolding of this life continues to surprise the readers. Tituba survived the witch trials, and was released when a Jew, Benjamin Cohen d'Azevedo, came to the prison to pay off her debts when the magistrate of the town of Salem decided that the drama of the witch hunt had gone on for long enough. The end of the big historical event, the Salem witch trials, however, is not the end of her colourful narrative. She lived on to have other adventures and experiences. She went to live with the Jew and almost became a Jew herself; she met rebel groups and was somehow involved in their revolutionary campaigns. She was finally arrested with the rebels and it was then that she was sentenced to death. In the narrative, Tituba herself commented: "I was the last to be taken to the gallows. All around me strange trees were bristling with strange fruit."[10] This "last statement" given by the protagonist in her own voice is somewhat strange because it is the very last moment of her life and one can hardly imagine Tituba lining up for the gallows and writing this at the same time. The intervention of a biographer in this case seems to be necessary and functional.

But more surprises follow. The hanging of Tituba with the group of rebels is not the last event recorded in the narrative, and not the last we hear of her voice. After the hanging scene, there is an epilogue to the narrative, and it starts with: "And that is the story of my life. Such a bitter, bitter story. My real story starts where this one leaves off and it has no end."[11] Although it is not clearly spelt out, we have reason to believe that it is still the voice of the protagonist Tituba, speaking in her post-mortem status. This statement alone overthrows what we have in mind concerning the autobiography and the biography, and leaves us wondering how to read the text, even when the protagonist has already died and the story is coming to an end. Here, the protagonist, for reasons not explained, was still there, summarizing the story of her life, and even commenting on the nature of her life, as if she stood apart from it. What is more disturbing is perhaps the expression "my real story starts (. . .)"[12] because it seems to suggest that what has happened before is not the real story at all. Imagine the readers reaching the end of the narrative, expecting to find a conclusion or a closure, but see that the protagonist herself has totally rejected what she has been telling us before in the previous narrative.

And what about this "real story"? The only thing that we know at this point is that it has no end. But this real story is the real *life* story of the protagonist. There might be different reasons why a life story has no ending; maybe the protagonist is still telling his/her own story, maybe he/she has died before the proper ending of the story, or it may be a deliberate authorial choice made by the protagonist who is also the author. Or, more uncanny, the story has no end simply because the life of the protagonist can be infinitely prolonged, that he/she will not die; or that the dead manage to speak from the grave. What reason did she give about her story having no end? During her partnership with the rebel Christopher, she had envied him for having a song which recorded his merits and made him "immortal" among the people. But now after her death, she was pleasantly surprised to find that "there *is* a song about Tituba!" too.[13] Having a song to her name is important because it is a record of her life, and the nature of a song can spread across geographical, cultural, age, gender, and other spaces. Its power to spread is even greater than words on paper. And now, her physical stage of life finished, she found her fulfilment in the alternative status of this song.

The song, carrying Tituba's name and life, is not only a righting of the wrongs done to her in the past – her forced anonymity and even deliberate obliteration of her history and her country. The fact that she now has a song to her name means to her a new level of existence because it is a recognition of her gifts. The introduction of a song as record of her life is another transgressive feature in this basically patriarchal form – the song is a fluid and shapeless mode of existence. Moreover, as suggested in Alice Walker's essay, "In Search of Our Mothers' Gardens", the *notion of a song* carries the weight of the unrecognized gifts/genius of the black women ancestors, such as Phillis Wheatley:

> [a] woman who still struggled to sing the song that was your gift, although in a land of barbarians who praised you for your bewildered tongue. It is not so much what you sang, as that you kept alive, in so many of our ancestor, the notion of song.[14]

Seen in this way, the song is essentially the medium of the oppressed, for it goes beyond the requirement for education and is not limited to a special class, age, gender, religion, or politically affiliation. It is a good symbol not only of black women's genius, but of a very individual kind of genius as stated by Alice Walker in response to Virginia Woolf's early 20th century essay, and challenges the conventional authority of the written word and the book of life written by educated people.

Towards the end of the narrative, Tituba's voice comments that "Yes, I'm happy now. I can understand the past, read the present, and look into the future."[15] The "spirit" of Tituba, now free of physical and temporal restrictions, has finally come to herself by transgressing all those barriers which have stopped her before. Although she has aborted her own baby at one point of her life, thus leaving no biological inheritance, the end of her own first-person narrative is a note of positive confirmation and a sense of continuation. She has "adopted" a girl called Samantha, who:

> has learned to recognize my presence in the twitching of an animal's coat, the crackling of a fire between four stones, the rainbow-hued babbling

of the river, and the sound of the wind as it whistles through the great trees on the hills.[16]

Ending the personal narrative with the girl and her instinctual recognition of the spirit Tituba has become, projects a sense of continuation of her own existence into the next generations. Tituba holds this power because she is now bodiless, and has merged with the elements of the natural world such as the water, the sky and the fire.

The women's bond in this narrative is another feature which complicates the nature of the first-person narrative. The narrative starts with the name of the protagonist's mother, and ends with the name of her adopted daughter – in-between is the protagonist's life and her encounters with various personalities which form this life she is retelling. Her life is structured by the various liaisons she makes with different women: Mama Yaya, who became her first surrogate mother, Judah White who taught her about different herbs, Hester Prynne who was a fellow victim in her days of imprisonment, but who liberated her from the confinement of silence. In Tituba's experiences, the woman-woman bond has served her as a source of power and liberation in the suffocating puritanical regime in Salem village. And this new form of power comes from the discovery/invention of a new type of language, not the language of the patriarchal puritans, which identifies with one strict god, which denounces all pleasures and enjoyment from life.

Instead, this new language is consistently associated with the women in the narrative. Abena was hanged when Tituba was still very young, because she attacked a white man in self-defence. Her last recorded words, however, are "The cutlass! Give me the cutlass!"[17] This is a call for a weapon of self-defence, because she refused to be insulted or treated as a sexual object any more. Witnessing her mother's hanging has planted in Tituba "a feeling that was never to leave me, a mixture of terror and mourning".[18] This primary loss, and the terror stimulated by the loss, shapes Tituba's life and how she deals with it. Her next refuge, a Nago whose name was Mama Yaya, showed her the "tradition of solidarity among slaves"[19] and not only took care of her, but initiated her into the language of nature by teaching her the qualities of the herbs, the sea, the mountains, and the hills. Finally she initiated Tituba into "the upper spheres of knowledge",[20] which opened the door that connected the living world and the world beyond. This knowledge of the natural world functions like a language which pierces the barrier between the human world and the natural world, bringing her across the barriers of ignorance. By the time Mama Yaya's body followed the law of nature, Tituba had already mastered this route of communication between this world and beyond, and did not cry for her death.

Tituba's encounter with Hester in prison is as important to her life as it is in the nature of the narrative. Hester Prynne is a character in Nathaniel Hawthorne's novel of 17th century New England society.[21] She had to wear the scarlet letter *A* on her breast as a mark of her being an adulterer while her partner in sin was sheltered from disclosure. Although she was white, and did not share Tituba's multiple oppressions; her sexuality was made the cause of her exile from human community, and she had to bear the consequence of her passion alone. While a lot had been prepared at the beginning of the narrative to ensure readers' acceptance that Tituba is a real historical personality, and that the information included in this narrative is of high authenticity because it is exclusive, the arrangement for Tituba to meet Hester and to establish an ambiguous female-female relationship with her complicates the nature of the narrative by questioning what the narrative itself seems to be trying to do at the beginning.

While it may be possible to distinguish between "real life" characters such as Samuel Parris, Sarah Osborne, John Willard, John Proctor and Tituba who are actual historical figures whose presence and participation in the Salem witch hunt had been officially documented,[22] and probably imaginary characters such as Mama Yaya, and Yao (Abena's husband) and the Jewish family headed by Benjamin, Hester's presence in the first-person narrative of Tituba makes the textual space complicated. Although it is easy to dismiss Hester as just another fictional character, her fictionality is slightly different from the others. Hester has the "reality" of a fictional text on her back, and she has the symbolic identity of a white woman whose sexuality has been silenced and punished by patriarchal society. Her story has gone down in literary history and has become part of a tradition – in feminist perspective, an oppressed figure who cannot tell her own story.

Hester's voice here is not only a textual rescue of a character who had not received fair treatment in another context. Her presence and interaction with Tituba in this text may be seen as a self-reflexive gesture to draw our attention to the creative nature of the text itself. While the textual Tituba in Condé's writing laments that there was only a sentence or two in some official document to give her historical presence, such as "Tituba, a slave originating from the West Indies and probably practicing 'hoodoo'",[23] and regretted that she had not played a more active role in the witch trials, Hester's presence here shows how the "reality" of her life is actually constructed by a "story", which she turns around for her own purpose in this present text. Instead of bearing the shame quietly and giving birth to an illegitimate child (a girl called Pearl in Hawthorne's 1850 novel) outside of her wedlock, Hester made a statement by planning and executing the death of her own baby. Yet this is not simply a description of a cruel mother. With our knowledge of Hester's fictional history, her actions here take on meaning from the previous self we know of her. Hester becomes "real" because we have all read her story, told in fiction by another author.

Tituba's post-Salem life is also a complex textual space where different levels of realities and fictionalities meet. Benjamin the Jewish merchant, who came to pay off her debts to the prison and brought her home, represents the universally homeless people who do not have a country to their name. Tituba may or may not have met a Jew in her free life, but the inclusion of a Jew here gives the chance to a homeless individual to voice his conditions and his feelings about his homelessness. For the author of this narrative, the Jewish character may be just a chance encounter at the time of the writing of the book, but it may equally be a reality for many readers who share similar memories and stories in their own cultures. After the episode with Benjamin, the Jew, Tituba's involvement with the rebels who finally led to her death for the cause also takes Tituba's life out of the 17th century which is the historical time-frame of her existence. This "I" who was telling her personal story is more than just Tituba, the black female slave condemned to be a witch, but a politically conscious person who was willing to make a point even if that put her life in risk.

What does this complicated text say about authorship in autobiography? This text itself, which is certainly not an autobiography in the most conventional understanding of the term, nor a totally fictional text, lies somewhere in the mysterious unknown between the two fuzzy genres. What this ambiguous status seems to be doing is to reawaken the readers to a process which I would like to call "a self coming into existence" as the readers are receiving the unfolding narrative. The unfolding of the narrative is not a fixed truth revealing itself through a gradual linear development to a definite end, but is itself a process of composition as the readers come into contact with different voices and facets of the narrative.

In particular, in this autobiographical narrative penned by a third party, the highlighting of the complex relationship between the author, the protagonist, the other characters, and the readers puts the nature of a first-person narrative in the foreground. While it seems that the time of the protagonist's birth, the historical incidents involved and the imaginary nature of some of the characters dismiss the authenticity of the first-person narrative and the authority of the narrative voice, this delicate merging of fact and fiction creates spaces for other things than a single authority to tell a story. The narrative becomes a ground for voices of representation, while the intervention of the author facilitates the merging of the personal and the collective, the known and the unknown, and shows how these differences are all a matter of the construction of the text.

Although the death of the author has been announced, the proliferation of personal narratives in different forms seems to have released something new into the autobiography as a genre. It has become more varied and the boundaries have become fuzzy. The uniqueness, the distinct nature of a person, the way one imagines oneself, the materials with which we construct ourselves, the linear flow of time which we see as marking the natural development of the self, all these basic concepts which were once viewed as the principles of an autobiography written by the person himself, have been challenged. An autobiography is no longer a pure form, but contaminated by the very complex and hybrid nature of identity as we recognize today. Although Condé's work may sit more comfortably in the shelves of fiction, the delicate merging of various strands of the narrative has come together to question, to explore, and to test how much they can do to move across different boundaries.

So, finally here is the "I", the "Tituba", and the "Black Witch" of the narrative. The "I" is the term of self-reference Tituba uses, but it is also very much the "I" of the author, Maryse Condé, whose cultural identity has given her chances to observe the postcolonial status of citizens in the contemporary world. The "Tituba" is the historical figure who has been denied a full record of her story, but who has returned with renewed vigour, who details for us not only her birth, her adventures, but also her death and her post-mortem life. It is also a Tituba who is aware of the various partial pictures of her life and times as recorded in other fictional texts, and who goes on to incorporate these other people's stories into her own version of the story of her life. The "Black Witch" comes across as an enlightened feminist who is not only aware of the multiple oppressions from which she is suffering due to her marginalized status, as a witch, a black woman, and a slave, but who also sees the empowerment of female sexuality. She understands the exhibitionist pleasures the young girls enjoy from their frantic seizures and shouts, and she appreciates the comfort of sexual contact with both male and female companions.[24] Among her relationships, her ambiguous liaison with Hester initiates her into the full subjectivity of womanhood. Motherhood is a choice, and sexuality is a mark of her independence. Class and racial oppressions give her the ability to identify with other marginal peoples, such as the Jews and the anti-government rebels. United by a common anonymity, these various identities all come forth and avenge their silence through the creation of this new text form, the song of life. Although not written like the meticulously recorded court details, the song goes beyond the printed page, and reaches even the most oppressed and restricted lives, bringing a voice to the most marginalized. It is this nature of the song, and its capacity to embody such a deprived existence such as Tituba's that adds a new dimension to the genre of stories of the self.

NOTES AND REFERENCES

1. Born in 1958 in Shanghai, Wong Kai Wai moved to Hong Kong with his parents at the age of five. He entered the Hong Kong industry as a screenwriter. He claims that his non-linear style of story-telling is inspired by the late Argentinian writer Manuel Puig's novel titled *The Buenos Aires Affair.* He belongs to the mid-1980s Second New Wave of Hong Kong filmmakers who continued to develop the innovative and fresh aesthetics initiated by the original New Wave. The Second Wave, which includes directors such as Eddie Fong, Stanley Kwan and Clara Law, is often seen as a continuation of the first as many of these directors worked as assistants to First Wave directors such as Tsui Hark, Ann Hui and Patrick Tam (with whom Wong worked and collaborated).
2. The plot of this 2004 production picks up right at the end of *In the Mood for Love* (2000). After Su Lizhen (Maggie Cheung) leaves, Zhou Muyun (Leung Chiu-Wai) becomes a very lonely writer. He meets a prostitute (Zhang Ziyi) and spends a night with her at room 2046, the very same room he had an affair with Su Lizhen. Then he starts writing a novel called *2046*, in which he reunites with Su Lizhen. In terms of plot and character development, the film may be seen as a sequel to *In the Mood for Love.*
3. The 1997 Handover was a planned transition of Hong Kong from a British colony to a Special Administrative Region of China. Much of the detail had been laid down in an international agreement, the Joint Declaration, signed between Britain and China in 1984 and the Basic Law, 1990. The agreement was signed on 19 December 1984 in Beijing by the Chinese Premier and the British Prime Minister. The Joint Declaration sets out the basic policies of the People's Republic of China regarding Hong Kong and provides that these basic policies will be stipulated in the Basic Law of the Hong Kong Special Administrative Region. After more than 150 years of British rule, Hong Kong ceased to be a British dependent territory at midnight on June 30, 1997, when it officially became a Special Administrative Region of China with a high degree of autonomy. The Joint Declaration embodies the concept of "one country (China), two systems" and sets out how the fabric of Hong Kong's capitalist way of life is to be preserved.
4. The systems practiced in Hong Kong are prescribed by the Basic Law, the constitutional document of the HKSAR which came into effect upon its establishment on July 1, 1997. The Basic Law was adopted by the Seventh National People's Congress of the People's Republic of China on 4 April 1990. It stipulates that the Chief Executive shall be elected by a broadly representative Election Committee in accordance with the Basic Law and appointed by the Central People's Government. Under Hong Kong's constitutional document, the Basic Law, the existing economic, legal and social system will be maintained for 50 years. The SAR enjoys a high degree of autonomy except in defense and foreign affairs.
5. In Chinese, this policy is condensed into a five-character slogan: *Wu shi nian bu bian* (no change in 50 years).

6. After the signing of the Joint Declaration, in the period leading to the 1997 handover, the local cultural scene had shown its responses to the situation through an overwhelming amount of nostalgic expressions. Remembrances of times past, retracing a specific "Hong Kong" local history, re-examining our colonial identity, and foreseeing the return to a rightful "Chinese" identity are all part of the flowering of local consciousness.
7. Set in the straitlaced and gossipy Hong Kong of the early sixties, *In the Mood for Love* (2000) features two married neighbors who share a contagious secret. Recent émigrés from mainland China, Mr. Chow (Leung), a journalist, and Mrs. Chan (Cheung), a secretary for a shipping company, have rented adjacent boardinghouse rooms in the close-knit Shanghai section of Hong Kong. Eventually, through a slow, undeniable accumulation of clues, the two surmise that her husband and his wife are having an affair, and their own burgeoning rapport acquires an erotic charge.
8. The popularity of keeping a personal blog, for example, has meant that an individual has more and more chance of sharing his/her personal life and stories with other people, even total strangers living on the other side of the globe.
9. Maryse Condé, *I, Tituba, Black Witch of Salem*, trans. Richard Philcox, (Charlottesville: University Press of Virginia, 1992), p. 3.
10. Ibid., p. 172.
11. Ibid., p. 175.
12. Ibid.
13. Ibid.
14. Alice Walker, *In Search of Our Mothers' Gardens: Womanist Prose*, (Orlando: Harcourt, Inc., 1967), p. 237.
15. Condé, p. 178.
16. Ibid., p. 179.
17. Ibid., p. 8.
18. Ibid.
19. Ibid.
20. Ibid., p. 9.
21. Nathaniel Hawthorne's novel, *The Scarlet Letter*, tells the story of an adulteress, Hester Prynne, who was punished for daring to trespass beyond her marriage and give birth to a girl when her husband was away. She had to wear a scarlet letter "A" on her bosom to indicate her crime and sin. Although a quiet and peaceful character in Hawthorne's novel, Hester in Condé's rendition embraces feminist visions and principles, and makes Tibuta conscious of her oppressions and even to fight back.
22. Paul Boyer and Stephen Nissenbaum, *Salem Possessed: The Social Origins of Witchcraft*, (Cambridge, Massachusetts: Harvard University Press, 1974).
23. Condé, p. 149.
24. In this respect of sexual awareness, Condé's work shares a common concern with Arthur Miller's dramatic rendition of a similar event in his 1952 play *The Crucible*. Abigail, the "leader" of the girls who started the witch scare, is

described having had a sexual encounter with one of the accused, but who was later rejected. Her accusations were thus significantly an act of revenge. In Miller's play, the "girls" who started the mayhem were all in their late teenage years, similar to Condé's rendition. Ann Petry's 1964 nouvella, *Tituba in Salem Village*, however, makes the girls much younger and removes the sexual perspective from the story all together.

Contributors

Alessandro Portelli, Dipartimento di Anglistica, Università degli Studi di Roma "La Sapienza", Italy.

Abhai Maurya, Central Institute for English and Foreign Languages, Hyderabad, India.

Suchitra Mathur, Department of Humanities and Social Sciences, Indian Institute of Technology, Kanpur, India.

Sharmistha Lahiri, Department of Germanic & Romance Studies, University of Delhi, Delhi, India.

Remo Cesarani, University of Bologna, Italy.

Manfred Stassen, Johns Hopkins University, USA.

Margit Köves, Department of Slavonic and Finno-Ugrian Studies, University of Delhi, Delhi, India.

Carmen Ulrich, Ludwig-Maximilians-University, Munich, Germany.

Dorethea Jecht, former DAAD Visiting Faculty in Department of Germanic & Romance Studies, University of Delhi, Delhi, India.

Dirk Wiemann, Institut für fremdsprachliche Philologien, Otto-von-Guerricke-Universität, Magdeburg, Germany.

Romit Roy, Department of English & Other Modern European Languages, Visva-Bharati, Santiniketan, West Bengal, India.

Rosy Singh, Department of Germanic & Romance Studies, University of Delhi, Delhi, India.

Patrizia Raveggi, Italian Cultural Centre, New Delhi, India.

Sanja Roić, Department of Italian Studies, University of Zagreb, Croatia.

Swantje Lichtenstein, Department of Social and Cultural Studies, University of Applied Sciences, Düsseldorf, Germany.

Kathleen Kerr-Koch, University of Sunderland, England.

Amy Wai-Sum Lee, Hong Kong Baptist University, Hong Kong.